LUTON SIXTH FORM COLLEGE

-9 JUL 1990

This book is due for return on or before the last date shown above.

3123

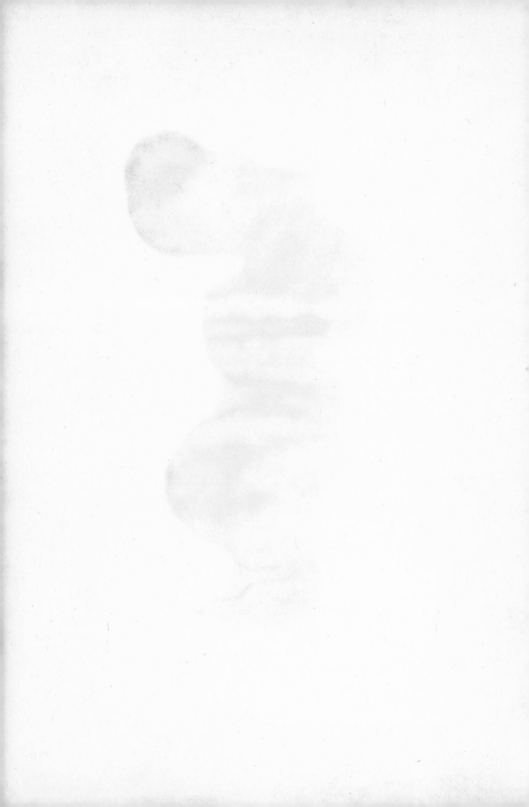

THE

WIND

B·A·N·D

Its

LITERATURE

and

TECHNIQUE

GREENWOOD PRESS, PUBLISHERS
WESTPORT, CONNECTICUT

Grateful acknowledgment is hereby made for permission to quote from copyright(ed) works as follows:

Bands of America. Copyright © *1957* by H. W. Schwartz. Reprinted by permission of Doubleday & Company, Inc.

Military Music. By H. G. Farmer. New York: Chanticleer Press, Inc., *1950.*

An Invitation to Band Arranging. By Erik Leidzen. Copyright(ed) *1950* Oliver Ditson Co., used by permission.

"Ceremonial Music." By Virgil Thomson. New York *Herald Tribune,* July *13, 1947.*

The Music of Gustav Holst. By Imogen Holst. New York: Oxford University Press, *1951.*

Prairie Overture, for Concert Band. By Robert Ward. © Copyright, *1960* by Highgate Press.

March from "Egmont." By Ludwig van Beethoven, arr. by Roger Smith. © Copyright *1960* by Beekman Music, Inc., New York. N.Y. Published by Mercury Music Corporation by special arrangement.

"Brookville," A Tone Poem for Band. By William Russo. © Copyright *1961* by Sam Fox Publishing Company, Inc., New York, N.Y. Used by permission.

A
Note of Thanks

⟦ A NOTE OF THANKS ⟧

This book is the result of much thought about the band, going back to my childhood, and of thirty years of experience as a professional musician and as a teacher. But both my thought and my experience have been influenced by the exchange of ideas with many colleagues in all branches of music, and I should like to express to them all my profound gratitude.

Programs, facts about their bands, and other helpful information have been generously provided by many of these colleagues for this book, and I should like to express my thanks to them:

The Officers of the College Band Directors National Association, and especially its President (1960), Mr. James Neilson, Director of Bands, Oklahoma City University.

Dr. William D. Revelli, Director of Bands, University of Michigan.

Mr. Mark Hindsley, Director of Bands, University of Illinois, and his Assistant Director, Mr. Guy M. Duker.

Dr. Frederick Fennell, Conductor of the Eastman Symphonic Wind Ensemble, Eastman School of Music.

Mr. Herbert N. Johnston, Conductor of the Philco Band.

Mr. Al G. Wright, Director of Bands, Purdue University.

Mr. Jonathan Elkus, Director of Bands, Lehigh University.

Mr. Arthur L. Williams, Professor of Wind Instruments and Music Education, Oberlin College.

Mr. Leonard B. Smith, Conductor of the Belle Isle Concert Band, Detroit.

[A NOTE OF THANKS]

Colonel George S. Howard, Chief of Bands and Music and Conductor of the United States Air Force Band, and Captain Harry H. Meuser, his Assistant Conductor.

Major Robert L. Bierly, Leader of the United States Army Field Band, and his predecessor, Lt. Colonel Chester E. Whiting, ret.

Mr. Herbert Hazelman, Director of the Greensboro, N.C., Senior High School Band.

Mr. Bruce Houseknecht, Conductor of the Joliet, Ill., Township High School Band.

Mr. Marion Jacobs, Director of the Grand Junction, Colo., High School Band.

For material help of another kind, I should like to express my obligation to my composer-colleagues Robert Ward, Henry Cowell, Vincent Persichetti and Erik Leidzen, as well as to Dr. Hugo Weisgall for information about John Holloway, and to Edward N. Waters for material about Victor Herbert.

I am greatly indebted to my associates Roger Smith, Assistant Conductor of the Goldman Band, and Robert Leist, Conductor of the Princeton University Band and arranger for the Goldman Band, for reading the manuscript and making many helpful suggestions, a task in which my wife also was indispensable. Finally I wish to express my thanks to Miss Sheila Keats for her invaluable help in the preparation and editing of the manuscript, and to Mr. Nelson M. Jansky and Mrs. Ruth S. Rischin of Allyn and Bacon, for their enthusiastic helpfulness.

My greatest debt is of course to my father, from whom I learned about bands, and of whose wisdom and experience I had the benefit. It is therefore both as a filial and a professional gesture that I dedicate this book to his memory.

R. F. G.

Contents

x

[CONTENTS]

[CONTENTS]

Part Two

TECHNICAL PROBLEMS OF THE BAND

Part Three

THE REPERTOIRE OF THE BAND

⟦ CONTENTS ⟧

Part Four

IMPROVING THE BAND

List of Illustrations

PLATES

I   Victor Herbert in uniform as leader of the Band of the Twenty-Second Regiment of New York. Courtesy, The Library of Congress

⟦ CONTENTS ⟧

[CONTENTS]

PROGRAMS, SCORES, DRAWINGS

〖 CONTENTS 〗

⟦ CONTENTS ⟧

part one

THE

B A N D

as a

musical institution

1

INTRODUCTION:

the

B · A · N · D

today

〖 THE BAND TODAY 〗

The wind band today is not only a musical phenomenon of greater interest than it was at any previous time in its history, but it also represents an activity of considerable sociological interest in the musical scene, especially in the United States. Despite the lamentations of those who talk about the good old days of Sousa, Pryor, or even Gilmore, it is a fact that there is greater activity in band music today, and activity of greater musical importance, than there was fifty or even twenty-five years ago. One need only recall that there are in the United States today about *20,000* school and college bands, and a grand total of all types of bands which perhaps approaches *30,000*. (This estimate may well be on the conservative side.) That the band has not lost any of its popularity seems obvious. But that its efforts are channeled in new directions is perhaps not quite so obvious. The wind band is decidedly not what it used to be, although superficially it may appear to be continuing in the simple line of its own tradition. Many new factors have entered the band picture in the twentieth century, and despite the continued popularity of band music and the ever greater activity in the field, there are many aspects of the wind band that are not too clearly understood, even among bandsmen.

The principal cause of confusion is, I believe, the changed orientation of band music in our century. H. W. Schwartz, in his excellent book, *Bands of America,* has shown that the peak of the popularity of the professional band was reached around *1910*. At no time, before or since, were there so many professional bands active, touring so widely, attracting such large audiences, and enjoying so universal a popularity. Later in this volume we shall look into the causes of change. But for the moment, it suffices to recall that the band in the United States, until at least *1925*, was primarily a professional or military undertaking, and that its aim was almost exclusively entertainment. Since the middle *1920*'s, however, the sponsorship of band music in the United States has shifted, in large measure, to the schools and colleges. This has produced not so much a musical revolution in band music as a social re-orientation. The primary aim of band music, except for the few remaining professional or community bands, can no longer be entertainment. Certainly, no one would seriously defend the idea that our schools and colleges are, or should be, in the entertainment business, even though we know that there are many borderline cases, and that such activities as college football, for example, are not easy to defend as being purely "educational."

There is, of course, considerable confusion in American education today between education and entertainment. While this problem, in its widest sense, is beyond the scope of this book, it is nevertheless necessary that its existence be recognized, for it is one of the conditions creating a certain confusion in the field of band music. Posed in another fashion, the question might be: if the aim of band music in the schools cannot be entertainment, then what can and should it be?

This is not an abstract question. In the overall picture of American education, it is in fact a challenge. But even in the smaller field of music and of music education, it has some interesting ramifications. For the break between the two band traditions, that of the professional-military and that of the school-college, is by no means a clear one. The school and college band has inherited much, in repertoire, instrumentation and other matters, from its historical predecessors. The curious results of this combination have never been the subject of serious study or discussion, so far as I know; but it is time that such a discussion were undertaken. I believe that it may help greatly to clarify many things about bands and band music today, especially in the United States.

An old Webster Dictionary gives the following interesting definition of a band: "A number of musicians who play together upon portable musical instruments, especially those making a loud sound, as certain wind instruments (trumpets, clarinets—also drums and cymbals)." I suppose that the definition needs little comment today; more modern dictionaries and encyclopedias give varying degrees of light according to newer usages. One can find the brief entry, "A company of musicians" in an abridged dictionary for college students, or essays of a thousand words or more in encyclopedias published in the last ten years.

As it happens, a definition of a band is still fairly difficult, and for many reasons the difficulty seems to be increasing. Primarily, there are many types of bands, and for general use perhaps the old Webster Dictionary definition will do as well as another. We assume that we are talking about the *wind band,* with its various aspects of military band, concert band, football band, high school band, and lately wind ensemble. These all really do consist of "a number of musicians who play together" and they all do include trumpets and clarinets, drums and cymbals; but all the instruments are no longer necessarily portable, nor are they all selected primarily for their loud sound.

Historically, the wind band was entirely functional. It existed to provide music for specific occasions and needs, military and civic. In this, it is completely different from the orchestra, which developed because of the demands of *art*—that is to say, of serious composed music. The wind band or ensemble had no such force behind it. It existed to make noise, to perform simple types of popular music, to sound hours, to give cadences for marching, and to perform other useful duties.

Only toward the latter part of the eighteenth century did its repertoire begin to change, with the addition of a few bits of more carefully thought-out written music, and the beginnings of arrangements of popular airs, chiefly operatic. Only at this time do we begin to hear of popular concerts given in parks by bands, the beginning of the concept that band music can provide entertainment, rather than serve only a purely utilitarian function.

The distinction between a purely *musical* reason for being, and an almost purely *useful* one is important. Again, it explains much of the present ambiguous situation of bands and band music. Our concert bands today want to believe that they exist for musical reasons. But why then do so many of them still wear uniforms? On the other hand, our football and marching bands are quite obviously still relics of the old functional band. And our in-between types, which include *the majority*

〖 THE BAND TODAY 〗

of bands, combine or try to combine all of the possible functions: concert (art music), entertainment (popular or light music), marching and ceremonial, and so on. By and large, the band today does not exist on a purely artistic level similar to that of the orchestra, although it is striving in that direction. Yet it retains these curious holdovers from the past, so that in many ways it is held back both by public opinion (it is still hard to get large sections of the musical public to take bands seriously) and by its own traditions of instrumentation and its association with parades and other non-musical activities.

There have been many other factors at work, especially in the past twenty-five years. During most of the nineteenth century, the band could quite honestly be accepted as a sort of poor man's symphony orchestra. It had a genuine educative function to fill, bringing music of the masters to large audiences who could not be reached directly by orchestral concerts. But radio and recordings, not to mention the increase of live orchestral concerts (there are over *120* orchestras in the United States!) have absolutely and permanently removed this function from the band's range in our times. When Wieprecht, in the *1840's*, arranged most of Beethoven's symphonies for band, he was doing a great and valuable musical and social service. But who today wants to hear a band play a Beethoven symphony, when for a small sum he can have a superb recording by Toscanini, Bruno Walter or any number of other conductors, with the greatest orchestras in the world? Or when he can hear these works if he is within range of a good FM station, and sometimes even on commercial AM stations? At no cost whatever!

The entertainment picture has changed too. The mechanical considerations apply equally in this field, but even more important, the nature of the truly popular instrumental combination has changed. Popular dance music and more or less serious jazz have evolved new styles of playing and new instrumental ensembles. These have further narrowed the scope of the military or concert band in the area of popular entertainment, and forced it to seek new avenues. Sousa himself foresaw this clearly. In his often-stated dislike of "jazz" and "rag-time," he was expressing his awareness of the inroads these new combinations were

⟦ THE BAND TODAY ⟧

certain to make in the sphere of activity of the professional touring band.

The background of the modern band involves one other consideration of importance, besides that of function. This is the matter of the instrumental composition of the band as a performing organization. It is obvious that anything termed generally a "wind band" consists either entirely or for the most part of wind instruments. This is understood to be true whether we speak in terms of wind band, concert band, military band, symphonic band, or merely "band." But we must ask why, and we must again draw certain conclusions from history and tradition, from the conditions of the band's development.

Why, originally, did "bands," both military and civic, consist entirely of winds? The reasons are simple enough: wind instruments are (*1*) portable and (*2*) loud. Portability is clearly desirable, even necessary, if a group is to play while marching, or even if it is to move from place to place in the course of discharging its duties. And if it is to play outdoors, it must be heard! Electrical amplification has no doubt modified our ideas about all this, but we must remember that it didn't always exist. It is quite true that a gaggle of 'cello players today could sit in a comfortably heated room, and provide loud enough music via a PA system to reach all parts of a community at once, with parades in all quarters. But this couldn't be done fifty years ago.

The point surely does not need to be underlined. But it seems that some bandmasters have had their feelings hurt by being reminded that volume or sheer noise is a very real part of the band tradition. Until fairly recently, bands played in the open air. They competed not only against open-air acoustics, but against man-made incidental noise. In parades and ceremonies, they had to be heard at middling to great distances, and usually over the sound of horses' hoofs or marching feet.

In other words, the composition of the band was *practical* before all else. It served a purpose. And this purpose was not the agility of execution, refinement of tone and subtlety of nuance that we think of as purely musical *desiderata;* it was power and manoeuverability first and foremost.

Historically speaking again, the band started playing on its feet.

⟦ THE BAND TODAY ⟧

It marched; it stood in public squares; it moved from place to place. Apparently it took several centuries before it occurred to anyone that a band might sit down to play, and that people might want to listen to the playing just for enjoyment. Or that they might stop to listen to a band apart from a parade or other ceremony. But this is more or less what happened. At first, all of the bands performing in parks or public squares were regimental bands. This is important for one reason only, but that reason is a vital one in the history of the band: the instrumentation remained that of the regimental band, and was still determined by the considerations governing the band's marching and other military functions. In other words, although the band was seated and playing a "concert," it still used only portable instruments producing ample volume.

This is a crucial point in understanding the modern band. For later on, in the nineteenth century, bands developed whose connections with the military were more remote, and which concentrated more and more on purely concert-giving activities. We see in today's bands such instruments as string basses (non-portable) and flutes (not notably loud), even harps (neither portable nor loud), and must wonder why not violas? Why was the basic wind character preserved?

This is indeed an interesting question, and it is by no means an easy one to answer. H. G. Farmer suggests that the instrumentation and technique of the band give it qualities such as "lucidity of expression and clarity of rhythm" which appeal to large masses of people. It is clearly along these lines that the explanation is to be found. The band appeals *musically,* as a sound and as an idiom, to a very large number of people. And this is an appeal that is wholly independent of comparisons; in other words, it does not relate to the sound of the orchestra or of any other large body of performers. It exists in its own right as a musical phenomenon.

Otherwise, it remains somewhat difficult to explain or to justify the somewhat arbitrary constitution of the wind band in the past or present, insofar as concert-giving activities are concerned. In a later chapter we shall examine in greater detail the development of wind band

⟦ THE BAND TODAY ⟧

instrumentation, and note the constant changes that have taken place throughout its history. Any instrument that can be blown has at one time or another been used in wind bands, and the proportion of instruments, or groups of instruments, one to another, has varied fantastically. Some of the experimentation has undoubtedly been carried on in a spirit of musical disinterestedness: how to make the wind band produce a better, more flexible and more varied sound. But some of the changes have been for non-musical reasons, either military tables of organization, or simple restlessness and a desire to change. As new instruments have been invented and manufactured, each has had its vogue; some, like the saxophones, have become fixtures in the ensemble; others, like the batyphone, have been tried and discarded.

What remains is the conclusion that the instrumentation of the band is still somewhat arbitrary or even capricious. One must remember that the instrumentation is governed by a tradition growing out of military usage, and guided by a variety of other considerations. The orchestra, as has been stated, developed under the command of the composer: one plays a Beethoven symphony with the instruments indicated in the score, *and no others.* It is true that Beethoven might have written for other instruments if they had been available in his time, but this is a fruitless argument; it is also true that his horn and trumpet parts might have been different had our modern instruments been invented a hundred years earlier. But again, we do not change these horn and trumpet parts for this reason. The orchestra in the hands of Richard Strauss, Mahler and their contemporaries grew to a huge assemblage of instrumentalists; but this orchestra is not used for performances of Haydn. The band, on the other hand, simply grew; and it presents exactly the opposite picture. Lacking a great repertoire of its own, it has put instrumentation first, and made the music fit the combination rather than the other way round. This is one of the roots of the problem of band music at the present time.

The second major problem is the nature of band music in the overall social and musical picture today. The band, as has been seen, no longer can justify itself, or exert its one-time immense appeal, as a substitute orchestra, purveying the "classics" to an audience which would otherwise not hear them at all. It does not compete with the dance band or jazz combination on a more obviously popular level. Just where, then, does it belong in the musical picture? Obviously, it is still the outdoor mobile unit par excellence. Nothing will replace a band at football games or for parades. But what about the concert band? Again, we come back to its justification on the basis of its unique and attractive sound. But to this we must add one further qualification: the sound must be put to the service of a repertoire that is also interesting, and that should be unique as well.

I cannot insist sufficiently on this point, although I am quite certain that most progressive bandmasters are in complete agreement about it. With the easy availability of the entire orchestral, operatic and chamber music repertories, via live performance, radio and LP recordings, the band must find its own musical niche not only as to uniqueness of sound, but also as to the music it plays. This is true not only in the field of professional practice (where the band can no longer be excused for playing a Beethoven symphony); it is also true in the educational field. Can a school or college director claim that he is adding to the *musical experience* or education of the student by performing a standard orchestral work that should be familiar to the student in its original form? In certain instances, it is possible to give an affirmative answer; but in general, it is fair to say that the best musical interests of both student and audience are not being served.

The most important factor in the world of bands and band music today is the growth of a new and original repertoire. I feel, after living with band music since early childhood, and with thirty years of professional experience behind me, that I can make this statement categorically and without reservation. This question of repertoire takes precedence over all discussions of the band's instrumentation, over methods, over all of the other questions that arise. For it is this repertoire, which exploits the *sound* of the wind band in all its possibilities and is designed for the type of audience that is attracted to the band, that will give the band an even more secure place in the musical community, and that will once and for all settle the question of band vs. orchestra, and

⟦ THE BAND TODAY ⟧

most of the other questions, both musical and social, that are raised about the band.

The band, until very recently, has had only the march as its own indisputable musical *genre,* and perhaps also the cornet solo. Not that these are to be dismissed lightly; they are still basic in the band's repertoire, and they are still, at least so far as a general audience is concerned, by far the most popular items the band plays. The military march goes back for centuries; the cornet solo begins almost the moment the modern instrument was invented; even before that, there were virtuosi such as Ned Kendall who played the keyed bugle. What associations there are for bandsmen in the names of the great march composers and the great cornet soloists! And how much they have contributed to the enduring popularity of the band! These forms of music are valid, not only because they are unique, but because they are interesting. The cornet solo, as a display of virtuosity, is easy to understand; and virtuosity with a simple content never fails to appeal. The military march, too, has developed into a minor art form, and in the hands of Sousa may be considered comparable to the waltz in the hands of Johann Strauss. It is a stylized expression, absolutely suited to the band, because conceived from first to last in band terms, and it is the one form of music that no other type of musical organization can ever play as effectively.

This is what is necessary for the remainder of the repertoire. I think that Sousa himself recognized this, although he never stated so, directly, when he played one of his own marches after each programmed number at almost all of his concerts. Not only were the marches by far the most popular pieces played, but they represented *real* band music, first, last and foremost. Sousa did not encourage or perform much original band music other than his marches; but perhaps he did not have to. The people came to hear the marches, and the cornet solos, and the trombone solos; the rest really did not matter very much. And as for serious musicians, they felt the same way: the Sousa Band was Sousa's marches, which they admired then, and probably always will.

If then, these problems of repertoire and instrumental constitution remain to be further studied and explored, we have perhaps at least

〖 THE BAND TODAY 〗

stated them as a background to further investigation of the nature and status of the band in America today. It should be apparent that the problems of the professional and the amateur band, the military and the high school band, the community and the university band, are not always the same. Even though their instrumentations may all be the same (this is, of course, only more or less true), and although their repertoires may vary only slightly, and that more in degree than in kind, there still remains an important question: for whom, and under what circumstances, do they play?

It is here that the differences become more important than the resemblances. Professional bands play to entertain an audience, the larger the better; in the old days, they also hoped to make money. Community bands in general also exist to entertain, although many of them contain amateur players who play simply for enjoyment. The amateur band, in general, plays simply for the fun of ensemble playing; unless it is extraordinarily good, its efforts are not really directed at an audience, except one of friends and relatives.

Bands in educational institutions, always remembering that these are today both numerically and culturally the most important in America, are, properly speaking, amateur bands. I trust that no one will take offense at this statement; I do not mean to imply that some of our university bands, and even some of our high school bands, do not play better than some professional bands. They do! However, the players are students; they are not paid for playing, and they spend considerably more time in rehearsal than in actual performance. They are not, as a rule, repertoire organizations playing many concerts in a single season, with a variety of different programs. They exist, at least theoretically, for the instruction of the players, the development of their skills, the extension of their musical experience and their training as teachers.

These are important differences, which must be discussed at some length. However, before going on to this, it should be noted that all of these bands, professional, military, school or college, *do* give concerts. And there are important similarities of repertoire and audience relations among all of them. For *in every one of its manifestations,* the band remains an instrument of what our sociologists call "popular culture." That is to say, it does not respond to the same needs or conditions as does the symphony orchestra, which is essentially a vehicle of minority or "high-brow" culture, as is the string quartet. The music played by the wind band does not, ordinarily, demand the kind of concentration (by audience or performers) required by the performance of orchestral or chamber music works of the highest artistic level. The wind band operates on the level of the orchestral "pops" concert at best; on the level of the salon orchestra most of the time; and from time to time on the level of the dance orchestra or the novelty ensemble. Some of its functions are more "popular" than "cultural"; some, in fact, cannot be called "cultural" at all: the marching band or the football band, for example. The concert or "symphonic" band does, however, represent a genuine contribution to musical culture; it is still essentially popular, but it also has the potential of elevating the level of popular taste and musical enlightenment.

So far as band music in our colleges, and even more particularly in our secondary schools, is concerned, it is this last potential that is of paramount importance. For the immense amounts of time and energy, and the large financial investment, that go into band activities in our educational institutions, must be justified by results that actually go beyond simple entertainment or group activity. There must be a musical end; perhaps it is not too far-fetched to suggest that there must even be an artistic end in view. On an obvious level, it is certainly true that all bands play music. But what kind of music? For whom? The question is being asked, and will be asked more insistently in the future: are the students acquiring more than a physical or manual skill through playing an instrument? Is the band in reality part of the calisthenics or physical education program? Does the band contribute anything of real value in the educational sense?

Put it another way: the band in the school is certainly a form of social activity. Music itself is essentially a social activity. Music can, under many conditions, be enjoyed in solitude; but this is not always true, and it is generally not true at all of young people. There is all the difference in the world between practicing in solitude and performing with or for others. Young people unquestionably enjoy, as do most of their elders, the social aspects of musical performance, at any level. But however pleasurable music may be as a social activity, two questions remain: is it always music? is it always properly a form of education? These questions are bound to be asked, and everyone in the band field must be prepared with honest answers. There is no use today in trying to avoid the issues. The people who are concerned about "frills" and other forms of decay in our educational system are neither fools nor villains. They are not out to destroy jobs in music education, or to subvert the American way of life, or to ruin the band instrument business. They are serious people, from Dr. Conant on down to many less authoritative teachers and citizens. It should be pointed out that the questions about the band are not exclusively the result of an increased emphasis on the sciences; they are the result of a reconsideration of our whole educational "philosophy" and practice.

The band *does* have a place in the school, for the band can do more than provide light entertainment or pleasant group activity or the opportunity to get dressed up in fancy uniforms. These aspects of the band can and should be utilized, of course; they appeal to youngsters, as do parades and games. But they cannot be the end of the activity, only the means. It is proper that the band, rather than the orchestra perhaps, be a part of a public school program, for our schools are essentially popular institutions for all of the people, and no longer exclusive institutions for a privileged few. The band is more truly a reflection of the culture of the public school system. But at the same time, the band in the school must constantly try to improve and *to educate*, for that is the function of any school, public or private, large or small.

The band of course can do this, and can thus justify its place in an educational system. I would go so far as to say that the band *must* do this if it is to hold its place in the years ahead. The band in the school and college must more than ever emphasize *musical* values rather than physical skill or group activity. There are many types of group activity which are less expensive and less demanding in terms of hours. The band must provide values that these other activities do not. Team play, the sense of pride in "belonging," the idea of cooperation—all these are common to group activities of many sorts. The band's values must be derived from participation in music not as a group activity *but as a musical activity.* From the standpoint of education, the importance of band music is that it convey to the student some sense of music, not simply as a matter of playing a saxophone or a trombone, but as an art, however limited that sense may be in terms of the student's capacities or inclinations. It is first of all through the quality of the music which bands play that this can be accomplished. Repertoire is a central consideration, but even more important is the question of how the repertoire is approached: what values are sought in music? Repertoire in the school band will always be determined in part by the capacity and ability of the band; but whatever the band's technical level may be, its abilities should be directed toward some reasonable and defensible educational end.

It seems to me that every school band should be part of a general music program. I do not want to use the term "music appreciation," since that has become associated with a melange of fairy-tales and musico-historical baby-talk, but perhaps the term "music discrimination" might serve. In any case, the band program should include a genuine involvement with an appreciation of music, of a directed and technical type, based on performer's problems, general repertoire, interpretation and *trained hearing.* The band should not be the only musical experience either; students in bands should be made aware of the treasures of music beyond the band repertoire, and their musical curiosity should be aroused and encouraged. Educators from Plato onwards have recognized the value of music in education as a means of developing sensitivity and of promoting intellectual growth. Schiller went so far as to propose education in the arts as the basis for moral development. Perhaps these ideas seem high-flown in the face of the daily realities of teaching instrumental music; yet they form a useful, in fact an indispensable background, for

[THE BAND TODAY]

our thinking about *the aims* of music education, and of bands in particular. With our educational practices being subjected to increasingly serious scrutiny, it is surely better to aim too high than too low in the field of band music in school and college. And while everyone agrees that band music is fun, that it is entertaining, and that it is a wholesome part of the popular cultural milieu, it is more than ever true that its place in our schools must be considered in terms of its actual and potential contribution to the *general education* of its participants.

2

+ + + + + + + + *European* + + + + + + + +

ORIGINS

of

the modern band

[EUROPEAN ORIGINS]

The wind band, as an artistic unit, is an invention of fairly recent times. Its origin can, as a matter of historical fact, be placed precisely in *1789*, with the formation of the band of the National Guard in Paris. This group of forty-five players was incontestably the first modern wind band, in terms of size, of function and of repertoire. To be sure, there had been some small bands previously that had engaged in concert-giving activities on a more or less regular basis, but it was the French Revolution, with its great emphasis on popularization and democratization, even of the arts, that produced the Band of the National Guard and the forward movement of band music from that time on.

The modern band's ancestors were those groups, usually small, of wind players employed to provide music for outdoor functions and ceremonies, both military and civic. One could no doubt stretch a point and find the ancestry of the wind band in early historic or even pre-historic times, but this is hardly useful or enlightening. We do not know what tune or what trumpets were used against Jericho, or whether the Roman legions favored *2/4* or *6/8* marches; fortunately, these questions are not relevant. The wind band as we know it is of course a part of the history of western European music, but the emergence of any musical phenomena that have any pertinence to our discussion cannot be dated earlier than the twelfth century. In more practical terms, we know actually very little of wind instrument performance, repertoire or function before the fifteenth century. We assume, on good evidence, that horns or trumpets of various sorts, and possibly double reeds as well, were used to accompany marching troops and to sound battle signals, and that wind instruments of many sorts were used in popular music for singing and dancing; but we have no evidence to suggest that there were regularly organized bodies of players, with fixed instrumental groupings, traditional repertoire or regularly assigned functions during the Middle Ages.

We do know, however, that there were "military bands" of a sort in the sixteenth century. Toward the end of the century, groups of players on trombones and cornetts (*zinken,* wooden instruments played with a cup mouthpiece) performed at San Marco in Venice, and presumably elsewhere. Most important, we can begin to trace the rise of

〚 EUROPEAN ORIGINS 〛

Stadtpfeiffer (town fifers) and *Thürmer* (tower musicians) in Germany from approximately this time. Artistically, the most impressive and enduring music by far was that composed by Giovanni Gabrieli and others of the Venetian and Roman schools for trombones and cornetts. Fortunately much of this music is preserved, and in our century it has once again received some of the attention it so markedly deserves. Yet this music, and this tradition of composition, did not establish itself permanently in terms of use; it did not spread outside of Italy, and it did not influence the course of what we can call *band* music.

For a fuller history of the development of the band and its instrumentation, I refer the reader to the account given in my book *The Concert Band* (Chapter 2, pp *18-54*). A distinction should be made here, however, between what we shall have to call, for want of a better term, "art" music and popular music. The wind instrument pieces of Gabrieli, Massaini, Marini and others belong, of course, in the first category. These works are serious musical expressions of the utmost sophistication and skill, with elaborate counterpoint and highly developed form. They stand among the most advanced expressions of their times. Further, they were performed by a specified instrumentation, or at the very least a specified division of parts, and were of course played from notes. They have no relation at all to the band music, civilian or military, of their period. For this band music was haphazard at best: presumably it was seldom played from written notes; there is no evidence of any organized or settled instrumentation; and all the evidence we have leads us to believe that the repertoire was limited to fanfares, military signals, simple chorales and popular dance tunes, including marches. This is, for better or for worse, the tradition of band music up to the time of the French Revolution.

The development of wind instruments, and of wind instrument music on a serious plane, was carried on within the general framework of musical composition. The wind ensemble, or band, as such, was as a rule merely a reflection, on a practical and popular level, of the usages developed in other areas of musical activity. In the period before the perfection of the violin family, the winds enjoyed more or less equality with the strings; perhaps it would be more accurate to say that they were used in no less a casual manner. The blending of different families of instruments must have caused considerable trouble, for the tradition in any case generally called for the use of instruments in related families. The consort of viols, becoming popular in the sixteenth century in England, or the ensemble of double reeds, or the groups of trombones and cornetts in Italy and Germany are examples of this usage, which reflects of course the prevailing style of writing for voices. Part-writing for voices gives the greatest possible homogeneity of sound, and probably also for a long time established an ideal of sonority that was imitated as far as possible in instrumental ensembles.

It has become customary to speak of "orchestration" as beginning at the very end of the sixteenth century and the beginning of the seventeenth, in the works of Giovanni Gabrieli, Claudio Monteverdi and their German pupil Heinrich Schütz. There is, however, also some misunderstanding about this. It is true that toward *1580,* Andrea Gabrieli and others began to specify instruments for performance, and that in the years immediately following there were many fascinating advances in the handling of instrumental sonority. But the large orchestra used by Monteverdi in his *Orfeo,* so often cited as an example, actually was employed in separate sections; the total ensemble did not play at one time. In other words, Monteverdi, although a daring experimenter, actually used groups of small "consorts" for contrast, but did not combine them all in the sense of a modern orchestra. Nevertheless, it is certain that the Gabrielis and Monteverdi showed what could be done with instruments in terms of sonority and effectiveness, and this is no less true with respect to the winds than to the strings.

What should be remembered is that the art music of the seventeenth century established the primacy of the violin family, and that the great instrumental literature of the period is for strings. The perfection of the violin at the hands of Gasparo da Salò, the Amatis and the Stradivari was, of course, a vital factor in this development. In any case, the daring experiments and the adventures of the late Renaissance and early Baroque composers were not pursued. Frescobaldi and Scheidt returned

⟦ EUROPEAN ORIGINS ⟧

to the practice of writing instrumental parts "for any sort of instrument," it being generally understood that *similar* instruments were to be used. There is little art music specifically for winds in the middle and late Baroque.

The wind instruments were, however, influenced by the example of the developed strings, and attempts were made to create more orderly families in the different categories of winds. Thus we have sets of schalmeys, or shawms, cornetts and other instruments, from treble to bass, performing part-music with presumably a more agreeable sound than that produced by earlier helter-skelter assortments. The *Stadtmusiker* (town musicians) and *Thürmer* in Germany seem to have reflected this development, and in the seventeenth century we have the first and last surviving music of any importance that was written specifically for them. These are the collections of Johann Pezel (or Pezelius) containing music in five parts for *zinken* (the old cornetts) and trombones, published in Leipzig in *1670* and *1685,* and the collection of *Quatricinia* (four-part music) by J. G. Reiche, published in Leipzig in *1696,* for one cornett and three trombones.

These pieces reflect the practice of writing for families of kindred instruments (although technically speaking, the cornett and trombone are of different types). Of the same nature, we have the marches and other little pieces composed and collected by Lully for the band of Louis XIV, and *Les Libertés* of André de Rosiers, all scored for a four-voiced family of oboes (*tailles*), and such works as the *Lustige Feldmusik* ("Joyous Open-Air Music") of J. P. Krieger (c. *1690*) for oboes and bassoons.

Although the German *Stadtmusiker* survived into the nineteenth century, the *Thürmer* seem to have disappeared from the musical scene some time around the second decade of the eighteenth century, coincident with the eclipse of the cornett and the trombone. These instruments fell into disuse, the cornett permanently, and the trombone for the greater part of the eighteenth century. They were replaced in general use by the horn and the bassoon, both in the town bands and in the developing orchestra. The town and regimental bands for a time went through an evolutionary phase in which one finds eccentric and irregular combinations of instruments. The trumpet, once an instrument "reserved" for the use of the nobility and played only by members of a strictly-regulated trumpeters' guild, begins to appear from time to time in the small in-strumental combinations. With the evolution of the clarinet, still another useful instrument makes its appearance. It was certainly in fairly com-mon use by *1725*, although it received its greatest impetus in the works of the Mannheim composers somewhat later than this. New percussion instruments, introduced from Turkey via Poland and Russia, created a great impression toward the middle of the century, and were quickly adopted not only by regimental bands, but also by orchestral composers. The great vogue of *alla Turca* music dates from this time; the term refers to the use of triangles, cymbals and others of the new instruments which so charmed western Europe.

It is in the eighteenth century that the modern orchestra and the art of orchestration as we know it really begin, with the basic string choir firmly established, and with the addition of increasing complements of wind instruments. It is also after the middle of the century that bands again begin to assume a definite shape. The typical mid-eighteenth cen-tury band was a double quartet of oboes, clarinets, horns and bassoons, to which were added, irregularly, one or two flutes, a trumpet, basset-horns, serpent or contra-bassoon, and drums. In about *1763*, Frederick the Great of Prussia stabilized Prussian regimental bands in the form of the octet of oboes, clarinets, horns and bassoons. It is this combination that is used by Mozart in the beautiful Serenades in E♭ (K. *475*) and C minor (K. *488*) and in the second act of *Don Giovanni*, as well as in works by Haydn, Pleyel, J. C. Bach, and later by Beethoven and Schubert. This combination is what might be called the "standard band" of the period, and the music written for it by these masters is characteristically "band" music: serenades, divertimenti and marches.

It is also around this time that the organization of the regimental bands became more firmly established. The oldest tradition of military music found the musicians employed by individual commanding officers at their own expense; but toward the end of the eighteenth century, some regular tables of organization were established, authorizing specific numbers of musicians for specific regiments. The payment of the musicians still, however, often depended on the regimental officers, who contributed to a band fund at their discretion.

By the end of the eighteenth century these newly-organized regimental bands had made a small but secure place for themselves in popular concert life. There are records of public concerts in parks and city squares in most of the countries of western Europe, with bands of from eight to twelve players. For court events, larger bands were occasionally assembled by the merger of several small units. In *1782,* a band of thirty-six players provided the music for a fête held at the Trianon Palace in honor of the Grand Duke Paul of Russia. In *1783,* the Duke of York imported from Germany a band of twelve players for the Coldstream Guards: two oboes, four clarinets, two horns, two bassoons, one trumpet and one serpent. When trombones and drums were added to this group a few years later, it became one of the first truly "modern" bands.

The end of the eighteenth century closes what we may properly call "the early period" in band history for, as has already been noted, the "modern" band begins with the French Revolution. The band of the National Guard was organized on the initiative of a young musician, Bernard Sarrette (*1765-1858*), whose name should be venerated by bandsmen as one of the most important in the history of band music. The setting was, of course, exactly right for Sarrette's enterprise: stirring music was demanded for the large popular assemblies, demonstrations and ceremonies of the years following *1789.* Nor was Sarrette alone in his enthusiasm. Other bands came into being, often as a result of the combination of small regimental or civic groups. The free municipalities supported them generously. The National Guard band itself was augmented to seventy players in *1790,* quite the largest and most completely satisfactory band ever known up to that time, and its leadership was assumed by François Joseph Gossec (*1734-1829*), with Charles Simon

⟦ EUROPEAN ORIGINS ⟧

Catel (*1773-1830*) as assistant conductor. These men were among the leading composers of France; they not only served as bandmasters, but wrote the first real masterpieces of *original band music.*

The National Guard Band was dissolved in *1792* for reasons of economy, but Sarrette used it as the nucleus for a training school, the Free Music School of the Parisian National Guard which, when merged in *1795* with the old Royal School of Singing, became the French National Conservatory. Sarrette became the first Director of the Conservatory, and served in this capacity until *1814.* The Conservatory during all these early years continued to support, encourage and develop the growth of excellent military music, and played a vital role in band history. In fact, it would be fair to say that no institution or period has been more important in the entire historical development of bands and band music.

To emphasize this, I should like to quote three sentences from the leading English historian of military music, H. G. Farmer, who, in his little volume *Military Music,* states: "What contributed most to France's pre-eminence in military music was *the need for it.* Secondly, *it had composers of the mettle of Gossec, Catel, Méhul and Cherubini in command.* Thirdly, the band of the National Guard was composed of 'the greatest *virtuosi* in Europe.'" The italics are mine; these points are as important today as they ever were, and deserve most thoughtful and constant consideration by all who are seriously interested in the welfare of bands and band music.

French military bands, of course, had their ups and downs; they became larger or smaller as economy dictated, but they never lost the impetus that had been given them, and for years they set the example for all of Europe. Bands in England and Germany soon grew in size and capability. Early in the nineteenth century, leading regimental bands in England had grown from groups of eight to twelve players to ensembles numbering up to thirty-five. The score of Beethoven's *Military March* in D, composed in *1816,* calls for a minimum of thirty-two players. By *1825,* nearly all the standard infantry and artillery bands in Europe consisted of between thirty and forty performers.

⟦ EUROPEAN ORIGINS ⟧

After Sarrette and the Band of the National Guard, the greatest forward movement in band music came from the celebrated Wilhelm Wieprecht (*1802-1872*) and his reorganization of the military music of Prussia. Wieprecht not only made excellent recommendations concerning the instrumentation and proportions of bands, but decisively demonstrated the advantages of using horns and trumpets equipped with valves. Wieprecht's first successes took place in the *1830*'s. The invention of the valve mechanisms is usually credited to Charles Claggett, in about *1813;* Adam Carse, however, contends that they were actually developed by the German, Stoelzel, and later improved by his countryman, Bluehmel, and by Wieprecht himself. Wieprecht had experimented also with the keyed bugle, developed around *1810* by James Halliday, an English bandmaster, and improved by John Distin, who became one of the most celebrated of the early virtuosi on this instrument. Wieprecht, however, soon abandoned this instrument in favor of those with valve mechanisms, as did most other progressive bandmasters. The keyed bugle was played as late as the *1850*'s in the United States by Ned Kendall and Joseph Greene; it was Patrick Gilmore who once and for all demonstrated the superiority of the newer instruments for American bands.

Much of band history centers on the development and improvement of instruments. There are many treatises on this subject, and it is surely safe to say that musical instruments are still, and perhaps always will be, in a state of evolution. The contributions of Wieprecht, the Belgian Adolphe Sax and the German Theobald Boehm were, however, outstanding, and they have left a mark not only on the design and manufacture of the instruments themselves, but on all subsequent band music.

Wieprecht's contribution went beyond reforms in the area of instruments and instrumentation. He was also one of the founders of the nineteenth century band repertoire. Mention has already been made of his transcriptions for band of Beethoven symphonies; in addition to these he arranged two complete symphonies of Mozart, as well as dozens of overtures of the Classic and Romantic composers, and innumerable operatic excerpts and potpourris. His example was widely followed in other countries, and the basis of the band repertoire for almost the next hundred years was firmly established.

By *1850* or thereabouts, the band was in every important respect very much the band that we know today. There were, of course, as there still are, arguments about the "correct" or the "best" instrumentation, arguments that were as inconclusive then as they are today. The sizes of bands varied, usually because of budgetary considerations and military tables of organization. In general, the various countries of Europe engaged in a wholesome rivalry as to the size, proficiency and uniforming of their principal bands, and bands became a colorful manifestation of musical nationalism. This nationalism of course was also reflected in the patriotic nature of much of the repertoire, as it still is today.

The mid-nineteenth century also saw the birth of massed-band festivals and of band contests, the precursors of those now presented by American schools and colleges. Wieprecht staged a grand massed band festival as early as *1838,* with the combined bands of sixteen regiments, totalling over *1000* performers, plus *200* extra side drummers. This was in honor of the visit to the King of Prussia of the Russian Emperor Nicholas. According to accounts, the uniforming of the performers was magnificent, but Wieprecht himself almost ruined the show by conducting in civilian clothes. This so annoyed the Emperor that Wieprecht was rushed to a military tailor who, it is said, fitted him out with proper gorgeousness for the repeat performance four days later. This little anecdote may be taken as the reader wishes; it may add some light on the historical status and function of bands.

Perhaps the greatest band contest of all time took place in Paris in *1867*. Bands from France, Austria, Prussia, Belgium, Spain, Russia, Holland, Baden and Bavaria took part, each playing a required piece (Weber's *Oberon* Overture) and one of its own choice. It is interesting to note that the Belgian and Dutch bands included string basses. They were apparently the first bands to do so. The selected pieces give a clear picture of the kind of music favored by bands of the era, and the list should be of considerable interest to bandsmen today:

〖 EUROPEAN ORIGINS 〗

Baden: Finale of *The Lorelei*   Felix Mendelssohn
Spain: Fantasy on National Airs
Prussia: Fantasy on *The Prophet*   G. Meyerbeer
Austria: Overture, *William Tell*   G. A. Rossini
Belgium: Potpourri on *William Tell*   G. A. Rossini
Bavaria: Introduction and Bridal Chorus
     from *Lohengrin*   Richard Wagner
Holland: Fantasy on *Faust*   Charles Gounod
Paris Guards: Bridal Chorus and Wedding
     March from *Lohengrin*   Richard Wagner
Russia: Fantasy on National Airs
Paris Guides: Fantasy on *The Carnival of Venice*

The judges of the contest, who were among the most distinguished musicians of the time, included Hans von Bülow, Félicien David, Ambroise Thomas, Léo Delibes, Eduard Hanslick and Georges Kastner. (Kastner was a composer of operas much esteemed in his day, and the author of the first modern treatise on instrumentation, which appeared some years before that of Berlioz.) The judges apparently had a difficult time, and in order to avoid starting a nineteenth century World War, divided the first prize among the bands of Prussia, conducted by Wieprecht, Austria, conducted by Zimmermann, and the Paris Guards, conducted by Paulus. Wieprecht's band was the largest participating, with a roster of eighty-five; the other bands averaged sixty players each.

The instrumentation of Wieprecht's band for this occasion deserves noting in full, not only because of its size, but because of the extremely interesting distribution. The modern reader will note particularly the emphasis on the top and bottom registers of the band:

     4 flutes and piccolos
     4 oboes (and English horn)
     1 A♭ clarinet (sopranino)

[EUROPEAN ORIGINS]

 4 E♭ or F clarinets
16 B♭ clarinets (8, 1st; 8, 2nd)
 6 bassoons
 4 contra bassoons
 4 B♭ cornets
 4 E♭ cornets (altos)
 8 trumpets (in G, F, E♭, E and D)
 4 French horns
 4 tenor horns
 2 baritone horns
 8 trombones
 6 bass tuba
 6 percussion

English bands were not represented at the *1867* contest, but comparable progress had been made in that country. As a result of the many differences in organization, instrumentation, and even of pitch, a unifying agency was instituted in a Military Music Class at Kneller Hall, near London, in *1857*. The prime movers in this establishment were James Smyth, leader of the Royal Artillery Band, and Henry Schallehn, a former bandmaster of the Seventeenth Lancers. The Class began to train bandmasters for the service, and received official status in *1875*. In *1887*, it became known as The Royal Military School of Music, but is still familiarly known to bandsmen as Kneller Hall.

Many nineteenth century English bandmasters achieved lasting fame. Among them should be mentioned J. A. Kappey (Chatham Marines) (*1826-1906*), Ladislao Zavertal (Royal Artillery) (*1849-1942*), Sir Daniel Godfrey (Grenadier Guards) (*1831-1903*), and Carl Boosé (Royal Horse Guards) (*1815-1869*). Godfrey was conductor not only of the Grenadier Guards, but also for many years conducted the municipal orchestra at Bournemouth. He made many band arrangements which still rank among the finest of their kind, and which are still in use in both England and the United States.

[EUROPEAN ORIGINS]

The instrumentation of the band of the Grenadier Guards under Daniel Godfrey (c. *1888*) may be of interest, especially in view of the tendency toward standardization taking place at the time in England:

1 piccolo	6 cornets
2 flutes	2 trumpets
2 oboes	4 French horns
4 E♭ clarinets	1 baritone horn
14 B♭ clarinets	3 trombones
1 E♭ tenor (alto?) clarinet	4 euphoniums
1 B♭ bass clarinet	6 bombardons
2 bassoons	3 percussion
1 contra bassoon	

Total: 57 players

The reader will note here, as with Wieprecht's band, the attention given to the top and bottom registers, and the minimizing of the over-strength of the alto and tenor registers.

The relationship among the sometimes complicated factors in band music received a happy solution in England in the nineteenth century, owing to the intelligence and good will of bandmasters, military authorities and publishers. Until the middle of the century, little band music was available in published form. Bandmasters, or their assistants, made arrangements as required or desired; bands having more talented arrangers were clearly the most fortunate. There was a certain amount of circulation and copying of manuscript arrangements, but this could obviously be of limited scope, at best. It was largely through the efforts of Carl Boosé that regular publication of military band arrangements was undertaken. In *1846*, the firm of Boosey and Company undertook the regular issuance of *Boosé's Journal,* with Boosé himself as editor. The *Journal* met with such success that other publishers soon followed suit. The entrepreneur Jullien commenced a regular band series with Charles

Godfrey, Sr. as editor. These journals of band music had the immediate effect not only of providing a good supply of well-arranged band music, but also the most important one of accelerating a tendency toward a uniform instrumentation, one designed to take advantage of the intelligently executed arrangements offered in these publications. Thus, for the first time, a *musical* unifying force was brought to bear on the practice of all British bands. The editions of Boosey and Company, and later of Chappell's *Army Journal,* also instituted during the nineteenth century, exerted a very strong influence on the instrumentation and repertoire of bands in the United States, as well as those of the British Empire.

3

H ★ I ★ S ★ T ★ O ★ R ★ Y

of

BAND

music

U ★ S ★ A

⟦ BAND MUSIC, U.S.A. ⟧

REVOLUTION TO THE CIVIL WAR

It is only natural that American bands should in general have followed English models, not only in Colonial times but throughout most of their history until the very recent past. Some small units accompanied British troops in the early days, and the American settlers themselves brought their own recollections of music in England. Later, the men who made the modern band in America, among them Patrick Gilmore and Allen and Harvey Dodworth, came from England or Ireland. A primary factor from *1846* on, as has been noted, was the availability of the excellent editions of Boosey and later of Chappell and Schott, which provided American bands with their principal sources of printed music, and which, of course, were issued with British bands in view.

The earliest American bandmaster of whom we have record is Josiah Flagg (*1738-1794*) of Boston. Flagg was an energetic musician and entrepreneur; his *Collection of the Best Psalm Tunes* (*1764*) had been engraved by Paul Revere. He organized many sorts of concerts, including one in *1771* advertised as featuring vocal and instrumental music "accompanied by French horns, Hautboys etc." to be given by the band of the *64th* Regiment. This is the earliest reference to a regimental band (obviously British) to be found on this side of the Atlantic. Flagg formed a band of his own in *1773*, and gave some concerts in Faneuil Hall. Lacking adequate records, we cannot be sure what sort of band it was, although it is reputed to have numbered fifty players. Secular music, as we know, was not greatly encouraged in New England, and it is probable that Flagg's career as bandmaster was short-lived. He disappears from view soon after *1773*.

Bands are said to have given outdoor concerts in other parts of the new country during and immediately after the Revolution. There were adequate, although not abundant, resources for all sorts of musical endeavors by *1800*. (The first mention of French horns in America, for example, is made by Benjamin Franklin, who wrote in *1756* of the fine music provided by flutes, oboes, French horns and trumpets, accompanied by the organ, in Bethlehem, Pennsylvania.) In *1798*, New York saw the establishment of the "Columbia Garden Summer Concerts," but we do not know what sort of band or orchestra was employed. Oratorio and opera performances were given in both Philadelphia and New York with some regularity, and various musical societies were active in all of the principal cities.

We have, unfortunately, very little real information about American bands before *1800*, and must assume their existence from indirect evidence. Thus, we know that the *Federal March*[1] of Alexander Reinagle (*1756-1809*) was performed, presumably by a band, in *1788*, for the Fourth of July procession in Philadelphia, celebrating the ratification of the Federal Constitution by ten of the states. Similar inferences as to band performance may be made with respect to *The President of the United States March* (*1789*) by Stephen Sicard, as well as *General Washington's Grand March*[2] and others of the period. Among typical quicksteps may be cited the *Massachusetts March* (Boston, *1791*) by Frederick Granger and *General Pinckney's March* (Charleston, S.C., *1799*) by a Mr. Foucard. We know also that James Hewitt (*1770-1827*), composer of the opera *Tammany,* produced in *1794* in New York, and of the famous "military sonata" *The Battle of Trenton,* composed a *New York Rangers March* (New York, *1799*) and that he was for several years "director of all the military bands in New York." Unfortunately, we do not know very much about the bands themselves. But we have, at least, evidence that they existed, and we may conjecture that they were rather small.

There is, however, information about two bands formed before *1800*, that constitute a glorious portion of American band history. The Massachusetts Band was formed in Boston in *1783*; it was known from about *1812* as The Green Dragon Band, changing its name again in about *1820*, to the Boston Brigade Band. It was this band that became, in *1859*, Gilmore's Band, the first great American band and undoubtedly one of the finest that has ever played. The second is the United States Marine

---

[1] See *Landmarks of Early American Music*, edited by the author and Roger Smith (New York: G. Schirmer, Inc., 1943), for reconstructed arrangements of this and the march of Sicard.
[2] The author's performance edition of this march appears in *Two Marches from Revolutionary America* (New York: Mercury Music Corporation).

⟦ **ILLUSTRATION I** ⟧

Title page of the first edition of "Battle of Trenton." From the author's collection

⟦ **ILLUSTRATION II** ⟧

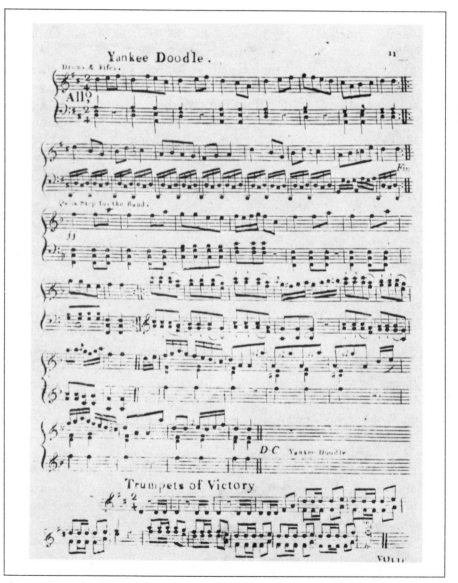

A page from the first edition of "Battle of Trenton." From the author's collection

⟦ BAND MUSIC, U.S.A. ⟧

Band, officially organized in *1798,* with William Farr as drum major. The original instrumentation is unknown, but by the end of the year *1800,* the Band consisted of two oboes, two clarinets, two horns, a bassoon and a drum. It thus resembled the regulation small bands of the eighteenth century in Europe.

The Marine Band has been the Presidential band since its inception, and has been heard by every President except George Washington. It has always been a feature of the capital, not only through its appearances at ceremonials and state affairs, but by its public concerts which were first given as early as *1800.* The instrumentation and size of the band grew slowly, and for many years it was not as proficient or as versatile musically as many of the civilian bands. It was not, in fact, until *1861* that its strength was authorized as thirty musicians, and not until *1899* that sixty musicians were authorized. Musically speaking, the Marine Band made its greatest strides under the direction of its most famous leader, John Philip Sousa, from *1882* to *1892.*

Most of the early nineteenth century bands were attached to local militia regiments. They were thus partly military, but on the whole should probably be considered civilian bands, since their personnel were not regularly involved in military duties and the bands were relatively independent units. They of course participated in all local parades, drills and ceremonies, but they also gave many concerts. Among the earliest of these bands were the Salem (Mass.) Brigade Band (established *1806*), the Militia Band of Bethlehem, Pa., and the *11th* Regiment Band of New York (established *1810*). Complete records of all these bands in their early days are not available. They were probably all mixed bands of irregular instrumentation, for we know that many, if not most of them, converted themselves to brass bands a few decades later. The original instrumentation of the Salem Brigade Band, for instance, consisted of five clarinets, two bassoons, one trumpet, triangle and bass drum; a few years later one French horn, two trombones and a serpent were added.

Additional light on the instrumental constitution and repertoire of American bands in the first two decades of the nineteenth century comes from the examination of publications such as the *Washington*

⟦ BAND MUSIC, U.S.A. ⟧

Guards March (*1804,* composer unknown), *Jefferson's March* (Philadelphia, B. Carr, *1805*) by Reinagle, and other popular quicksteps such as the *Bangor March* and the *Bristol March,* both given in Oliver Shaw's compilation *For the Gentlemen* (Dedham, Mass., *1807*) in a scoring for flute, two clarinets and bassoon. Samuel Holyoke's *Instrumental Assistant* (Exeter, N.H., *1807*) gives other quicksteps such as the *Massachusetts March* in a larger scoring for oboes, clarinets, horns and bassoons. Shaw (*1778-1848*) and Holyoke (*1762-1820*) were two of the most prominent early New England psalm-tune composers and among the few who wrote secular music. Holyoke's collection (in two volumes) is among the earliest musical publications in score to appear in the United States. Other early publications of interest to bandsmen are the *Military Music of Camp Dupont* (Philadelphia, George E. Blake, *1816*) and Robinson's *Massachusetts Collection of Martial Music* (*1818*).

The New England brass bands enjoyed their most active and prosperous period from the early *1830*'s to the outbreak of the Civil War, although some, like the American Band of Providence, R.I., remained active long afterwards. The Boston Brass Band was founded in *1835,* with Edward (Ned) Kendall (*1808-1861*), the most famous virtuoso of his time on the keyed bugle, as leader. His brother, James Kendall, almost equally celebrated as a performer on the "clarionet," was for some years leader of the Boston Brigade Band. The American Band was founded in *1842,* with W. F. Marshall as "conductor" and Joseph Greene, formerely of the Boston Brass Band, as 'leader." This band attained its greatest fame after *1866,* when its leadership was assumed by one of America's great bandmasters, D(avid) W(allis) Reeves (*1838-1900*).

An equally famous brass band was that of Easton, Pa., formed in *1830*, with Peter Pomp as leader. From about *1849*, its leader was Thomas Coates (*1818-1895*), another of America's most celebrated bandmasters. Pennsylvania was a center of great activity in band music, a not surprising fact in view of the musical traditions of the Moravian communities. The oldest civilian concert band still performing in the United States today was formed in Allentown in *1828;* in length of continuous existence, it is second only to the Marine Band. Other early and famous bands that

⟦ ILLUSTRATION III ⟧

HOLLOWAY'S FAREWELL CONCERT.
VOCAL AND INSTRUMENTAL.
MASONIC TEMPLE.

Saturday Evening, March 11th, 1837.

THE following gentlemen have kindly offered their valuable services, viz: Messrs. T. Comer, Williamson, W. B. Oliver, C. Stedman, A. Denton, S. G. Adams, Lathrop, Thomas, and the MEMBERS OF THE BOSTON BRASS BAND. Also, by the kind permission of Mr. Pelby, the members of the Orchestra attached to the National Theatre.

Solo Performers—Messrs E. Kendall, T Ryves and J. Hollo

Vocal Performers– Messrs T. Williamson, T. Comer, W. B. Oliver, C. Stedman, A. Denton, S. G. Adams, Lothrop and Thomas.

Leader of the Brass Band—Mr E. Kendall.
Leader of the Orchestra—Mr J. Holloway.

PART I.

Overture: Bronze Horse· Full Band. Auber.
Solo: E flat Bugle, by E. Kendall: Air Cinderella: received with rapturous applause at Mr Knæbel's Concert. Knæbel.
Quick Step. Lafayette Guards: Brass Band. J. Holloway
Song. By Mr Williamson: 'I have gazed on Beauty's Brow from the Bronze Horse. T. Comer
Glee and Chorus. 'When the wind blows,' from the 'Miller and his Men,' by W. B. Oliver, C. Stedman, A. Denton, S. G. Adams, Lothrop, Thomas. Bishop.
Quick-Step. Winslow Blues: Brass Band. J. Holloway
Solo. Trumpet Air and Variations by T. Ryves. S. Knæbel.
Quick-Step. 'Woodup,' composed and respectfully dedicated to the Washington Light Infantry. J. Holloway.

PART II.

Overture. Tancredi: Brass Band. Rossini.
Solo Violin. (First time in Boston) Scotch Air and Variations: J. Holloway, composed by A. Romberg.
Tucker's Quick Step New England Guards: Brass Band. S. Knæbel.
Song. Mr Williamson. 'The Warrior's Triumph,' (first time) Trumpet Obligato, by T. Ryves. A. Bennet.
Quick Step. 'The Roarers,' (1st time) composed: arranged and respectfully dedicated to the Rifle Rangers, by J. Holloway.
Song. 'The Sea,' by Wm B. Oliver. Neukomm.
Quick Step. Mechanic Riflemen: Brass Band. J. Holloway.
Laughing Trio. T. Comer, Williamson and W. B. Oliver.
Finale. Holloway's Farewell Quick Step, performed for the first time, by the Boston Brass Band, composed, and respectfully dedicated to the Military Companies of Massachusetts by J. Holloway.
☞ Performance to commence at o'clock precisely.
Tickets 50 cents each, may be had at Messrs Prentiss, Ashton and Wade's Music and at the door of the Masonic Temple on the evening of the performance. 3t m9

⟦ BAND MUSIC, U.S.A. ⟧

should be mentioned include the Barrington (N.H.) Band, founded in *1832;* the Rohrersville (Md.) Band, founded in *1837;* and the Stonewall Brigade Band of Staunton, Va., founded in *1845.*

Although the Allentown Band is the earliest civilian band which has continued to exist, the Independent Band of New York, founded in *1825,* was the first important completely professional band of its time. This band was extremely active from the very start, and had the good fortune to number among its members during its early years Thomas Dodworth and his son Allen. The Dodworths, with another son, Harvey, were among the most progressive and energetic musicians of the city, with admirable ideas about instrumentation and performance. All were performers, conductors and composers; in addition they were in business both as music publishers and as importers of instruments. In *1834,* Thomas Dodworth persuaded the Independent Band to change its instrumentation to brass exclusively, and to change its name to the City Brass Band. In *1836,* this band split, and part of it continued as the National Brass Band under the leadership of Allen Dodworth. Shortly afterward this organization became known as Dodworth's Band. For many years, in fact until Gilmore's arrival in New York in *1873,* Dodworth's Band was the finest in New York.

It was perhaps because of the prestige and influence of the Dodworths that most of the famous bands of the country became brass bands during the *1830's.* The Salem Brigade Band became the Salem Brass Band in *1835* or *1837;* the Boston Brigade Band became a brass band in *1838.* Some of the other famous all-brass bands have already been mentioned. A program of the Boston Brass Band, newly formed with Ned Kendall as leader, illustrates the type of music one might have heard at band concerts of this period. The concert, a farewell for the popular quickstep composer John Holloway (b. *1812*), took place in Boston on *March 11, 1837.*[3] (See page *40.*)

The American Band of Providence, like the Boston Brass Band, was a brass band from the start, and its instrumentation is typical of the period. Here is its roster, as given in a program of March *10, 1851:*

---

[3] Spellings in all programs reflect the style of the times.

〖 ILLUSTRATION IV 〗

The Boston Brass Band with its "new uniforms" and "improved instruments."   *Courtesy, The Bettmann Archive*

[[ILLUSTRATION V]]

First Eb cornet part of John Holloway's "Wood Up."

Courtesy, Family of John Holloway

⟦ BAND MUSIC, U.S.A. ⟧

W. J. Marshall, Conductor

J. C. Green, Leader, E♭ Bugle

E. A. Paine, E♭ Cornett

J. Lothrop, B♭ Bugle

B. G. West, Post Horn

W. W. Hull, Trumpet

L. W. Simmons, Alto

E. K. Reynolds, Alto

B. J. Bliven, Tenor

E. F. Paine, Tenor

S. R. Sweet, Baritone

H. E. Barney, Bass

Thos. Thorpe, Bass

T. D. Paine, Bass

O. W. Keach, Side Drum

H. A. Potter, Bass Drum

W. L. Reynolds, Cymbals

Few of the bands of the time gave concerts without the assistance of vocal and instrumental soloists, who were often accompanied by a piano rather than by the band. The American Band's concert of February *3, 1851,* was no exception. The soloist was Miss Emily B. Carpenter, and the program shown on page *45* was a typical one.

The programs of these bands founded prior to *1850* are instructive, and obviously constitute our best source material for the band repertoire of the time. See page *47* for another American Band program.

These programs are quite typical of the period prior to the Civil War. One will look in vain for more substantial repertoire than that represented by the few Verdi or Rossini overtures (with some by Auber, Cherubini or Mercadante) and the dozens of polkas, galops, quadrilles and waltzes by Labitzky, Gung'l and other fashionable composers. Among the pieces by native composers we find more of the same, plus some patriotic medleys and a few good marches. The names of these early American march composers are now almost forgotten, but their works are authentic musical Americana and they deserve a place in our band history.[4]

Among the most celebrated band pieces of the period were two by John Holloway, the *Wood Up Quickstep* and the *Winslow Blues Quickstep. Wood Up* was a great show-piece as a cornet (or rather, keyed-

[4] The author has prepared new editions of many of these pieces. Some are now available; more will follow. The Goldman Band has recorded a few for Capitol records.

〚 ILLUSTRATION VI 〛

Howard Hall.

AMERICAN BRASS BAND'S CONCERTS.

This Association respectfully announce that their Third Concert of the Course will be given in

HOWARD HALL

Monday Evening, Feb. 3, 1851.

On which occasion they will be assisted by

MISS EMILY B. CARPENTER,

And

MR. C. A. ADLER.

CONDUCTOR, W. F. MARSHALL,
LEADER, J. C. GREENE,
PIANO FORTE, C. A. ADLER.

PROGRAMME.

PART I.

1. ELFIN QUICK STEP—Band,..............................*W. F. Marshall.*
2. SONG OF AMERICA—Miss Carpenter,............ ....*Carl. Lobe.*
3. CORNET SOLO—(accompanied by Orchestra)—Mr. J. C. Greene,....*Romaine.*
4. PAS DE FLEURS—Band,................................*Max Maretzek.*
5. ROMANZA—"Sounds so entrancing,"—Miss Carpenter,......*Andreas Randel.*
6. OVERTURE—Donna del Largo——Band,..........................*Rossini.*

PART II.

1. GRAND WEDDING MARCH—From Mendelshon's Opera—
   "Midsummers Night Dream,"—arranged expressly for the
   Band, by W. F. Marshall,............... ....*Mendelshon,*
2. SONG—"Let the bright Seraphim,"—Miss E. B. Carpenter,—
   with Trumpet Obligato by Mr. J. C. Greene,....................*Handel.*
3. SEPTETTE—From Anaille—("Rest Spirit, Rest,)—Miss Carpenter.....*Rooke.*
4. POLKA—Band,..*A. Dodsworth.*
5. CAVATINA—"Twas no vision," —From I. Lombardi—Miss
   Carpenter, ...*Verdi.*
6. EVERGREEN GALLOP—Band,...............................*Labitzky.*

Tickets for two or more 25 cts each.   Single Tickets 37.

N. B.—Holders of Season Tickets are requested to exchange them at the door for an Evening Ticket to the remaining Concert.
☞ The FOURTH and *LAST CONCERT*, will take place about Feb. 24th.

Doors open at 6 1-2 o'clock.   Concert commence at 7 1-2.

〖 ILLUSTRATION VII 〗

Howard Hall.

LAST GRAND CONCERT OF THE COURSE,

BY THE

AMERICAN BRASS BAND

The Band respectfully announce their FOURTH CONCERT will be given in

HOWARD HALL

ON MONDAY EVENING, MARCH 10, 1851,

They will be assisted by

Miss Emily B. Carpenter.

MR. C. A. ADLER,

Will preside at the Piano Forte.

W. F. Marshall, Conductor,	E. F. Paine, Tenor,
J. C. Greene, Leader, Eb Bugle,	S. R. Sweet, Baritone,
L. A. Paine, Eb Cornett,	H. E. Barney, Bass,
J. Lothrop, Bb Bugle,	Thos. Thorpe, Bass,
B. G. West, Post Horn,	T. D. Paine, Bass,
W. W. Hall, Trumpet,	O. W. Keach, Side Drum,
L. W. Simmons, Alto,	M. A. Potter, Bass Drum,
E. K. Reynolds, Alto,	W. L. Reynolds, Cymbals.
B. J. Bliven, Tenor,	

PROGRAMME--PART I.

1. GRAND KOSSUTH MARCH—Band..................................*Lenschow*
2. SERENADE—"On the Adria's Sea,"—Miss CARPENTER................*Linbad*
3. GRAND CONCERT WALTZES—respectfully dedicated to the
   American Brass Band to the subscribers and patrons of their
   Concerts of 1850—51, composed expressly for this occasion by. *W.F.Marshall*
4. ARIA—From Mansadiere.—"With what rapture."—Miss CARPENTER.....*G. Verdi*
5. AIR—"We can love no more," and Polacca,—Band,..................*Grafulla*
6. SONG—"Lament of the Alpine Shepherd Boy,"—with Flute,
   Miss CARPENTER,..*I' H. Brown*

PART II.

1. GRAND OVERTURE—de la Opera Faniska,—arranged by.....*W F. Marshall*
2. SONG—"O steal to my lattice,"—Miss CARPENTER,................*Rodwell*
3. CELEBRATED DRUM POLKA, (by request,)........................*Strauss*
4. KAZNEAU'S QUICKSTEP—Band,...............................*F. H. Brown*
5. SCENA AND CAVATINA from Ernani—Miss CARPENTER,..........*G. Verdi*
6. AIR—Bonny Deli and Shaker Song, Fi! Hi! Hi!—Band,................

DOORS OPEN AT 6 1-2 O'CLOCK......CONCERT COMMENCE AT 7 1-2 O'CLOCK.

TICKETS 25 CENTS—To be had at the usual places.

Printed by A. C. GREENE; 15 Market Square.

[**ILLUSTRATION VIII**]

Howard Hall.

AMERICAN BRASS BAND'S CONCERTS.

The Band respectfully announce their FIRST Concert of the Course will be given at

HOWARD HALL

On Monday Evening, Dec. 30th,

They will be assisted by

MD'LLE. LOVARNY,

Who will sing some of her favorite

ARIAS AND BALLADS.

MR. C. A. AADLER,

Will preside at the Piano Forte.

The **GRAND PIANO** used will be of **Chickering's** celebrated Manufacture and used by **JENNY LIND** at her Concerts.

PROGRAMME.

PART I.

1—**Napoleon's Grand Coronation March,**
    The first piece performed in public by the Band after its organization.
2—**By the Sad Sea Waves**—Md'lle Lovarny,.........*Benedict.*
3—**Solo**—Eb Bugle—Thema Gramachree—J. C. Greene, .*S. Knœbel.*
4—**Arnhiem Quick Step**—Band,.............*W. F. Marshall.*
5—**On the Banks of the** Gaudalquivir, Md'lle Lovarny, *Lavenue.*
6—**Cavatina**—Una Voce poco fa—Band,..............*Rossini.*

PART II.

1—**Overture**—N'l Opera Tancredi—Band,.............*Rossini.*
2—**Coming thro' the Rye,**—Md'lle Lovarny,.........—
3—**Quartette**—From Semiramide—Cornett, Alto, Bari-
    tone and Bass Tubas,...........................*Rossini.*
4—**Zephyr Polka**—Band,.....................*W. F. Marshall.*
    [This Polka is just published for Piano Forte and for sale at Leland's.]
5—**The Swiss Girl,**—Md'lle Lovarny,.................*Linley.*
6—**Winslow Blue's Quick Step,**.............*J. Holloway.*

**Tickets for the Course $1. Family Tickets for three or
    more, 25cts.   Single Tickets, 37½ cts,**
To be had at the Book and Music Stores and at the door.

Doors open at 6 1-2 o'clock.   Concert commence at 7 1-2.

A. C. GREENE, Printer, 15 Market Square, Providence, R. I.

bugle) solo, in addition to being a band piece. It was, in fact, *Wood Up* that was used as the competition piece in the famous solo contest held in *1856*, between Ned Kendall, playing the keyed bugle, and Gilmore, playing the new-fangled cornet. Holloway's *Mechanick's Quickstep* was almost as popular. All these pieces were written in the *1830*'s and remained popular for many years. They were published only in piano editions; presumably each band made its own arrangement.

Another famous and enormously popular piece of the period was *The Wrecker's Daughter,* a quickstep by Conrad Fay. Like *Wood Up,* this was also used as a bugle solo. The same is true of *Money Musk,* a favorite of Kendall and Greene. W. F. Marshall and the Dodworth brothers wrote many quicksteps and dance pieces, Allen Dodworth's *Jenny Lind Polka* being characteristic. The piano edition of the latter advertises that the *Polka* was featured by "Dodworth's Famous Cornet Band."

Other prominent and popular composers of quicksteps and miscellaneous band pieces during the period *1830-1860* include James Hooton, B. A. Burditt, Tom Comer, Charles Zeuner, George Farmer and, somewhat later, the bandmasters D. L. Downing, D. W. Reeves and Thomas Carter. Henry Schmidt, piano teacher of William Mason, also wrote some fine marches. Many of these pieces have for us a quaint period charm, a kind of gay innocence and nostalgic appeal. They should be restored to the repertoire, not only for the variety they lend a program, but as reminders of the old days of American band music.

GILMORE AND HIS TIMES: 1829-1892

The man who changed the history of band music in America, Patrick Sarsfield Gilmore, arrived in Massachusetts in *1848*. Gilmore was born in County Galway, Ireland, on December *25, 1829*. As a very young man he joined a regimental band, with which he traveled to Canada, coming from there to the United States at the age of nineteen. He soon

⟦ BAND MUSIC, U.S.A. ⟧

established himself as the greatest cornet virtuoso yet heard on these shores. It was Gilmore, in fact, who established the superiority of the cornet over the keyed bugle, besting the great Ned Kendall in a spectacular contest which at once proved the superiority of both the player and the instrument. Soon after his arrival, Gilmore became active as a bandmaster, serving as leader of the Boston Brass Band from *1852,* and assuming the leadership of the Salem Brass Band in *1855.*

Gilmore did not form a mixed reed and brass band until *1859.* The credit for reversing the trend to the all-brass band belongs to two New York bandmasters, Kroll and Reitsel, who in *1853* reorganized the New York Seventh Regiment Band as a mixed woodwind and brass ensemble. (The Dodworth Band must have added reed instruments at about the same time, for it is known that the Dodworths were importing saxophones and other woodwinds.) The Seventh Regiment Band was merged in *1860* with another famous New York group, the Shelton Band, led by one of the finest of the early bandmasters, C. S. Grafulla, an outstanding arranger and composer of marches and characteristic pieces which were tremendously popular in their time. Under Grafulla, the band of the Seventh Regiment consisted of about sixty players, and rivalled Dodworth's in excellence. A third celebrated New York band of this time was that of the Ninth Regiment, under D. L. Downing, also well known as a composer and arranger of band music.

In *1859,* Gilmore was invited to become leader of the Boston Brigade Band. He accepted the invitation on condition that the band would really be *his* band: that it would henceforth be known as *Gilmore's Band,* and that he would run it as a completely professional and proprietary affair, just as Dodworth's Band was run. In other words, Gilmore wished to assume not only the conductorship, but the financial responsibility and risk as well as the profits, the complete power to book engagements, and to conduct all other musical and non-musical affairs. Gilmore's conditions were accepted without hesitation, and a new chapter in American band history was begun. The original Gilmore Band of *1859* consisted of thirty-two players, freshly uniformed and equipped by Gilmore, who rehearsed regularly and fulfilled a strenuous schedule of engagements. Gilmore also began building the library of band music for which American bands are still indebted.

It must be remembered that in the days of Gilmore, and in fact until the early years of the twentieth century, the so-called "military" band not only performed at concerts and parades and public ceremonies, but also provided dance music and music for social entertainments. In other words, the band had a varied field in which to operate for profit. Gilmore took full advantage of this. He provided music for anything and anybody with money to pay for his services, and would provide a band of any size or shape to suit the occasion. But it is important to remember that the music that he had to perform for the various types of engagements did not actually vary to any important extent; the polkas, waltzes, quadrilles and even the marches were dance music as well as general repertoire.

Gilmore's band business—and it was a *business!*—was interrupted by the outbreak of the Civil War, which channeled his energies in other directions for several years, but also gave him the opportunity to demonstrate on a much wider scale his enormous talents for organization and leadership. The Gilmore Band enlisted as a unit in October, *1861,* with the *24th* Massachusetts Volunteer Regiment, serving with distinction, and providing a model for other bands until the dissolution and mustering-out of all volunteer bands in August, *1862.* Gilmore and his musicians returned to Boston, where they began giving concerts to sustain morale at home, one of the historic functions of bands during all wars. At the same time, he was asked by the Governor of Massachusetts to re-organize the state's military bands. Gilmore organized and sent out a number of new bands, accompanying one of them to New Orleans, where he was asked by General Banks to take charge of the music in his command. Oddly enough, however, Gilmore was not called on when, in *1862,* the War Department formed an advisory board on bands. This board was composed of Gilmore's leading contemporaries: Harvey Dodworth, Thomas Coates, C. S. Grafulla and D. L. Downing.

It was while he was occupied with military band matters in New

⟦ BAND MUSIC, U.S.A. ⟧

Orleans that Gilmore conceived the first of the mammoth band festivals that made him a national celebrity. For the inauguration of Governor Michael Hahn, Gilmore, at the request of General Banks, assembled a "Grand National Band" consisting of some *500* Army bandsmen plus a number of additional drum and bugle players, and obtained permission to organize a chorus of *5000* school children. The event took place in Lafayette Square on March *4, 1864.* The program consisted largely of patriotic tunes, ending with *Hail, Columbia.* For this finale, Gilmore added thirty-six cannon, which he fired by electric buttons from the podium. This was his first taste of spectacular effect of this sort, and it evidently gave him an appetite for more—which was so fulsomely gratified in the later festivals in Boston.

Gilmore returned to Boston after the New Orleans triumph, and gave regular concerts for several seasons, as well as fulfilling any and all other engagements that he could secure. A typical Gilmore program of this period is one of December *23, 1868* (page *52*), presented by a band of twenty-five pieces, but still billed as "Gilmore's Grand Boston Band." Admission was fifty cents; reserved seats seventy-five cents.

The National Peace Jubilee of *1869* brought to fruition a dream which Gilmore had held for many years. His driving ability, enthusiasm and persuasiveness won over almost all the staid and conservative doubters of Boston and, in fact, of the entire country. The National Peace Jubilee was infinitely grander than anything brought off up to that time. It combined the showmanship and musicianship of Jullien, with appeals to Patriotism, Education and just about every other sure-fire cause. The forces assembled included an orchestra of *500,* a band of *1000,* a chorus of *10,000* and a vast array of soloists. Ole Bull served as concertmaster, Edward Everett Hale gave the invocation at the opening concert, Oliver Wendell Holmes provided words for a *Hymn of Peace,* Lowell Mason gave the proceedings his blessing, and President Grant and his entire Cabinet lent the prestige of their attendance.

The Jubilee opened on June *15, 1869,* and continued for five days. After the grand opening concert came a symphony and oratorio concert, then a "People's Day." The fourth concert was for the "high-

J. C. GREENE'S CONCERTS.

The public are respectfully informed that the first Concert of J. C. Greene's Second Annual Course, will be given in the

CITY HALL,

— ON —

WEDNESDAY EVENING, Dec. 23d, 1868,

— BY —

Gilmore's Grand Boston Band,

(TWENTY-FIVE PIECES,)

P. S. GILMORE, Conductor,

With the following eminent Soloists:

Mr. M. ARBUCKLE,

The Celebrated Cornet Player,

Herr SCHMIDT,

The Distinguished Clarinet Player,

Miss ANNA GRANGER,

The Excellent and Admired Soprano Vocalist,

Who has just returned from Europe.

⟦ ILLUSTRATION IX ⟧

PART FIRST.

1. GRAND OVERTURE—"Poet and Peasant." ....LUPPE.
   Gilmore's Orchestra.

2. CORNET SOLO—Sixth Air et Varié. ....DE BERIOT.
   M. Arbuchle.

3. POT POURRI—"Bohemian Girl." ....BALFE.
   Gilmore's Military Band.

4. NIGHTINGALE SONG—"The Marriage of Jeannette."...MASSE.
   Miss Anna Granger.

5. CLARINET SOLO—Thème et Varié. ... .SCHMIDT.
   Herr Schmidt.

6. SAILOR'S SONG—With Cornet Obligato.............C. KREBS.
   Cornet by M. Arbuchle, Sung by Miss Anna Granger.

⟦ ILLUSTRATION IX ⟧

PART SECOND.

7. OVERTURE—"William Tell."...................... Rossini.
Military Band.

8. CORNET SOLO—"Carnival de Venice."............Paganini.
R. Arbuckle, accompanied by Orchestra.

9. GRAND CORNET WALTZ—"Soldaten Lieder.".........Gungl.
Military Band.

10. ENGLISH SONG—..
Miss Anna Granger.

11. GRAND MEDLEY—"The Rage in London."............Riviere.
(Introducing Popular Melodies of the Day.)
Military Band.

Tickets, including Reserved Seats, 75 Cents each.

Tickets of Admission, - - - - - 50 Cents each.

The Front Seats *only* of the Gallery are reserved.

Doors will be open at 6½ o'clock.   Concert will commence at 7½.

☞ The next Concert of the series will be given in City Hall, on WEDNESDAY
EVENING, January 13th, upon which occasion the instrumental music will be furnished by the far-famed GERMANIA ORCHESTRA AND MILITARY BAND, and
the superb Soprano Vocalist, Miss ANNA S. WHITTEN, will appear here for the
first time, and sing some choice selections, with orchestral accompaniment.

〚 BAND MUSIC, U.S.A. 〛

brows" (Beethoven's *Fifth Symphony*) and the final concert featured a huge chorus of school children. The program of the "People's Day" concert is reproduced on pages 56-57.

But excitement and triumph, even on this scale, were not enough for Gilmore. The noise of the Jubilee had hardly died down when he began to plan an even larger "World Peace Jubilee," on a scale exactly double. This grand event took place in *1872*, and offered, just as Gilmore had promised, twice as much of everything. Not only that, but Gilmore had secured the participation of orchestras and bands from Europe, including the Band of the Grenadier Guards, under Daniel Godfrey; the Emperor William's Household Cornet Quartette; the orchestra of Johann Strauss; the Kaiser Franz Grenadier Regiment Band, under Heinrich Saro; the National Band of Dublin under Edwin Clements; and the Garde Républicaine Band under Paulus. There were also bands from the United States, including the Marine Band, under Herman Fries, and New York's Ninth Regiment Band, under D. L. Downing. The chorus for the *1872* Jubilee consisted of *20,000* voices, the band numbered *2000* and the orchestra almost *1000*. As soloists, a distinguished "bouquet of artists" participated. The expected cannon, anvils and other trimmings were all twice as big and twice as numerous. The Festival continued for ten days, and it is safe to say that nothing like it has been seen before or since. The program of the fifth day ("Austrian Day"), June *21, 1872* is shown on page *58*.

The "World Peace Jubilee" was another triumph for Gilmore. As an organizer and promoter, he was one of the greatest of all time. But it should be remembered that despite the vaudevillean character of some of his most famous exploits, he did a great deal of valuable work in the popularization of good music. This much was admitted even by his severest critics. Gilmore was to the band in America almost what his contemporary, Theodore Thomas, was to the orchestra.

The Jubilee of *1872* had one other result. The European bands had impressed all who heard them by their obvious superiority to any American bands. They thus set a standard of performance and repertoire

⟦ ILLUSTRATION X ⟧

THIRD DAY'S

Concert of the National Peace Jubilee.

<hr>

PART I.

1. OVERTURE, "Fra Diavolo." · · · · · · · · · · AUBER

   Arranged for Orchestra of One Thousand Performers, Fifty Trumpeters
   performing the solo part.

2. CHORAL, "Judgment Hymn." · · · · · · · · LUTHER

   Chorus, Organ, and Orchestra.

3. GRAND MARCH, "Peace Festival." · · · · · · · JANOTTA

   Composed for this occasion, and arranged for Grand Orchestra and
   Military Band combined.

4. ARIA, *Robert, toi qui j'aime.* · · · · · · · · MEYERBEER

   Sung by MADAME PAREPA ROSA.

5. SCENA, from "Il Trovatore," introducing the Anvil Chorus. · · VERDI
   With Chorus, Band of One Thousand, One Hundred Anvils, several Drum
   Corps, Artillery, Bells, &c. The Anvil part will be performed by
   One Hundred Members of the Boston Fire Department.

6. OVERTURE TRIOMPHALE, on the American National Air, "Hail
   Columbia." · · · · · · · · · · C. C. CONVERSE

   Introducing the Full Chorus, accompanied by the Orchestra, Military
   Band, and other accompaniments.

<hr>

INTERMISSION FIFTEEN MINUTES.

[ILLUSTRATION X]

PART II.

1. MARCHE MILITAIRE, "Prince Frederick." - - - - - - BILSE
   Band of One Thousand Performers.

2. NATIONAL AIR, "The Star Spangled Banner."
   Sung by MADAME PAREPA ROSA, with Chorus and Orchestral accompaniment.

3. ARIA FOR TRUMPET, from "Il Bravo." - - - - - - MERCADANTE
   Performed by M. ARBUCKLE, with Orchestra accompaniment.

4. THE HARP THAT ONCE THRO' TARA'S HALLS. - - - - - MOORE
   Arranged for Full Chorus, Grand Orchestra, Military Band and Organ.

5. OVERTURE, "Stradella." - - - - - - - - - - - FLOTOW
   Reed Band of Five Hundred Performers.

6. CHORAL, One Hundredth Psalm.
   Chorus, Organ, Orchestra, Military Band, &c. The audience is respectfully invited to join in the last verse.

The Vocal parts are led by the following eminent Soloists.

SOPRANOS:

Mrs. H. M. Smith,   Miss Graziella Ridgway,   Miss Nelly Fiske,
Mrs. Sophia Mozart,   Mrs. D. C. Hall,   Miss Lizzie M. Allen,
Miss L. M. Gates,   Miss S. W. Barton,   Miss Hattie M. Safford,
Miss Annie M. Granger   Mrs. J. W. Weston,   Miss Emma A. Hamlin.
Miss A. L. Whitten,

ALTOS:

Mrs. Drake,   Mrs. A. C. Monroe,   Mrs. W. H. Wadleigh,
Miss Addie S. Ryan,   Mrs. John J. Henry,   Mrs. Logan,
Mrs. Chas. A. Barry,   Mrs. Louisa A. Sharland,   Mrs. C. A. Guilmette,
Mrs. T. H. Emmons,   Mrs. S. Shattuck,   Mrs. J. T. Beers.

TENORS:

W. H. Daniel,   W. H. Davis,   D. F. Fittz,
James Whitney,   Geo. W. Hazlewood,   Allen A. Brown,
H. L. Whitney,   James P. Draper,   Dr. Langmaid.
L. W. Wheeler,   Edward Prescott,

BASSES:

P. H. Powers,   Signor Ardavani,   M. W. Whitney,
Charles H. McLellan,   J. E. Perkins,   Dr. C. A. Guilmette,
E. B. Fairbanks,   J. J. Kimball,   Hiram Wilde,
J. R. Rudolphsen,   Henry M. Aiken,   George W. Dudley.
H. C. Barnabee,

⟦ ILLUSTRATION XI ⟧

PROGRAMME.

PART I.

1. **NATIONAL HYMN.** "Angel of Peace," . . . . *Keller.*
Words by Dr. O. W. Holmes.
Chorus, Organ, Orchestra, and Bands.

2. **OVERTURE.** "Kaiser," . . . . *Westmayer.*
[Dedicated to the Emperor Francis Joseph I. of Austria.]
Orchestra.

3. **CHORUS.** "See, the Conquering Hero Comes." Judas Maccabeus, . *Handel.*
Chorus and Orchestra.

4. **GRAND ARIA.** (Selected.)
Madame Peschka-Leutner.

5. **SOLO FOR CORNET.** 7th Air E varie, De Beriot.
Mr. M. Arbuckle.

6. **CONCERT WALTZ.** "Kunstler Leben," . . . . *Strauss.*
Orchestra.
Conducted by Herr Johann Strauss.

PART II.

1. { *a.* OVERTURE. "Semiramide," . . . . *Rossini.*
   { *b.* SELECTION. Reminiscences of Meyerbeer.
Selected from Le Prophete, Les Huguenots, Robert le Diable, l'Etrole du Nord, &c.
Solos for Euphonium, by Mr. Lawford ; Cornet by Mr. Ellis ; Clarionet by } *Meyerbeer.*
Mr. Spencer.
BAND OF THE GRENADIER GUARDS.
(Scond appearance), Mr. Dan Godfrey, Leader.

2. **CHORUS.** "Sleepers Wake." "St. Paul," . . . . . *Mendelssohn.*
Chorus and Orchestra.

3. **PIANO SOLO.** (Selected.)
Madame Arabella Goddard.

4. **SEXTETTE.** FROM "LUCIA," Chi ma Frena, ... *Donizetti.*
Bouquet of Artists, Operatic Chorus, and Orchestra.

5. **FOUR PART SONG.** "Farewell to the Forest." (By request.) . *Mendelssohn.*
[Unaccompanied.]

6. **HYMN.** "Coronation," . . . . *Holden.*
The audience will please sing the 3d and 4th verses.

1. All hail the pow'r of Je-sus' name! Let an-gels prostrate fall; Bring forth the roy-al di - a - dem, And
2. Ye chosen seed of Israel's race, Ye ransom'd from the fall, Hail him who saves you by his grace, And
3. Let ev' - ry kindred, ev' - ry tribe, On this ter- res- trial ball, To him all ma- jes - ty as- cribe, And
4. O that with yonder sacred throng, We at his feet may fall; We'll join the ev - er- last- ing song, And

crown him Lord of all. Bring forth the roy - al di - a - dem, And crown him Lord of all.
crown him Lord of all. Hail him who saves you by his grace, And crown him Lord of all.
crown him Lord of all. To him all ma - jes - ty as - cribe, And crown him Lord of all.
crown him Lord of all. We'll join the ev - er- last-ing song, And crown him Lord of all.

for the American bands to take as a goal. Gilmore himself had already begun on this path with his own band, and the influence he exerted on all other American bands of his era was great and beneficent. This influence extended to both instrumentation and repertoire. Gilmore himself, aside from his taste for extravaganzas, was a sound leader and musician.

One more Gilmore program should be of interest. This one is dated December *9, 1876* and has been reproduced on pages *60-61.*

Gilmore unquestionably had the greatest soloists ever to appear with a band. Miss Lillian B. Norton was, of course, none other than the great singer who later achieved fame under the name of Nordica. Gilmore "discovered" her, and was the first to present her to the public.

Gilmore's greatest work was done after *1873,* when he accepted the leadership of the *22nd* Regiment Band of New York, on the same conditions he had imposed when he accepted the leadership of the Boston Brigade Band in *1859.* Under Gilmore, the *22nd* Regiment Band (universally known as Gilmore's Band) became the greatest of its time, and probably one of the greatest of all time. He had a roster of virtuoso musicians, including both Matthew Arbuckle and Jules Levy as cornet soloists. Trombonist Frederick Innes played in Gilmore's Band, as did dozens of America's (and Europe's) most brilliant wind instrumentalists. Gilmore toured the United States and Canada several times, and in *1878,* took his band on a tour of Europe. The band was hailed as the equal of any in the world at the time. Its instrumentation for the tour was as follows:

2 piccolos	2 bassoons
2 flutes	1 contrabassoon
2 oboes	1 E♭ soprano cornet
1 A♭ sopranino clarinet	4 B♭ cornets (1st and 2nd)
3 E♭ soprano clarinets	2 trumpets
16 B♭ clarinets	2 flügelhorns
(8, 1st; 4, 2nd; 4, 3rd)	4 French horns

PROGRAMME.

◆

PART FIRST.

◆

1.—OVERTURE, "Stabat Mater,"   - - - -   Rossini.

GILMORE'S BAND.

2.—PICCOLO SOLO, "Canary Polka,"   - - - DeCarlo.

Signor DE CARLO.

3.—ANDANTE, FIFTH SYMPHONY,   - - Beethoven.

GILMORE'S BAND.

4.—CORNET SOLO, "Fantasie Original," - - - Hartmann.

Mr. M. ARBUCKLE

5.—PIANO SOLO, "Paraphrase on Themes from Rigoletto," - Liszt.

Master HERMANN RIETZEL.

6.—SONG, "Good Bye, Sweetheart,"   - - - - Hatton.

Mr. W. H. STANLEY.

PROGRAMME.

PART SECOND.

7.—GRAND OPERA FANTASIE, - - - - MEYERBEER.

Including the gems of Le Prophete, L'Africaine, L'Etoile du Nord, Les Huguenots and other Operas.

GILMORE'S BAND.

8.—SCENA FROM IL TROVATORE, - - - VERDI.

Miss LILLIAN B. NORTON.

9.—SAXOPHONE SOLO.—Variations on " Casta Diva," - BELLINI.

Mr. E. A. LEFEBRE.

10.—OVERTURE,—" Jubel," - - - - - - WEBER.

GILMORE'S BAND.

Conductor, - - P. S. Gilmore.

The hall doors will remain closed during the performance of the last selection.

The Pianos used in the Gilmore Concerts are from the WEBER warerooms, Fifth Avenue and 16th street, New York. The Cabinet Organs are furnished by MASON & HAMLIN, of Boston.

〖 BAND MUSIC, U.S.A. 〗

1 alto clarinet	2 E♭ alto horns
1 bass clarinet	2 B♭ tenor horns
1 soprano saxophone	2 euphoniums
1 alto saxophone	3 trombones
1 tenor saxophone	5 bombardons (basses)
1 bass (baritone?) saxophone	4 percussion players

Total: 66 players

Gilmore trained his ensemble meticulously. The instrumentation he adopted, especially in the matter of proportion of reeds to brasses, is still the basic pattern for the concert band in America, and his choice of repertoire opened new vistas. His programs were considerably in advance of anything that had been attempted in this country up to the time. Along with the popular quadrilles, polkas and medleys of the time, Gilmore offered good transcriptions of standard orchestral overtures, and excerpts of works of the masters, from Mozart to Wagner. In the way of repertoire, no nineteenth century band advanced beyond the point attained by Gilmore, and in fact no great change in the character of the repertoire can be noted until the *1920*'s, with those introduced by Edwin Franko Goldman.

Other bands flourished in the period after the Civil War. Many new ones were established, and concerts in parks became a fixture in many cities. Concerts were given regularly in New York's Central Park as far back as the *1850*'s by the Thirteenth Regiment Band under Harvey Dodworth, and later by other regimental as well as proprietary professional bands. The two established Service bands, the Marine Band of Washington and the band of the United States Military Academy at West Point, began to expand and develop during these years. Gilmore's band served all these groups as the inspiration and example.

Illustrations *13* and *14* will serve as examples of what typical bands provided as musical fare. The Fort Adams program is interesting

FORT ADAMS R. I.

Programme.

I.	QUICKSTEP,	GRAFULA.
II.	ARIA and CHORUS, "Die Vier Haimonskinder."	BALFE.
III.	SONG, "When May Breezes,"	KRAPE.
IV.	WALTZ, "Dreams of the Ocean,"	GUNGLE.
V.	OVERTURE. "Norma,"	BELLINI.
VI.	SCHOTTISCHE, "Jessie,"	DOWNING.
VII.	SELECTION, "Nabuco,"	VERDI.
VIII.	MARCH,	COATES.

I. *Carriages upon entering the Fort will turn to the right and will not be reversed while inside the Fort.*

II. *All driving or riding must be at a walk.*

III. *Keep off the Grass.*

By Order of Brevet Major General SHERMAN.

JAMES M. LANCASTER.
Brevet Captain and 1st Lieut. 3rd Artillery.
ADJUTANT.

⟦ **ILLUSTRATION XIV** ⟧

J. C. GREENE'S

CONCERTS!

The public are respectfully informed that the SECOND CONCERT of
Mr. J. C. GREENE's SECOND ANNUAL COURSE,
will be given in

CITY HALL,

——on——

WEDNESDAY EVENING, JANUARY 13, 1869,

——BY THE——

Boston Germania Orchestra,

AND MILITARY BAND,

Assisted by the distinguished Sophrano, of Boston.

MISS ANNA S. WHITTEN.

C. H. EICHLER, LEADER OF ORCHESTRA.
ANTON HEINICKE, LEADER OF MILITARY BAND.

MR. FRANK TINGLEY will preside at the Pianoforte.

〚 **ILLUSTRATION XIV** 〛

PROGRAMME.

PART I.

1. OVERTURE to "Orpheus."................................*Offenbach*
2. GRAND CONCERT WALTZ, "Romance of the Vienna
   Forest,......................................*Strauss*
3. CAVATINA FROM LUCIA,......................*Donizetti*
   MISS ANNA S. WHITTEN.
4. VIOLIN SOLO,..............................*David*
   MR. CARL EICHLER.
5. ANDANTE from the Surprise Symphony,.............*Haydn*
6. PARTRIDGE POLKA,..........................*Koppitz*

PART II.

7. OVERTURE to "Zampa."........................*Herold*
8. SERENADE,................................*Gounod*
   MISS ANNA S. WHITTEN.
9. FLUTE SOLO,..............................*Furstenaw*
   MR. L. R. GOERING.
10. TRAUMBILDER, "Visions in a Dream."............*Lumbye*
11. SONG "Come into the Garden Maud."............*Parker*
    MISS ANNA S. WHITTEN.
12. MARCH DU SACRE, "from the Prophete.".........*Meyerbeer*

☞ MR. J. C. GREENE *will, by request, play* "WOOD UP"
in the course of the evening.

Tickets including Reserved Seats, - - 75 Cents each.
Tickets of Admission, - - - - 50 Cents each.

The Front Seats only of the Gallery are Reserved.

The Grand Pianoforte, used on this occasion, is from the celebrated Manufactory of
CHICKERING & SONS, furnished by their Agents, Messrs. CORY BROTHERS.

Doors will be open at 6 1-2 o'clock.   *Concert to commence at 7 1-2.*

for the inclusion of works by Grafulla, Downing and Coates, leading bandmasters and band composers of the period.

Many bands also doubled as orchestras. The Germania group was an excellent ensemble, and greatly impressed its audiences by its polished performances. The reader will note that Mr. Greene was still performing the *Wood Up Quickstep* (by popular demand) *on the keyed bugle* as late as *1869.*

One final program, from *1877,* of the American Band under its celebrated leader D. W. Reeves, composer of *The Second Connecticut Regiment March,* is shown in Illustration *15.*

Gilmore continued active until the day of his death; he was in fact on tour with his band when he died in St. Louis, Missouri, on September *24, 1892.* After some dispute about the succession to the leadership of the band, and some internal dissension among its members, Victor Herbert was chosen as the new leader. Reeves had been chosen by one faction of the membership, but withdrew in the face of many obstacles that appeared insurmountable.

Herbert re-organized the band and threw himself into a career as band leader with all the vigor he brought to his other pursuits. He toured with the band, wrote and arranged music for it, played 'cello solos with band accompaniment, got himself outfitted in a resplendent uniform, and in general was the complete bandmaster. Many of Herbert's marches, written about this time, are masterpieces; they are too little known and too seldom played today. He even became a journalist, and at the request of Anton Seidl, its editor, prepared a statement on "Artistic Bands" for the two-volume *The Music of the Modern World,* published by D. Appleton & Co., *1895-1897:*

The important part that military bands have taken in the development of musical knowledge in America can not be overstated. . . . It would be interesting to analyse the popular preference for bands over orchestras, if space permitted, but the fact can be clearly demonstrated. There are to-day large and expensive concert bands which travel from

[**ILLUSTRATION XV**]

—OF—

Franklin Lyceum Entertainments.

Wednesday Evening, October 17th, 1877.

American Band Concert,

WITH SOLO TALENT.

EDWARD HOFFMAN, - - - - Accompanist.

PROGRAMME.

OVERTURE—" Semiramis," - - - - *Rossini.*
AMERICAN BAND.

FANTASIE—" Auf den Alpen," (Alpine Echoes,) - - *Hereforth.*
AMERICAN BAND.

CORNET SOLO—"Old Folks at Home," - - - *Salcedo.*
MR. J. SALCEDO.

SHADOW SONG from Dinorah, - - - *Meyerbeer.*
MISS EMMA C. THURSBY.

CORNET SOLO—" Fantasie Brilliante, - - - *Arban.*
MR. D. W. REEVES.

OVERTURE—" Lodoiski," - . - - - *Cherubini.*
BROWN & REEVES' ORCHESTRA.

CORNET SOLO—" Maud Waltz," - - - - *Levy.*
MR. J. SALCEDO.

CAPRICE MILITAIRE, - - - - - *Hertzeele.*
AMERICAN BAND.

SWISS ECHO SONG, - - - - - *Eckert.*
MISS EMMA C. THURSBY.

SELECTION —" Evangeline," · - - - *Rice.*
AMERICAN BAND.

FANTASIA—" A Day in Camp," - - - *Reeves.*
AMERICAN BAND.

The Piano used on this occasion is a "CHICKERING," from Cory Brothers, Sole
Agents for Rhode Island.

Providence Press Company, Printers

⟦ BAND MUSIC, U.S.A. ⟧

State to State over the entire continent, while orchestras have to limit their tournées.

From the old bands which depended on the local brasses and drums, all forced to their utmost to make the most noise possible, to the bands of the present day which interpret the works of the greatest so as to satisfy even the most exacting musician, has been a hard but glorious struggle up the steeps of Parnassus, and to Patrick Sarsfield Gilmore belongs most of the glory. Mr. Gilmore knew men and music, and through his knowledge of both he held the masses and led them. In each programme there was something that made each auditor a better man musically, and prepared him for another step ahead. . . .

Edward N. Waters, in his great biography of Herbert, quotes the entire article, and gives many colorful details of Herbert's seven years with the *22nd* Regiment. The band under Herbert played anywhere and everywhere, from amusement parks to the inauguration ceremonies for President McKinley. The programs were similar to those of Gilmore, but, according to contemporary critics, the standard of playing was, if anything, even higher. The first concert of the *22nd* Regiment Band under Herbert took place on November *26, 1893,* at the Broadway Theatre in New York, with a distinguished audience in attendance. The program is shown on page *69.*

The *1890*'s were a fabulous period in American band history. Not only were Sousa and dozens of other famous bandmasters active, but for a short time even symphonic musicians were band conductors. Herbert's good friend and colleague Nahan Franko, the first American-born conductor of the Metropolitan Opera, gave band concerts during the summers, and for a time acted as conductor of the New York City Police Band. All these bands gave concerts, participated in parades, and furnished dance music for society balls. This was the background in which young Edwin Franko Goldman grew up, and in which Sousa and his band began its glorious career. They were indeed in many respects the good old days!

⟦ ILLUSTRATION XVI ⟧

WAGNER	*Overture to "Tannhäuser"*
SCHUMANN	*Träumerei*
DELIBES	*Intermezzo from "Naïla"*
ROSSINI	*Grand Aria from "Mahomet II"*
	Chevalier Luigi Colonnese, baritone
{ HERBERT	*Badinage*
{ CHOPIN	*Nocturne in E Flat*
COSSMAN	*Tarantella*
	Victor Herbert, 'cello
DAVID	*Aria, "Thou Brilliant Bird," from "LaPerle Du Bresil"*
	Charlotte Maconda, soprano
LISZT	*Hungarian Rhapsody No. 2*
HERBERT	*Twenty-Second Regiment March (first time)*
DONIZETTI	*Romanza from "Maria Padilla"*
	Chevalier Luigi Colonnese
STRAUSS	*Pizzicato Polka*
GILLET	*Loin Du Bal*
{ NEVIN	*" 'Twas April"*
{ DELIBES	*"Les Filles De Cadix"*
	Charlotte Maconda
	Duo for Cornet and Trombone
	Herbert L. and Ernest H. Clarke
HERBERT	*American Fantasy*

[ILLUSTRATION XVII]

Engraving of a Saturday afternoon Band concert at Central Park, New York City. Courtesy, The Bettmann Archive

[BAND MUSIC, U.S.A.]

THE ERA OF JOHN PHILIP SOUSA
(1854-1932)

The facts of Sousa's career are generally well known to all who are interested in bands or band music, and we have, in addition, his delightful and informative autobiography as a permanent source of material. No one will dispute the statement that Sousa was the greatest march composer and the most popular and famous bandmaster who ever lived. The period in which Sousa flourished, roughly *1880-1925*, was, as H. W. Schwartz has pointed out, the heyday of the band as a popular musical attraction, and the most prosperous era for the professional touring band. It was part of Sousa's genius that he knew perfectly how to exploit the favorable setting for his activity.

The band had been developed by Gilmore in the United States and by the many great bandmasters in Europe into a flexible and brilliant musical instrument. Its instrumentation, although varied in detail from band to band, was essentially uniform and, most important, a large library of available English and German publications, and even a few American ones, provided a stock repertoire of familiar standard and light music. By this time, the march was coming into favor in an entirely new way, a way, of course, that Sousa himself did more than anyone else to develop. It was becoming stylized as a dance, and for several decades actually was a staple in the ballroom as well as in the parade. The result was an added kind of appeal for the "military" or wind band, an appeal it has never enjoyed in the same way since the two-step went out of fashion. And, to make the musical and social climate ideal for the activities of the band, it had the field of light entertainment and popular concerts of "light classical" music all to itself. There were no popular orchestral concerts except for those of Theodore Thomas (and somewhat later, those of Anton Seidl), and even these were just a shade on the "highbrow" side. In Sousa's most active period, from approximately *1892* to *1915*, there were not only no television or radio or LP records, but not even movies. (Young readers, I find, really have trouble believing this!)

[BAND MUSIC, U.S.A.]

In other words, there was no competition in the specific areas of popular culture and entertainment where the band operates best.

Sousa's early training was received in theater orchestras; as a very young man he played under Offenbach, among others, and his instrument was the violin. Unlike almost all other of the great bandmasters, Sousa was not an expert performer on any wind instrument. (In addition to the violin, Sousa played the piano, though not as a professional.) He was offered the leadership of the Marine Band in *1880,* when he was twenty-four years of age, and proceeded immediately to re-vitalize that organization. One of the first things he did was to *order music:* quantities of the new publications from England and Germany. He reformed the Band completely, and it immediately became evident that here was a new force in the world of bands. It was but a short time before the reputation of Sousa's Marine Band was national in scope. President Harrison gave Sousa permission to take the Band out on tour, and all parts of the country were soon familiar with this great organization.

In *1892,* Sousa left the Marine Band and organized his own business or proprietary band, the one ever since famous as Sousa's Band. Its first concert was presented at Plainfield, New Jersey, on September *26, 1892,* just two days after the death of Patrick Gilmore. It is a fitting touch in the story of American bands that Sousa's first concert with his new band should open with a tribute to his illustrious predecessor.

The make-up of that first band was as follows:

2 flutes	4 cornets
2 oboes	2 trumpets
2 Eb clarinets	4 French horns
14 Bb clarinets	3 trombones
1 alto clarinet	2 euphoniums
1 bass clarinet	4 basses
2 bassoons	3 percussion players
3 saxophones	

Total: 49 players

⟦ BAND MUSIC, U.S.A. ⟧

Sousa remained firm all his life on several points about the band, and these are points worth recalling. The first, which he stated repeatedly, was that the band was for entertainment, not for education. Sousa said that his function was to give the public what it wanted. The second point was that he adhered basically to the English style of band instrumentation. As late as *1930* he declared that bands in England had "nearly a correct band instrumentation." Sousa's band, like all other great bands, was not middle-heavy, nor was it too large. Of course its size varied, according to demands and circumstances. At its largest, it numbered about seventy-five, but normally it functioned with approximately sixty players.

6 flutes (piccolos)	1 baritone saxophone
2 oboes	1 bass saxophone
1 English horn	6 cornets
26 B♭ clarinets	(4, 1st; 2, 2nd)
(14, 1st; 6, 2nd; 6, 3rd)	2 trumpets
1 alto clarinet	4 French horns
2 bass clarinets	4 trombones
2 bassoons	2 euphoniums
4 alto saxophones	6 sousaphones (basses)
2 tenor saxophones	3 percussion

Total: 75 players

The repertoire and programming of the Sousa Band followed fairly closely the patterns set by Gilmore, with one notable addition: Sousa's own marches. Sousa had a fairly large number of arrangements made specially for his band, as did Gilmore. The heaviest "classics" were occasional Wagnerian overtures or excerpts; the lighter standard orchestral works were plentifully represented; there was a good deal of ephemeral music of the day; and there were lots of soloists. Sousa featured singers as well as his galaxy of star instrumentalists: Arthur Pryor on trombone; Herbert Clarke, Frank Simon, Walter Smith and others on cornet; J. J. Perfetto and Simone Mantia on euphonium; and countless others. The Sousa Band was an ensemble of the greatest wind instrument performers of the time, and many of these players went on to great careers as conductors of their own bands. Much of the Sousa repertoire and style of programming went with them.

It was perfectly possible for Sousa, as I have pointed out, to combine several useful and profitable missions with the type of programs that was characteristic of him. It will be remembered that when Sousa played for King Edward VII in *1901*, six of the ten numbers on the program were of his own composition, and two were by Pryor and Clarke. In addition, Sousa played several of his own marches that were not on the listed program. This was what people wanted to hear! The reader today must remember that on every Sousa program anywhere from four to six additional Sousa marches were played, usually interspersed among the listed numbers.

A few Sousa programs, from different periods of his career, give a good idea of the repertoire. (See Illustrations *18* through *21*.)

During the years spanned by Sousa's career, there were many other excellent and popular bands. By far the best account of these bands and their activities is given in Schwartz's *Bands of America*. One need only mention the bands of Arthur Pryor, Thomas Preston Brooke, Frederick Innes, Patrick Conway, Alessandro Liberati, Giuseppe Creatore, Bohumir Kryl, Jean Missud and Mace Gay to realize that never before or since have there been so many professional bands active on so wide a scale. Most of these bands traveled a good deal (though not all of them) and most of them found available seasonal engagements at popular parks or resorts, such as Willow Grove near Philadelphia, Atlantic City, and elsewhere. There were bands in most of the large cities, and many of the smaller ones, east, west, north and south. There can be no doubt about the breadth and universality of their appeal. Many of the conductors gave their own special color to their programs and performances, and many of them, notably Liberati, Creatore and Kryl, cultivated crowd-appealing eccentricities. But on an over-all basis, one is struck by the

⟦ ILLUSTRATION XVIII ⟧

𝔐𝔲𝔰𝔦𝔠𝔞𝔩 𝔓𝔯𝔬𝔤𝔯𝔞𝔪

BOSTON FOOD FAIR

MECHANICS BUILDING, OCT. 1 to 27 Inclusive—Open 10 a.m. to 10 p.m.

Grand Concert by Sousa and His Band

THURSDAY, OCTOBER 18, 1906
Afternoon, 2 to 4.

John Philip Sousa, Conductor.
Miss Ada Chambers, Soprano.
Miss Jeannette Powers, Violinist.

1. Overture, "Oberon" ....Weber
2. Quartet for Saxophones, "Rigoletto" ....Verdi
    Messrs. Schensley, Knecht, Schaich and Becker.
3. Scenes from "La Giaconda" ....Ponchielli
4. Violin solo, "Largo" ....Handel
    Miss Jeannette Powers.
5. Fantasie, "Siegfried" ....Wagner
6. Excerpts from the operatic works of Meyerbeer
7. a. Valse, "Espana" ....Waldteufel
    b. March, "Jack Tar" ....Sousa
8. Ballad for soprano, "Calm as the Night" ....Bohm
    Miss Ada Chambers.
9. Gems from "The Bride-Elect" ....Sousa

Evening, 8 to 10.

John Philip Sousa, Conductor.
Miss Ada Chambers, Soprano.
Miss Jeannette Powers, Violinist.
Herbert L. Clarke, Cornetist.

1. Overture, "Poet and Peasant" ....Suppe
2. Song for cornet, "The Lost Chord" ....Sullivan
    Mr. Herbert L. Clarke.
3. Songs of Grace and songs of Glory   Sousa
    (A collocation of hymn tunes of the American Churches
    introducing "Lead Kindly Light" and "Nearer, my God to
    Thee," the two favorite hymns of the late President McKinley.)
4. Aria for soprano, "Samson and Delilah" ....St. Saens
    Miss Ada Chambers.
5. Gems from "Lady Madcap" (new) ....Rubens
6. Second Polonaise ....Liszt
7. a. Caprice, "Paradise on Earth" (new) ....Einoedshofer
    b. March, "King Cotton" ....Sousa
8. Violin solo—prize song from "Die Meistersinger" ....Wagner
    Miss Jeannette Powers.
9. Overture, "William Tell"..Rossini

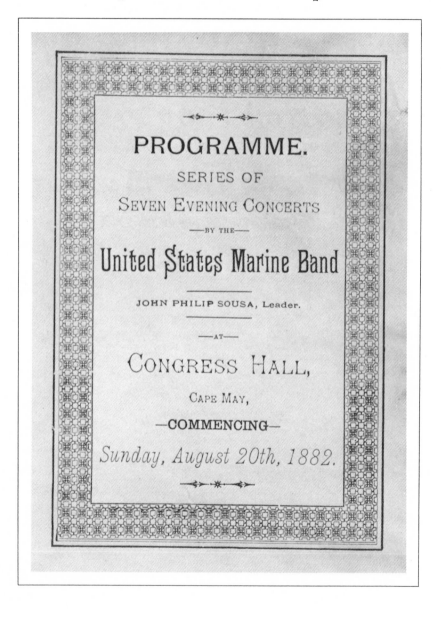

—PROGRAMME—

Sunday Evening, August 20th.

1.—MARCH, . . . SOUSA.
"Congress Hall,"
(Dedicated to Messrs. H. J. & G. R. Crump.)

2.—COLLOCATION, . GODFREY.
"Reminiscences of Mendelssohn,"
INTRODUCING—Overture from "Midsummer Night's Dream;" Pilgrims March from "Italian Symphony;" Song, "I am a Roamer;" from the "Son and Stranger;" Aria, "Jerusalem thou that Killest the Prophets;" Aria, I will sing of thy great mercies from "Oratories of St. Paul;" Allegro, from the "Scotch Symphony;" Duet, "I would that my love;" March from "Cornelius;" March from "Athalia;" "Bottoms March," and the "Wedding March" from "Midsummer Night's Dream."

3.—CORNET SOLO, . ROSSINI.
"Inflammatus,"
(By Mr. Wm. Jaeger.)

4.—SONG, . . . SULLIVAN.
"St. Agnes Eve."

5.—MOSAIC, . . . WAGNER.
"Lohengrin."

6.—GAVOTTE, . . CZISBULKA.
"Stephani."

7.—MARCH, . . . SOUSA.
"Funebre in Memoriam."

8.—COLLOCATION, . . VERDI.
"Il Trovator."

9.—HYMN, . . . MASON.
"Nearer My God to Thee."

Metropolitan Opera House.

Lessee, ... MAURICE GRAU OPERA CO.
Manager, ... MR. FRANK W. SANGER

SUNDAY EVENING, APRIL 22, at 8.15.

Grand Farewell Concert

....OF....

Sousa and his Band

(The Official American Band at the Paris Exposition),

Mr. JOHN PHILIP SOUSA, Conductor.

SOLOISTS:

MISS BLANCHE DUFFIELD,
Soprano.

MISS BERTHA BUCKLIN,
Violiniste.

MR. ARTHUR PRYOR,
Trombone.

PROGRAMME.

1. OVERTURE—"Imperial" (new), . HAYDN-WESTMEYER

2. TROMBONE SOLO— Air and Variations, . . PRYOR
   MR. ARTHUR PRYOR.

Programme continued on next page.

⟦ **ILLUSTRATION XX** ⟧

PROGRAMME—Continued.

3. (*a*) SLAVONIC DANCE, No. 2, ... DVORAK

   (*b*) HUNGARIAN DANCE, No. 6, . . . BRAHMS

4. SOPRANO SOLO—Waltz, "Maid of the Meadow," . SOUSA
         MISS BLANCHE DUFFIELD.

5. "CAPRICCIO ITALIEN" (new), . . TSCHAIKOWSKY

INTERMISSION.

6. IDYLL—"Ball Scenes" (new), ... CZIBULKA

7. (*a*) "RONDE DE NUIT" (new), . . . GILLET

   (*b*) MARCH —"The Man Behind the Gun" (new), . SOUSA

8. VIOLIN SOLO Adagio and Moto Perpetum,
                    from Third Suite, RIES
         MISS BERTHA BUCKLIN.

9 FANTASIE—"Good-Bye," . . . . SOUSA

Only Everett Pianos used at Sousa's Concerts.

⟦ **ILLUSTRATION XXI** ⟧

SOUSA AND HIS BAND

MR. JOHN PHILIP SOUSA, *Conductor*
Miss Grace Hoffman, *Soprano*
Miss Florence Hardeman, *Violinist*
Mr. Herbert L. Clarke, *Cornetist*

PROGRAMME

1—Prologue, "The Golden Legend"...Sullivan

In the scene depicted by the Prologue, the defeat of Lucifer is foreshadowed by an impotent attempt to wreck the Cathedral of Strasburg. The central figure of the scene is the Spire of the Cathedral. The time is night, and a storm is raging. Lucifer, with the Powers of the Air, is trying to tear down the Cross. According to the legend, he calls to and is answered by his allies as follows:

"Hasten! Hasten!
  O ye Spirits!
From its station drag the ponderous
  Cross of iron, that to mock us
Is uplifted high in the air!"

"Baffled! Baffled!
  Inefficient,
Craven Spirits! leave this labor
  Unto Time, the great Destroyer!
Come away, ere night is gone!"

"O we cannot;
  For around it
All the saints and guardian angels
  Throng in legions to protect it;
They defeat us everywhere!"

"Onward! Onward!
  With the night-wind
Over field, and farm, and forest
  Lonely homestead, darksome hamlet,
Blighting all we breathe upon."

They sweep away, and the Gregorian Chant is heard, the choir singing:
"Nocte surgente
Vigilemus omnes."

2—Cornet Solo, "Neptune's Court"...Clarke

MR. HERBERT L. CLARKE

3—Character Studies, "Dwellers in the Western World".....................Sousa

[a] The Red Man
"And they stood on the meadows
  With their weapons and their war-gear,
Painted like the leaves of autumn,
Painted like the sky of morning."

[b] The White Man

They sailed, they sailed. Then spoke the Mate,
"This mad sea shows its teeth to-night,
He curls his lips, he lies in wait,
  With lifted tusk, as if to bite."
  . . . Ah! that night!
Of all dark nights! And then a speck—

A light! A light! A light! A light!
  It grew, a startling flag unfurled;
It grew to be Time's burst of dawn;
  He gained a world; he gave that world
Its grandest lesson—"On and On."

⟦ ILLUSTRATION XXI ⟧

[c] The Black Man
"Now, de blessed little angels
Up in Heaven, we are told,
Don't do nothin' all dere lifetime
'Ceptin' play on harps o' gold."
"Now I think Heaben'd be mo' homelike
Ef we'd hyeah some music fall
F'om a real ol' fashioned banjo,
Like dat one upon de wall."

4—Soprano Solo, "Fors e Lui" (from "La Traviata") ....Verdi

MISS GRACE HOFFMAN

5—Largo, from "New World" Symphony ....Dvorak

The "New World" symphony expresses the state of soul of an uncultured Czech in America, the state of a homesick soul remembering his native land and stupefied by the din and hustle of a new life.

The "Largo" is the second movement, and in it Dvorak is said to attempt the suggestion of the mood in the story of Hiawatha's wooing, as told by Longfellow. The chief and romantic theme is sung by the English horn over a soft accompaniment. The development is extended. After the theme is sung by two muted horns there is a change to minor, and a short transitional passage on a contrasting theme leads to the second theme in the wood-wind over a bass counterpoint. There are several melodies in this movement; but, while the sentiments are diverse, there is no abruptness in contrast. There is a return to the first theme in the English horn. The "Largo" ends pianissimo with a chord in the bass section alone.

INTERMISSION

6—En Passant, "A June Night in Washington" ....Nevin

Outside the garden,
A group of negroes passing in the street,
Sing with ripe lush voices,
Sing with voices that swim,
Like great slow gliding fishes,
Through the scent of the honeysuckle:
  My love's waitin',
  Waitin' by the river,
  Waitin' till I come along!
  Wait there, child; I'm comin',
  Jay-bird tol' me,
  Tol' me in the mornin',
  Tol' me she'd be there to-night,
  Wait there, child; I'm comin'.

Wave of dream!
Spell of the summer night!
Will of the grass that stirs in its sleep!
Desire of the honeysuckle!
And further away,
Like the plash of far-off waves in the fluid
  night,
The negroes singing:
  Whippo'—will tol' me,
  Tol' me in the evenin',
  "Down by the bend where the cat tails
    grow,"
  Wait there, child; I'm comin'.
Lo the moon,
Like a galleon sailing the night;
And the wash of the moonlight over the roofs
  and the trees!

7— (a) Serenade, "Aubade Printaniere" ....Lacombe
    (b) March, "The New York Hippodrome" (new) ....Sousa

8—Violin Solo, "Spanish Dances" ....Sarasate

MISS FLORENCE HARDEMAN

9—Introduction to Act III, "Lohengrin" ....Wagner

⟦ **ILLUSTRATION XXII** ⟧

THE INNES BAND OF NEW YORK

Afternoon Program

1. Anglo-Americana, Folk Song Fantasy	Baetens
2. a. Offertory in F	Battiste
b. For Flag and Country	*Innes*
(New—First Time)	
3. Cornet Solo—Showers of Gold	Clark
Ernest Pechin	
4. Second Hungarian Rhapsody	Liszt
5. a. Cavatine, Op. 85, No. 3	Raff
b. Minuet, Op. 14	Paderewsky
6. Aria for Soprano, from Faust—The Jewel Song	Gounod
Ethel Richardson	
7. Overture, Poet and Peasant	Suppe

AMERIC·A

Night Program

1. Kermesse Scene, from Faust	Gounod
2. a. Serenade	Innes
b. Patrol of the Allies	Innes
3. Irish Rhapsody	Herbert
4. Solo for Violin—Appassionata	Vieuxtemps
David Ednor	
5. a. Intermezzo, from The Jewels of the Madonna	Wolf-Ferrari
b. A Moment Musical	Schubert
6. Aria for Soprano—Polonaise from Mignon	Thomas
Ethel Richardson	
7. Overture—Tannhauser	Wagner

AMERICA

⟦ ILLUSTRATION XXIII ⟧

AFTERNOON

1st Concert, 2.30 to 3.15

1. Overture, "Tam O' Shanter" ....Drysdale
2. Airs from "The Magic Melody" ....Stromberg
3. Three Arabian Dances ....Ring
   a. Caravan
   b. By the Fountain
   c. Bedouin
4. Baritone Solo, "Sole Mio" ....Di Capua
   Mr. Carlo Ferretti
5. March from "Suite in D Minor" ....Lachner

Electric Fountain Display, 4 o'clock

2nd Concert, 4.30 to 5.30

1. Overture, "La Gazza Ladra" ....Rossini
2. Scenes from "Ruddygore" ....Sullivan
3. Suite, "Silhouettes" ....Hadley
   a. Spanish
   b. French
   c. American
   d. Irish
4. Soprano Solo, "The Bells of St. Mary's,"
                                        Adams
   Miss Vahrah Verba
5. Songs of Scotland ....Lampe

EVENING

3rd Concert, 7.45 to 8.30

1. Overture, "Ruy Blas" ....Mendelssohn
2. Cornet Solo, "Russian Fantasia" ....Levy
   Mr. Ernest F. Pechin
3. Scenes from "Carmen" ....Bizet
4. Soprano Solo, "Little Grey Home in the
   West" ....Lohr
   Miss Vahrah Verba
5. Three Light Pieces ....Fletcher
   a. Lubly Lulu
   b. Fifinette
   c. Folies Bergere

Electric Fountain Display, 9.30 o'clock

4th Concert, 9.45 to 10.45

1. Overture, "Aroldo" ....Verdi
2. Trombone Solo, "Carnival of Venice," Arban
   Mr. Pedro Lozano
3. Hungarian Rhapsody No. 6 ....Liszt
4. Baritone Solo, Barcarole from "La Gioconda,"
                                      Ponchielli
   Mr. Carlo Ferretti
5. Tone Poem, "The Evolution of Dixie"....Lake

similarities of these bands rather than by their differences. And this again is particularly true with respect to the programs.

Bands playing on tour often played two engagements in different places on the same day (often using the same program), while the bands performing at fairs or resorts never gave fewer than two different programs—and often as many as four—daily. Shown on page *82* are the two programs of a typical day's engagement of "THE INNES BAND OF NEW YORK (Forty-Two Performers)—The Whole Under the Personal Direction of FREDERICK INNES, Kenton Chautauqua, Afternoon and Night, Sunday, August *4, 1918*":

Bands playing engagements at Philadelphia's famous Willow Grove Park presented *four* concerts daily, although they were relatively brief ones. One day's program of Patrick Conway and his band at Willow Grove, Tuesday, May *15, 1923* is given on page *83*.

Band engagements of this type continued through the *1920*'s, but in the *1930*'s they began to diminish. The last band concert at Willow Grove took place in *1926*, and other resorts began to close down as the nation took to the automobile, and vacation and amusement habits changed. Pryor's Band continued to play at Asbury Park into the *1930*'s, as did Harold Bachman's Million Dollar Band in Tampa, Florida. Other bands continued active, though on a generally smaller scale. The old type of "business" band, able to tour profitably, began to yield to new developments, not only in the field of band music proper, but in the whole field of popular amusement. During the *1930*'s the character of band activity changed, with the emergence of a new type of professional band, the enlarged sphere of activity of the new Service bands, and the accelerated development of the band movement in education.

EDWIN FRANKO GOLDMAN (1878-1956)
AND THE NEW BAND REPERTOIRE

The new image of the concert band is largely the work of one man, Edwin Franko Goldman. It is in many ways difficult for me to write about

〚 BAND MUSIC, U.S.A. 〛

the work of my father, especially since I was professionally associated with him for many years; but it is obviously true that no book on bands can overlook or minimize his activities and accomplishments. Fortunately, a good many other authoritative bandsmen can be quoted. H. W. Schwartz writes:

A new kind of concert band has taken their [i.e., the old "business" bands] place, and the man who best typifies this new kind of band and marks this transition is Dr. Goldman. The Goldman Band survived the automobile, the phonograph, the movies and the radio, powerful forces which crushed the famous bands of yesteryear. For three decades it has stood as America's foremost symbol of what a modern concert band should be. . . .

Although the Goldman Band is a local band, through radio it has been shared with the nation. Furthermore the personal influence of the great conductor of the Goldman Band has spread from coast to coast. For many years he championed various movements of which the aim was to raise the standards of musical performance by the concert band. He battled for original compositions, written by eminent composers, expressly for band performance. He advocated improvements in the instrumentation of the concert band and in more adequate publication of band music.

In an article written in *1948,* Henry Cowell stated, after discussing the performances of the Goldman Band:

This is no slight achievement, but Dr. Goldman has made an even more significant contribution to music as a result of his determination to improve the quality of music available to the symphonic band, and his interest in keeping the Goldman Band in active touch with the living

〔 BAND MUSIC, U.S.A. 〕

*music of the day. That it is now possible to offer a program of fine art
music of great variety and interest, all written expressly for the band by
famous living composers, is very largely due to the efforts, influence and
persuasiveness of Dr. Goldman. No mean composer of lively marches himself, in the Sousa tradition, Dr. Goldman began many years ago to urge
the best known composers of Europe and America to contribute to the
repertory of good music for band by writing with wind instruments in
mind. His success in this undertaking has made it unnecessary for bandmasters to depend any longer on the artistically deplorable arrangements,
for winds, of music conceived for strings.*

Dr. Goldman received a serious musical training. He was one of
the very few pupils of the great and eccentric virtuoso Jules Levy, and he
studied under Antonin Dvořák at the National Conservatory. At the age
of seventeen, he became first trumpet player at the Metropolitan Opera
House (and it is interesting to note that at that time the trumpet parts
were played on cornets), playing under such conductors as Mahler,
Mancinelli, Toscanini. Like most members of the Metropolitan Opera
orchestra, he played in bands during the summer, and soon took his turn
conducting them. These bands were composed of excellent musicians,
but they seldom rehearsed, and the musicians themselves did not take
them very seriously except as sources of extra summer income. The idea
soon occurred to Goldman that an extraordinary band could be organized
with these musicians from the Met, the Philharmonic and other outstanding orchestras, if only they could be welded into a cohesive ensemble, well rehearsed, and with a pride in their organization.

This nucleus of musicians became the foundation of the Goldman
Band in *1911*. In *1918*, the famous series of summer concerts got under
way, on the Green of Columbia University, with funds raised by sub-
scription. In *1924*, Mr. and Mrs. Daniel Guggenheim and Mr. and Mrs.
Murry Guggenheim took over the support of the concerts, which have
continued since that time with the generous support of members of the
Guggenheim family, and since *1944*, of the Daniel and Florence Gug-

genheim Foundation. Although the concerts have been given since *1923* in Central Park and other city parks, they are not municipal concerts, nor do they receive any tax support.

The concerts themselves are certainly familiar to all who are interested in bands. Dr. Goldman had vigorous ideas on band instrumentation, and on how a band should play, but others have had just as strong convictions on these points. His greatest contribution lies unquestionably in the area of the band repertoire. He saw clearly the change in the band's status, and had the imagination to deal with it.

For the first season of Dr. Goldman's concerts (the band was known until *1920* as The New York Military Band) there was already a gala array of soloists, guest conductors and new compositions. The principal soloists were Ernest Williams, cornet; Jan Williams, clarinet; and Gardell Simons, trombone. Singers included Marie Tiffany of the Metropolitan Opera, Isabel Irving and a number of others. The New Choral Society of New York appeared at two concerts, with guest conductors including Percy Grainger, Arthur A. Clappé, principal of the Army Music Training School and a well-known bandsman, Gustav Saenger, N. Clifford Page, Albert Chiaffarelli and others, all of whom conducted new compositions specially written for band. Mr. Grainger, in addition to his own compositions, performed Liszt's *Hungarian Fantasy* (complete) in an arrangement by Rocco Resta.

The list of new works and specially made transcriptions presented by the Band under Dr. Goldman during the first twenty years of the Band's activity is indeed an imposing one, the more so in that nothing of the kind had ever been attempted before. The first American competition for a new serious band work was instituted by Dr. Goldman in *1920*. The judges were Percy Grainger and Victor Herbert, and the award went to Carl Busch of Kansas City for his Symphonic Episode, *A Chant from the Great Plains.* John Philip Sousa had been invited as a third judge, but was unable to accept because of his crowded touring schedule. The importance of the motives for the competition was clearly understood by all concerned. Victor Herbert, with his experience both as bandsman and composer, wrote:

⟦ BAND MUSIC, U.S.A. ⟧

The contest proves that a greater interest is being taken in bands and band music than ever before, and also that we are developing a branch of that art that has hitherto been neglected. *A contest of this kind . . . is doing a real service to the advance of our native music.*

Grainger wrote: . . . *All this is a most encouraging result of the knowledge that you are spreading of the great and beautiful possibilities of a finely organized modern military band.*

Grainger himself was one of the first to show the extent of these possibilities. His band works from *1918* on are among the classics of band literature in terms of imaginative and novel treatment and beauty of sonority. Most of these works were written for the Goldman Band and received their first performances at Goldman Band concerts.

In addition to the development and encouragement of a new repertoire of original music, Dr. Goldman also had innumerable arrangements and transcriptions specially made for his band, and extended the range of the transcribed literature into new regions. Bach, for example, was introduced to band audiences by Edwin Franko Goldman, who occasionally even presented whole programs of Bach and other "early" composers—earlier, that is, than the conventional Verdi and Tschaikowsky. Transcriptions of contemporary music, by Sibelius, Stravinsky and others, often with the approval or at the suggestion of the composers, also were featured by Dr. Goldman.

It would be untrue to say that there was suddenly a great surge of interest in composing for the band. Dr. Goldman had to work hard to persuade leading composers to take an interest in the medium, but little by little his enthusiasm and persistence were rewarded. An older generation of American composers were the first to respond; among them were Henry Hadley, Clarence Cameron White, Daniel Gregory Mason, Bainbridge Crist and Leo Sowerby. The first distinguished European composers to write works for Dr. Goldman were Ottorino Respighi, Jaromir Weinberger and Albert Roussel. But from the late *1930*'s on, it was apparent that the new repertoire was going to grow on its mo-

⟦ BAND MUSIC, U.S.A. ⟧

mentum and provide a real stimulus for composers, bandsmen and audiences alike.

By *1942*, for the first time, it was possible to present a complete and fairly well-balanced program of concert works originally composed for band, and on July *21* of that year the Goldman Band gave what is probably the first such concert in the history of band music. (Page *90*.)

In recent years, this repertoire has kept expanding at an ever-increasing rate, so that a new and original band repertoire of respectable proportions is now available. By the time of Dr. Goldman's death, on February *21, 1956*, it could be said that almost every American composer of reputation had composed at least one band work, many of them stimulated by commissions given by Dr. Goldman himself.[5] The movement has made its mark in other countries as well as in the United States.

The instrumentation of the Goldman Band under Dr. Goldman varied over the years. For the season of *1930*, the complement was sixty-two, distributed as follows:

4 flutes (piccolo)	4 cornets
2 oboes (English horn)	4 trumpets
1 E♭ clarinet	5 French horns
19 B♭ clarinets	6 trombones
(1st, 2nd, 3rd)	2 euphoniums
1 bass clarinet	4 tubas
2 bassoons	2 string basses
1 alto saxophone	1 harp
1 tenor saxophone	3 percussion players

Total: 62 players

In honor of Dr. Goldman's seventieth birthday, the League of Composers presented a historic concert in Carnegie Hall, with the Gold-

[5] See Chapter 8.

⟦ **ILLUSTRATION XXIV** ⟧

TWENTY-FIFTH SEASON

PROSPECT PARK———BROOKLYN

BY COURTESY OF FIORELLO H. LA GUARDIA, MAYOR OF THE CITY OF NEW YORK

The DANIEL GUGGENHEIM MEMORIAL CONCERTS

Given by

THE GOLDMAN BAND

EDWIN FRANKO GOLDMAN, Conductor
RICHARD FRANKO GOLDMAN, Associate Conductor

These Concerts are the gift of
THE DANIEL AND FLORENCE GUGGENHEIM FOUNDATION
for the benefit and enjoyment of the people of New York

IMPORTANT NOTICE

In order to preserve the unity and continuity of the programs given by the band, the attention of the audience is called to the new policy of interpolating no extra numbers among those on the printed programs. If the applause of the audience warrants, the band will gladly render extra numbers of a light nature after the close of the regular concert.

Silver Jubilee Year

Thirty-fifth Concert, Tuesday, July 21st, 1942
(Program subject to change without notice)

PART I.

ORIGINAL BAND MUSIC

1. CHRISTMAS MARCH ....**EDWIN FRANKO GOLDMAN**

This march is built on well-known Christmas songs and carols, all of which will be familiar to the listener. It opens with the tune of "Good King Wenceslas", followed by the hymn "Adeste Fideles" sounded by the brasses alone. "Dashing Thru The Snow" and "Jingle Bells" are followed by "O Tannenbaum", with the preceding tunes used as counter-melodies. Following this, Handel's famous air "Joy to the World" is heard, leading into the song, "It Came Upon a Midnight Clear". "Holy Night, Silent Night" is introduced as a counter-point. "The First Noel" and "Deck the Hall" are heard as the march proceeds. The ending introduces "Hark The Herald Angels Sing", with several of the preceding melodies woven into the harmonies. This March was composed early in 1940.

2. SPRING OVERTURE ....**LEO SOWERBY**
1895—

Leo Sowerby was one of the first eminent American composers to become interested in writing for the concert band. Having served as bandmaster in the U. S. Army in 1917-18, he has a first-hand knowledge of the medium. The "Spring Overture," designed along conventional musical lines, shows his skill and individuality in band instrumentation.

Mr. Sowerby was born in Grand Rapids, Michigan. He was graduated from the American Conservatory in Chicago, and received the degree of Doctor of Music from Rochester University. He was the first composer to receive a fellowship from the American Academy in Rome, and has won numerous awards for his compositions. His orchestral works and chamber music receive frequent performances. Mr. Sowerby is a member of the Advisory Council of the American Composers Alliance, and an Honorary Member of the American Bandmasters Association.

3. CANTO YORUBA ....**PEDRO SANJUAN**
Conducted by the Composer

Pedro Sanjuan, distinguished conductor and composer, is Basque by birth. As a young man he moved to Madrid, where he pursued his musical studies with Joaquin Turina. For a time he was bandmaster of the Guardia Civil, later becoming conductor of the Madrid Philharmonic Orchestra. He lived for a number of years in Cuba, where he founded and conducted the Havana Philharmonic Orchestra. He is considered an outstanding authority on Cuban music. His compositions, most of which are based on Spanish or Cuban characteristics, have been performed throughout the world with great success. Mr. Sanjuan now lives in the United States.

The "Canto Yoruba" ("Yoruba Song") is described by the composer as follows: "The slaves of the Colonial period, who originally came from the West Coast of Africa (Yoruba region), continued to practice their ancient rites in Cuba. The religious practices of the 'initiated' are countless, but nearly all of them include an invocation to the ancestral deities, manifested in the form of ritual dances and magic songs. In all of these ceremonies, the drum is the sacred instrument. The chants and rhythms of these Afro-Cuban rituals form the basis of the present composition. The work is, however, not a reproduction of these, but is wholly the personal impression of the composer." The "Canto Yoruba" was written directly for band for performances at these concerts.

4. RHAPSODY, JERICHO ....**MORTON GOULD**
1913—

Morton Gould is one of the best-known of younger American composers and conductors. Many of his works, such as the often-played "Pavane," have achieved nation-wide popularity. "Jericho" is Gould's first large work written directly for band. It is a programmatic composition in the form of a rhapsody. The various sections are entitled: Prologue, Roll Call, Chant, Dance, March and Battle, Joshua's Trumpets, The Walls Came Tumblin' Down, and Hallelujah. The music is highly descriptive in character, and abounds in striking instrumental effects.

5. A LEGEND ....**PAUL CRESTON**
1906—

The name of Paul Creston is becoming increasingly familiar to American concert audiences through frequent performances and broadcasts of his music by leading orchestras and ensembles. Mr. Creston, one of the most talented of the younger American composers, has written works in many forms, in each of which he shows

Prospect Park, Brooklyn, on Tuesday, Thursday and Saturday evenings at 8.30. There will be no concert by the Goldman Band in Central Park on Friday evening, July 31st.

⟦ ILLUSTRATION XXIV ⟧

originality and masterly command of the medium. He has twice been the recipient of a Guggenheim Fellowship in composition, and has received many other important recognitions of his work. Mr. Creston was born in New York City, and received all of his musical training in the United States.

"A Legend" is the composer's first work written for band. No specific legend or story is illustrated by the music; the composer prefers that the music evoke for each listener such ideas or pictures as seem appropriate. The work was composed in 1942.

PART II

6. NEWSREEL..**WILLIAM SCHUMAN**
1910—

I. Horse-Race   **II.** Fashion Show   **III.** Tribal Dance
IV. Monkeys at the Zoo   **V.** Parade

William Schuman is one of the most gifted of the younger American composers. His works, which include at the present time four symphonies, three string quartets and a great number of compositions in large and small forms, have been performed by the New York Philharmonic, the Boston Symphony and many other outstanding groups. Schuman was born in New York City, and is at present a member of the faculty of Sarah Lawrence College. "Newsreel" is his first work written directly for band. It is a satiric suite in five movements: Horse-Race, Fashion Show, Tribal Dance, Monkeys At The Zoo, and Parade. The five movements are played without interruption. Those familiar with movie newsreels will appreciate the humor of the composer's musical interpretations.

7. FIRST SUITE IN Eb FOR BAND......................**GUSTAV HOLST**
1874—1934

Holst's First Suite for band was composed in 1909, and bears the opus number 28-A. The composer's use of the possibilities of the band is extremely striking, and shows great knowledge of the qualities of the different instruments. Holst was one of the first important composers to write directly for band.

The First Suite is composed of three movements: Chaconne, Intermezzo and March. Each movement is built on the same theme, varied rhythmically and harmonically. The Chaconne is an old dance-form, used frequently by Bach and his contemporaries. It is in ¾ time, with the melody in the bass.

8. FESTIVE OCCASION..................................**HENRY COWELL**
1897—

"Festive Occasion" was written especially for the twenty-fifth anniversary season of the Goldman Band by the distinguished American composer, Henry Cowell. The work is in the style of a grand march, although its prevailing spirit is one of gaiety and festivity.

Mr. Cowell has for many years been considered one of the most representative of American composers. His works, ranging from the daringly experimental to the almost conventional, have been performed in all parts of the world. In addition, Mr. Cowell is well known as a lecturer and musicologist. He is one of the first important American composers to turn his attention toward writing for band.

9. (a)   A CURTAIN RAISER and COUNTRY DANCE
RICHARD FRANKO GOLDMAN
1910—

(b)   "LOST LADY FOUND"........................**PERCY GRAINGER**
1882—

(a) "A Curtain-Raiser" was written in February 1941, and scored directly for band. The piece is of straightforward design, and was written as an attempt to provide a fresh sort of native material for American bands. The composition has no story or program, since the composer believes that the music should speak for itself.

Mr. Goldman's association with the Goldman Band makes it natural that his interest as a composer should turn to band music. He has written several other works for full band and for various combinations of wind instruments.

(b) "A Lost Lady Found" is the last movement of Mr. Grainger's "Lincolnshire Posy," a brilliant and colorful suite originally composed for the band medium. The entire suite is founded on folk-tunes from Lincolnshire, in England. They are treated in Mr. Grainger's inimitable way, and scored with the consumate skill always evident in his band scores.

10. ENGLISH FOLKSONG SUITE.................**R. VAUGHAN WILLIAMS**
1872—

I. March—Seventeen Come Sunday
II. Intermezzo—My Bonny Boy
III. March—Folk Songs from Somerset

Ralph Vaughan Williams is one of the most eminent of contemporary English composers, known throughout the world for his splendid choral and orchestral works. Like many modern English composers, he has found great inspiration in the study of folk music and in the work of early English masters such as Purcell. He has made his own the modal harmonies and striking rhythms found in the traditional folksongs of Norfolk and Somerset, but has formed an entirely individual style out of these elements.

Vaughan Williams' interest in the wind band has nowhere found more satisfactory expression than in this suite. The score is remarkable for its originality and masterful instrumentation. The musical subjects are all traditional, and reflect the composer's lifelong studies in the field of folk music. This Suite, originally written for band, has recently been transcribed for orchestra. The version played at this concert is the original.

man Band conducted by Walter Hendl in a program celebrating the maturity of the new band repertoire which owed so much to Dr. Goldman's work. The program is one of which any musician or musical organization might well be proud, for the solidity and substance of its musical content. (Illustration 25 on page 93.)

Of the works presented, the Milhaud, Schoenberg, Grainger, Cowell and Sanjuan all had received their first performances by the Goldman Band; the others, except for the Miaskovsky had received their first United States performances by the Goldman Band. It is certainly not unjustified to assert that a program such as this one marks a new era in band music.

NEW MUSICAL DIRECTIONS

When Lowell Mason was engaged in his pioneering work for the introduction of music in the public schools, he could not in his wildest flights of imagination have anticipated the extent to which music, instrumental as well as vocal, would some day be a part of the public school program in the United States. Nor could he have supposed that colleges and universities, public and private, would in the twentieth century have become centers of an immense variety of musical activity. Nevertheless, it is ultimately to Lowell Mason and other nineteenth century pioneers that we owe this extraordinary and peculiarly American development of musical performance (or "applied music," as the current phrase has it) in all branches of our educational system.

Music as a discipline had been recognized in classical times as a fundamental part of a rational curriculum. But the idea of musical performance in the general scheme of education is a comparatively new one and, it should be noted, one which is not often admitted outside of the United States. Today in the United States there are few schools that stand against the prevailing current in this respect. The idea of choruses, orchestras, bands, madrigal groups, brass ensembles, operetta groups, even dance orchestras—not as extra-curricular activities but as part of a cur-

[ILLUSTRATION XXV]

THE LEAGUE OF COMPOSERS
25TH ANNIVERSARY SEASON—1947-48

presents

A PROGRAM OF CONTEMPORARY MUSIC

WRITTEN FOR SYMPHONIC BAND

IN HONOR OF THE 70TH BIRTHDAY

OF EDWIN FRANKO GOLDMAN

January 3, 1948

Toccata Marziale	*Ralph Vaughan-Williams*
Suite Française	*Darius Milhaud*
Theme and Variations for Wind Band, Opus 43-a	*Arnold Schoenberg*
The Power of Rome and the Christian Heart	*Percy Grainger*
Shoonthree	*Henry Cowell*
Canto Yoruba	*Pedro Sanjuan*

Three Pieces written for Le Quartorze Juillet *of Romain Rolland*

a. La Marche sur la Bastille	*Arthur Honegger*
b. Prelude	*Albert Roussel*
c. Le Palais Royal	*Georges Auric*

FIRST PERFORMANCE IN AMERICA

Symphony No. 19 for Band *Nicholas Miaskovsky*

riculum in regular school hours—is so generally accepted that few ever question how they got there or why they should be there.

These musical activities did not become part of our school or college programs without a great deal of pioneering work by many people. In Lowell Mason's day, vocal music had been introduced into many schools, but by the end of the nineteenth century there was little activity in the instrumental field. The few groups that existed did so largely because of the enthusiasm of a few members of a given community, and with almost no exceptions these groups practiced and played after school hours. The first fruitful efforts to organize an instrumental program in a school system were those of Will Earhart in Richmond, Indiana, around *1900*. The time was finally ripe, and the movement for instrumental music in the schools gathered momentum rapidly. It was at about the same time, in *1905*, that Albert Austin Harding (*1880-1958*) began his work at the University of Illinois, remolding an informal college band into the model organization it became under his guidance.

Activity along these lines was pursued in many parts of the country, but especially in the mid-West. In *1918*, Joseph E. Maddy was made supervisor of instrumental music in the schools of Rochester, New York, the first educator to hold a post of this sort. Dr. Maddy's tremendous contribution to the cause of music education is too well-known to require recounting; all music educators in America must acknowledge their debt to him. School orchestras, rather than bands, received emphasis at first in most communities; but as support for school instrumental music grew, the band began to receive increasing attention. The work of men like A. R. McAllister in Joliet, Illinois, gave the band movement a great deal of impetus. McAllister began his work with the Joliet Band as far back as *1912*, and for many years the Joliet Band was synonymous with the most remarkable achievements in public school music.

By the early *1920*'s, the idea of bands and orchestras in the schools was gaining ground rapidly. A national contest for high school bands was organized by a group of wind instrument manufacturers in Chicago in *1923*. This event attracted much attention, and the idea of annual band contests aroused great enthusiasm. It was felt, however, that the sponsorship by instrument manufacturers might appear to have motives other than purely educational ones, and the contests of following years were conducted by the National Bureau for the Advancement of Music, working through and with the Committee on Instrumental Affairs of the Music Supervisors (later, Music Educators) National Conference. The first National Contest under this arrangement was held in Fostoria, Ohio, in *1926*, with *315* bands entered in the competitions. The National School Band Association was formed in this same year. The incredibly rapid growth of the school band movement can be gauged by the fact that by *1932* over *1000* school bands were taking part in national contests.

In the college field, Dr. Harding's work at Illinois was widely emulated. The Illinois Band first attracted attention for its spectacular performances while marching and deploying in intricate formations. But Dr. Harding also was developing a symphonic band of outstanding quality. For this band Dr. Harding made many transcriptions of large late-nineteenth century orchestral works, including compositions by Franck and Richard Strauss; these became a feature of his repertoire. In every phase of university band activity—marching, concertizing, repertoire and, not the least important, organization and management—Dr. Harding's Illinois Band became a model for others.

The Illinois Band was, under Dr. Harding, and still is, under his successor Mark Hindsley, large, both as a marching band and as a concert unit. The symphonic band uses over *100* players, with a very complete instrumentation. Illinois, in addition, maintains a Regimental Band, also of large proportions. A typical program of Dr. Harding is the following one, shown on page *96*.

SUMMARY

The preceding account of the development of bands and band music in Europe and in the United States brings us in all essentials up to the beginning of the *1960*'s. The band in the United States today exists

⟦ ILLUSTRATION XXVI ⟧

UNIVERSITY OF ILLINOIS CONCERT BAND

DR. A. A. HARDING, CONDUCTOR

March 16, 1948

PROGRAM

Overture to "The Wasps" of Aristophanes	RALPH VAUGHAN-WILLIAMS*
Excerpts from the symphonic poems "A Hero's Life" and "Death and Transfiguration"	RICHARD STRAUSS*
Symphony in B-flat minor, Op. 4 *Third Movement*	TIKHON KHRENNIKOV*
"Danse" (Tarantelle styrienne)	DEBUSSY-RAVEL*
"Psyché and Eros" from the symphonic poem "Psyché"	CÉSAR FRANCK*
Three Dances from the ballet suite, "Gayne"	ARAM KHACHATURIAN

INTERMISSION

Overture, "Vanguard" *Conducted by Mark Hindsley*	FREDERIC CURZON
Selection from "Brigadoon" *Conducted by Mark Hindsley*	FREDERICK LOEWE
Suite—Lieutenant Kije, Op. 60	SERGE PROKOFIEFE*
Symphony No. 5-1/2 (Symphony for Fun)	DON GILLIS*
Fantasy—Jingles All the Way	HOWARD R. CABLE
Selected marches from the pen of the "March King"	JOHN PHILIP SOUSA

* These works are manuscript transcriptions made especially for the University of Illinois Concert Band by Dr. Harding.

[BAND MUSIC, U.S.A.]

as the result of much thought and pioneering work on the part of many great bandsmen. It is no longer a haphazard offshoot of more seriously conceived musical enterprises, but a musical activity of vast proportions, involving more people as performers—and possibly also as audiences— than ever before.

We may divide the history of the band into a number of distinct phases, which may be useful for the student as a convenient reference:

I. *The early period, to* 1789, *characterized by small ensembles, almost purely functional in character, and generally attached to the military. The bands of* Stadtmusiker *and* Thürmer *should not, however, be forgotten.*

II. *The era of the growing concert band, to approximately* 1850, *aided by two principal factors: (a) the impulse given to democratization of the arts by the French Revolution and (b) the development of more flexible and perfect wind instruments.*

III. *The era of the popular "business" band, approximately* 1850-1920, *typified by Gilmore and Sousa in the United States, and by the concert activities of the great national bands in Europe. This is also the great era of transcribed light classics and popular idiomatic band music such as marches, cornet solos, potpourris and other such characteristic pieces.*

IV. *The present period, which may be dated as beginning in about* 1920, *characterized by the development of an important original band repertoire, pioneered by Edwin Franko Goldman, and by the phenomenal development under Maddy, Harding, McAllister and others, of the band in the schools and colleges, which has assumed a position of major importance in band music today.*

4

CONTEMPORARY

···

B A N D S

〔 CONTEMPORARY BANDS 〕

THE PROFESSIONAL BAND

It is unquestionably true that the professional band is no longer the dominant factor in band activity today. This dominance has clearly been assumed by the bands in our colleges and universities, and to some extent by those in the high schools. However, some purely professional civilian bands remain active, and there is evidence to indicate that others are coming to the fore. The Goldman Band, still perhaps the best-known of the "proprietary" professional bands, celebrated its fiftieth year of continuous existence in *1961*. The Service Bands are, of course, composed of professional musicians, but fall into a somewhat different category. Municipal bands of professional players exist in a number of cities. Most of these, however, are small, and not many of them play extended concert series. Changes in the economics of the music business, as well as in the general picture of band activity, have made it all but impossible today for the professional band to tour extensively or to maintain itself as did the Gilmore and Sousa bands. It is worth noting, in passing, that even Sousa's band lost money on its last tours, although it was certainly still popular and attracted large audiences.

Aside from The Goldman Band, the Belle Isle Concert Band of Detroit, conducted by Leonard B. Smith, may be cited as typical. This band was organized by Mr. Smith in *1946,* and gives regular seasons of thirty outdoor concerts each summer. It is a "proprietary" organization, that is to say, a personal undertaking, and not a municipal or tax-supported group. Its performances are made possible by funds provided through the Music Performance Trust Fund and by business support. The City of Detroit provides the band shell and the park facilities. The Belle Isle Concert Band (*1960*) consisted of fifty-three musicians, distributed as follows:

3 flutes (piccolo)	2 trumpets
2 oboes	5 French horns
1 bassoon	2 baritones

⟦ CONTEMPORARY BANDS ⟧

14 B♭ clarinets	5 trombones
1 bass clarinet	4 basses
4 saxophones	4 percussion
5 cornets	1 harp

Total: 53

A typical program of the Belle Isle Concert Band is shown on page *101*.

Band concerts in public parks are traditionally free concerts, as contrasted with indoor concerts where an admission fee is usual. This poses the problem of financial support for all organizations that are not tax-supported. The concerts given by the Goldman Band on the Mall in New York's Central Park, and in Brooklyn's Prospect Park, are still made possible by the generosity of the Daniel and Florence Guggenheim Foundation, and the concerts are known as The Guggenheim Memorial Concerts. The Goldman Band in *1960* was composed of fifty-two players, with the following instrumentation:

3 flutes (piccolo)	5 cornets
2 oboes (English horn)	2 trumpets
1 E♭ clarinet	4 French horns
*16 B♭ clarinets	2 baritones
1 bass clarinet	6 trombones
2 bassoons	3 basses
*2 saxophones	3 percussion

Total: 52

(As present conductor of the Goldman Band, I do not suggest that this is an ideal instrumentation, although of course I believe it is

* Alto clarinet, soprano saxophone and baritone saxophone are not used regularly, but are played by clarinetists who double when necessary and appropriate. Contrabass clarinet and contrabassoon are added when called for in specific scores.

⟦ **ILLUSTRATION XXVII** ⟧

THE BELLE ISLE CONCERT BAND

Sunday, June 12, 1960

PART I

WILLIAM WALTON
"Orb and Sceptre" (First Time)
A. CARLOS GOMEZ
Overture, "Il Guarany"
JOHANN SEBASTIAN BACH
Jesu, Joy of Man's Desiring
JOHANN SEBASTIAN BACH
Fugue ala Gigue
CLAUDE DEBUSSY
"Fetes" from "Three Nocturnes" (First Performance)

PART II

FERDE GROFE
"On the Trail" from "Grand Canyon Suite"
J. EDW. BARAT
Solo for Cornet "Fantasie in E♭" (First Performance)
Mr. Leonard B. Smith, Cornetist
CLARE GRUNDMAN
Blue Tail Fly
LEONARD B. SMITH
March "Hail, Detroit"
LEONARD B. SMITH
March "Town Crier"
JOHANN STRAUSS
Waltz "Acceleration"

basically sound for a group of this size. Any changes that may be made will undoubtedly be in the direction of greater strength at top and bottom, rather than in the middle registers. But here again, I can only suggest that this problem depends less on what I think is good in the abstract than on how composers and arrangers write for band. This problem will be discussed at much greater length in Chapters 5 and 6.)

The good professional band today is composed of highly proficient musicians and every part is played expertly. Under present-day conditions where rehearsal time is expensive, the musicians must also be excellent sight-readers, and I suppose it is not unjust to say that the conductor must not only be a good sight-reader but must be sufficiently sure of what he is doing so that no time is wasted. The conditions governing professional performance are very different indeed from those obtaining for any other type of band performance, and the nature of the performance technique also influences the question of suitable or proper size of the band as well as the specific instrumentation.

On the question of repertoire, it is apparent that the Belle Isle Concert Band, giving thirty concerts *in the same location* each season, or the Goldman Band, giving fifty concerts (thirty-six of which are in Central Park) must get through a lot of music without much duplication in the programs. This means not only a need for an extensive library, and much thought about program-building, but also a highly-developed rehearsal technique which can accomplish the maximum possible in the minimum time allowed. And this depends in the last analysis on the outstanding performance abilities of top-flight professional players.

Illustration *28* may be cited as typical of recent Goldman Band programming under my direction.

SERVICE BANDS

The United States Marine Band is by many years the oldest of the service bands, with only the band of the United States Military Academy

⟦ ILLUSTRATION XXVIII ⟧

THE GOLDMAN BAND

Prospect Park, Brooklyn

June 30, 1960

PART I

PHILIP JAMES
Festal March
LOUIS SPOHR
Nocturne in C
1. Marcia   2. Adagio   3. Polacca
BORIS BLACHER
Divertimento
(First Performance in America)
J. N. HUMMEL
Rondo, from Concerto for Trumpet
James Burke, Cornetist
NORMAN LLOYD
A Walt Whitman Overture

PART II

RICHARD FRANKO GOLDMAN
March, The Foundation
VITTORIO GIANNINI
Praeludium and Allegro
WILLIAM SCHUMAN
Overture, "Chester"
LUDWIG VON BEETHOVEN
"March" from Egmont
EDWIN FRANKO GOLDMAN
March, The Spirit of Peace
JOHN PHILIP SOUSA
March, The Free Lance

(All except Hummel and Beethoven are original band works.)

⟦ CONTEMPORARY BANDS ⟧

as a close second. The Marine Band, since Sousa was its leader, has been one of the world's outstanding bands, and has continued to function as the Presidential band. It is at present under the direction of Lt. Colonel A. F. Schoepper.

It was not until the close of World War I that large bands were authorized for the Army and Navy. The Navy Band was established in *1918,* and was functioning efficiently by *1923.* The Army Band, an outgrowth of the Expeditionary Force Band of the first World War, was officially organized in *1921.* Both of these bands are large units, and both have established excellent reputations as concert organizations. Lt. Commander Charles Brendler is the present leader of the Navy Band. The Army Band is now under the leadership of Major Hugh Curry.

The United States Air Force Band was organized in *1942,* and the Army Field Band (originally known as the Army Ground Forces Band) in *1946.* The former is led by Colonel George S. Howard, the latter by Major Robert L. Bierly, who succeeded the band's first leader, Lt. Colonel Chester E. Whiting, in October *1960.*

Most of these bands also maintain symphony orchestras, either through the use of extra string players, or through the use of players who double on wind and stringed instruments. All of them concertize extensively both in and out of Washington, and have been heard not only in the United States but in many parts of the world. They also have in common the fact that they are all large bands, with permanent bases, maintaining large staffs of arrangers, assistants and administrative personnel, and all are, of course, tax-supported. They have, in many respects, replaced the professional civilian bands as touring attractions. They are primarily "concert" bands, of course, although they are attached to branches of the military and naval services, and wear the uniforms of their respective branches. It is in this respect only that they trace their descent from the original types of "military" band.

The United States Air Force Band can be considered typical of the large service bands, in terms of size and activities. Its present instrumentation (*1960*) consists of:

⟦ CONTEMPORARY BANDS ⟧

1 piccolo	6 cornets
4 flutes	4 tenor trombones
2 oboes	2 bass trombones
1 English horn	3 baritones
16 B♭ clarinets	3 tubas
1 bass clarinet	6 cellos
2 bassoons	6 double basses
1 contrabassoon	5 percussion players
6 French horns	1 harp
2 trumpets	

Total: 72 players

The reader will note the unusual make-up of this band, which includes six cellos and *no* saxophones. Captain Harry H. Meuser, Assistant Conductor of the Air Force Band, has commented on its make-up as follows:

It is true we do not use saxophones in The Air Force Band. We feel that they take away the tonal qualities of oboes, English horns, bassoons and French horns. These voices are doubled usually by the saxophones and destroy the true qualities of these instruments. This necessitates rearranging but the end result is musically gratifying. It is not that we expect the band to sound like an orchestra; this to me is a ridiculous attempt. We try only to achieve a purer woodwind sound when playing transcriptions of orchestral compositions. When it is absolutely necessary in the performance of such numbers as "An American in Paris," or Bizet's "L'Arlésienne Suite No. 2," we do assign a clarinetist or clarinetists who double on the saxophone to cover the part. In other words, when the original compositions called for saxophones we incorporate them in the band; otherwise we do not.

The cello section of the band adds a richness in certain registers that cannot be duplicated by the euphonium or baritone horn. This is especially true in the accompaniment of vocal solos and solo flute, clarinet, oboe, English horn, bassoon and French horn.

The following program of the United States Air Force Band, presented in March *1960* while the band was on tour in Japan, is a representative one. (See pages *108-109.*)

The Army Field Band maintained the following instrumentation in *1960:*

3 flutes (piccolo)	10 cornets and trumpets
2 oboes	3 baritone and/or euphonium
1 English horn	8 French horns
3 bassoons	8 trombones
14 B♭ clarinets	4 tubas
1 bass clarinet	4 double basses
1 contrabass clarinet	6 percussion players
5 saxophones	

Total: 73 players

Aside from the major service bands stationed in Washington, there are some *250* smaller bands attached to the various services, operating on a total annual budget estimated at *$28,068,000.*

UNIVERSITY AND COLLEGE BANDS

If Illinois was the first important modern university band, it did not take others very long to follow suit and to establish reputations for marching and concert performance. There is hardly a college or uni-

⟦ CONTEMPORARY BANDS ⟧

versity today that does not have a full-time band and Director of Bands, engaged not only in providing music and entertainment at athletic events, but undertaking some sort of concert activity as well. Competition is keen among these bands in marching, in uniforming, in formations—and in performance. The College Band Directors National Association, founded in *1942* by William D. Revelli, Director of Bands at the University of Michigan, had a roster of over *300* active members in *1959*, and is regularly adding more. The C.B.D.N.A. does not include all of the band directors active in colleges, although it does represent most of those associated with the larger institutions and those with the most highly developed band programs. Its stated objectives are contained in the following Declaration of Principles:

We affirm our faith in and our devotion to the College Band, which, as a serious and distinctive medium of musical expression, may be of vital service and importance to its members, its institution, and its art.

To its members the College Band, through exemplary practices in organization, training, and presentation, should endeavor to provide effective experiences in musical education, in musical culture, in musical recreation and in general citizenship.

To its institution the College Band should offer adequate concerts and performances at appropriate functions and ceremonies, in the interests of musical culture and entertainment, and for the enhancement of institutional spirit and character.

To music as an art and a profession the College Band should bring increasing artistry, understanding, dignity, and respect, by thorough and independent effort within the band's own immediate sphere, by leadership and sponsorship in the secondary school music program, and by cooperation with all other agencies pursuing similar musical goals.

To these ends we, the members of this Conference, pledge our-

⟦ **ILLUSTRATION XXIX** ⟧

THE UNITED STATES AIR FORCE BAND

Colonel George S. Howard, Conductor

Captain Harry H. Meuser, Assistant Conductor

THE SINGING SERGEANTS

Captain Robert L. Landers, Director

March 2   PROGRAM   *1960*

Overture to the opera "Mignon"   *Ambroise Thomas*

Vocal Solo—"L'Arlesiana"   *Francesco Cilea, arr. Floyd Werle*

M/SGT. WILLIAM DU PREE, TENOR SOLOIST

Three Musical Paintings   *Henri René, arr. Floyd Werle*

Trumpet Trio—"Bugler's Holiday"   *Leroy Anderson*

M/SGT. ARTHUR WILL, T/SGT. JACK TARDY, S/SGT. LEIGH BURNS

Dawn Breaks at a Shinto Shrine   *Urato Watanabe, arr. Robert Cray*

Selections by The Singing Sergeants, "Americana"

CAPTAIN ROBERT L. LANDERS, DIRECTOR

Swanee

Red River Valley

⟦ ILLUSTRATION XXIX ⟧

St. Louis Blues

Swing Low, Sweet Chariot

Battle Hymn of the Republic

INTERMISSION

La Fiesta Mexicana	*H. Owen Reed*
Harp Solo—"Chanson de Nuit"	*Maurice Ravel, arr. Floyd Werle*

T/SGT. PHILLIP YOUNG, SOLOIST

Sleigh Ride	*Leroy Anderson*
A Bit of Scotland	

T/SGT. GEORGE LUCAS, AIRMAN WILLIAM LOGAN, SOLOISTS

Four Contrasting Marches	
Colonel Bogey England	*Kenneth Alford*
Flieger Germany	*Paul Dostal*
Akebono Japan	*arr. Robert Cray*
Stars and Stripes Forever America	*John Philip Sousa*
The Singing Sergeants	

CAPTAIN ROBERT L. LANDERS, DIRECTOR

U.S. Air Force Hymn	*Mary Baker, arr. Ivan Genuchi*
Serenade from "The Student Prince"	*Sigmund Romberg*

M/SGT. WILLIAM DU PREE, TENOR SOLOIST

⟦ CONTEMPORARY BANDS ⟧

selves to seek individual and collective growth as musicians, as teachers, as conductors, and as administrators.

The university band is, as indeed is the high school band, an entirely new departure in music, primarily because it attempts to combine education and entertainment in a completely new way. Despite attempts to prove the contrary, I cannot see that the football band belongs in any category other than that of entertainment—nor, for that matter, does football played before *90,000* paying customers. The emphasis on the several aspects of band activity in different colleges (and high schools) varies considerably. In some institutions, the marching band is the number one attraction; in others it is less important than the concert band. But by and large, the two may be said to co-exist comfortably, although they may attract both players and audiences for widely different reasons. The bibliography on marching bands and techniques is enormous, and reflects the preoccupation with the subject in the schools. And of course it need hardly be said here that the technique displayed (even by many high school bands) is often prodigious and amazing. The accomplishment represents a tremendous expenditure of time and effort. How "educational" it is will very likely be a subject for increasing debate as the many problems faced by all of our educational institutions become more severe.

The effort and expense that have gone into the development, equipment and maintenance of the large college bands are evident in the facilities that many of them enjoy. Separate band buildings, carefully designed for every aspect of instruction and performance, are not uncommon. But even where special band buildings are not found, most institutions provide ample space and special facilities to suit the band's requirements. Gone are the days when, in most institutions, the band rehearsed in the basement of the physics lab or the chapel, and kept its equipment in dormitory closets. Libraries, practice rooms, storage rooms and a variety of rehearsal rooms are now usually available, not to mention good auditoriums for concerts. Most institutions own a large variety

[CONTEMPORARY BANDS]

of fine instruments, and enough in the way of general property and equipment to require the services of a sizable staff. These staffs are usually composed, at least in part, of student band officers. In many institutions, in addition to a Director of Bands, there are assistant band leaders and professional instructors in various instruments. Often the marching band has a staff of its own. Full or part-time concert managers are also required in some instances to take charge of the band on tour or for off-campus engagements. All in all, the college band is today very often a large-scale business enterprise.

In considering the concert activities of the college bands, and the professional apparatus that most of them involve, it still should not be forgotten that they represent activities of educational institutions, and that their primary aim is the education of the students who play in the bands. It is this that is the unique aspect of their vast activity. This education is, moreover, a highly specialized type of training, for it is unlike the conventional conservatory training which has as its objectives the preparation of performers for professional concert careers. The college band provides training primarily for public school teaching, so far as much of its personnel is concerned, and a musical-social activity for many of the others. It is obvious that the training of professional musicians can hardly enter into the picture on this scale, since there is already no place for the professional musician to go.

The relation of the university band to the university music department is often a puzzling one. The band is often almost a department in itself, and in many cases far outweighs the music department in power and prestige. In some cases, the band and the music department are not on notably good terms. The band director is usually (not, however, invariably) a member of the music education department, in which he often has professorial rank, and in a good many instances, rather more than professorial salary and perquisites. The preponderant relation of the band is with this department rather than with the department of music. Many of the students making up the band are usually majors in music education. Some are majors in the music department itself, and as a rule a fairly large number will be majors in anything from agriculture to zoology, playing in the band in a purely avocational way. However, for the most part, the most proficient university bands are found in those institutions that have large departments of music education, for it is in this area that the band is unquestionably the most important performance activity.

The band as part of the music education curriculum is thus part of a pre-professional training of a special type. In a sense, it is a curiously closed circle. The band helps train music educators for the public schools, and in this way the entire band movement is kept more or less on its own terms, while maintaining a constant feeding process. This is obviously necessary and in most ways desirable, yet it presents one danger which is not always recognized and is seldom discussed. That is simply that the band movement itself may become more and more divorced from other musical studies and activities, and from the main stream of musical life. There is some awareness of this, and some signs of a feeling that music and music education departments should perhaps operate with somewhat better co-ordination than has been prevalent. But there are many factors, not all of them academic, that enter into this problem, and changes will probably not come quickly.

The average college band rehearses several hours a week, and generally presents three or four "formal" concerts during the course of an academic year. There is of course a wide variation in the amount of time spent in the preparation of these programs. In general, the college band today emphasizes the best possible performance of a selected group of compositions to be played in public, rather than a general reading of band literature. Performance, with many of the college and university bands, is on an extraordinarily high level. As has been previously stated, many of these bands play far better than many professional bands. They have the additional advantage of being able to provide the greatest variety of instrumentation, through the resources of a large body of willing student performers and the availability of college-owned instruments. Thus the director can, for example, assign a student to the E♭ clarinet, if he so wishes, and can provide not only the instrument itself, but also adequate instruction. He can thus maintain the kind of in-

⟦ CONTEMPORARY BANDS ⟧

strumentation he wants, at least most of the time, without worrying about where replacements will come from when star performers graduate. Needless to say, there will inevitably be some variation from year to year (as there will be in football teams), but this is not in practice very wide. The top college bands maintain a quite remarkable level of excellence, and of course are fed each year by the thousands of talented youngsters graduating from the high school bands.

Among the features of band activity in the colleges are the intercollegiate band festivals held in many states and regions. The college bands have never engaged in contests and competitions as have the high school bands, but there are a number of well-established festivals, for which the best players from a large number of bands are chosen to form an all-State or all-regional group. These selected bands usually meet for a three-day period, and present a chosen program, often under the direction of a guest conductor. The programs are usually chosen to show off the abilities of the band, and often include music that would be too difficult for many of the individual bands of the region. The Ohio Intercollegiate Band Festival, first organized in *1929,* is a representative example, as is the one held annually in Pennsylvania. The *1960* Pennsylvania Festival featured a band of about *120* players, chosen from no fewer than thirty-four colleges in the state. This group, which is selected as a representative one, met for a total of approximately twelve hours of rehearsal. Its performance, of an extremely long and very taxing program, was remarkable. The program was chosen, as is customary, jointly by the guest conductor and the committee in charge of the Festival. (Page *114.*)

In addition to festivals such as these, band activity in the colleges includes "clinics" and conferences on a variety of scales, from local and state-wide, to regional and national. The annual mid-West Band Clinic is among the best known. At these meetings, held primarily for the instruction of and exchange of information among bandmasters, guest speakers are heard, demonstrations are given, and the participation of one or more bands is featured. Occasionally special bands are made up for these occasions, including bands composed entirely of bandmasters. Many universities, and some of the service bands as well, also hold "read-

⟦ **ILLUSTRATION XXX** ⟧

PROGRAM

March with Trumpets — William Bergsma

Overture in C — Charles Simon Catel
edited by R. F. Goldman and R. Smith

La Boutique Fantasque — Rossini-Respighi
arr. by Godfrey-Leidzen

Symphony for Band — Vincent Persichetti

    I. Adagio-Allegro

    II. Adagio sostenuto

    III. Allegretto

    IV. Vivace

Intermission

Fantasia in G Major — Johann Sebastian Bach
arr. by R. F. Goldman and R. L. Leist

Praeludium and Allegro — Vittorio Giannini

Passion in Paint Suite — Henri Rene
arr. by F. Werle

    I. At the Moulin Rouge

    II. Persistence of Memory

    III. L'Absinthe

Prelude and Processional, from *"Henry VIII"* — Camille Saint-Saens
arr. by J. Elkus

The Foundation March — Richard Franko Goldman

The Invincible Eagle March — John Philip Sousa

ing clinics" at which new works are read and rehearsed. In many states there are also state-wide bandmasters associations, functioning independently of national organizations such as the C.B.D.N.A., although many bandmasters are simultaneously members of both or, indeed, of several others besides.

An entire volume would be required to give even a partially detailed account of the variety of activities characterizing the world of band music in the colleges. But all of these activities subserve the main purpose of the college band which is, after all is said and done, the performance of band music and the training of student musicians. Illustrations *31-34* will serve to illustrate characteristic repertoire of representative college bands. Instrumentation used by each of the bands is given below:

University of Michigan Symphony Band
William D. Revelli, Conductor

Instrumentation (*1960*): *17* flutes, *4* oboes, *2* English horns, *3* bassoons, *1* contrabassoon, *1* E♭ soprano clarinet, *25* B♭ soprano clarinets, *5* E♭ alto clarinets, *3* B♭ bass clarinets, *2* E♭ contrabass clarinets, *4* E♭ alto saxophones, *1* B♭ tenor saxophone, *1* E♭ baritone saxophone, *10* cornets, *4* trumpets, *8* French horns, *6* tenor trombones, *2* bass trombones, *4* euphoniums, *6* tubas, *2* string basses, *6* percussion players (Total: *117* players)

University of Georgia Symphonic Band
Roger L. Dancz, Director

Instrumentation (*1958*): *1* piccolo, *9* flutes, *2* oboes, *3* bassoons, *13* clarinets, *2* bass clarinets, *1* contrabass clarinet, *1* soprano saxophone, *5* alto saxophones, *2* tenor saxophones, *1* baritone saxophone, *5* French horns, *10* cornets, *5* trumpets, *4* trombones, *2* baritones, *6* basses, *1* string bass, *7* percussion players (Total: *80* players)

116

〖 CONTEMPORARY BANDS 〗

University of Illinois Concert Band
Mark H. Hindsley, Conductor

Instrumentation *(1953)*: *15* flutes and piccolos, *4* oboes and English horns, *6* bassoons and contrabassoons, *29* clarinets, *6* bass clarinets, *3* contrabass clarinets, *4* saxophones, *10* cornets, *4* trumpets, *10* French horns, *8* trombones, *5* baritones, *6* tubas, *4* double basses, *2* harps, *1* celeste, *7* percussion players (Total: *124* players)

Of special interest, it seems to me, is a program given by the band of a university that does not offer any major in music and that has no instrumental instruction or courses in music education. This is the band of Lehigh University, long famous as an engineering school. Its concert band, of approximately sixty musicians, nevertheless manages to muster a fine and well-balanced instrumentation, and to present programs such as the one on page *120*, under its gifted young conductor, Jonathan Elkus. Instrumentation used by the band is given below:

Lehigh University Concert Band
Jonathan Elkus, Conductor

Instrumentation *(1960)*: *3* flutes (piccolo), *2* oboes, *1* E♭ clarinet, *12* B♭ clarinets (*5, 1st; 4, 2nd; 3, 3rd*), *1* alto clarinet, *1* bass clarinet, *2* bassoons, *3* alto saxophones, *1* tenor saxophone, *1* baritone saxophone, *4* French horns, *6* cornets, *2* trumpets, *4* trombones, *3* baritones (euphonium), *3* sousaphones, *1* string bass, *5* percussion players (Total: *55* players)

The composition of the Lehigh marching band, from an academic viewpoint, seems to me most interesting. Of ninety-six members, sixty are in engineering curricula, twenty-nine in liberal arts, eleven in business administration, and the remainder in combined curricula such as arts-engineering or industrial engineering-business. The extent of interest in

⟦ ILLUSTRATION XXXI ⟧

UNIVERSITY OF MICHIGAN SYMPHONY BAND

William D. Revelli, Conductor

April 10   P R O G R A M   *1960*

LATHAM	*Three Chorale Preludes*
ROSSINI	*Overture to "La Gazza Ladra"*
CRESTON	*Concerto for Saxophone*

DONALD SINTA, ALTO SAXOPHONE

VERDI	*"Manzoni" Requiem (Excerpts)*

INTERMISSION

MUELLER	*Overture in G*
BRISBIN	*Gethsemane*
JACOB	*Original Suite for Band*
BACH	*Fantasia in G major*
STRAUSS	*Death and Transfiguration (Finale)*
SOUSA	*The Free Lance March*

118

UNIVERSITY OF GEORGIA SYMPHONIC BAND

Roger L. Dancz, Director

March 2   PROGRAM   *1958*

Canzon Quarti Toni	GIOVANNI GABRIELI
Military Symphony in F	FRANCOIS JOSEPH GOSSEC
Overture for Band	FELIX MENDELSSOHN
Trauersinfonie	RICHARD WAGNER
Royce Hall Suite for Concert Band	HEALEY WILLAN

INTERMISSION

Divertimento for Band	VINCENT PERSICHETTI
Chester—Overture for Band	WILLIAM SCHUMAN
West Point Suite	DARIUS MILHAUD
Fanfare and Allegro	CLIFTON WILLIAMS

This is the Fifty-third Annual Winter Concert of the University of Georgia Band. For the second consecutive year, the program includes only orginal compositions for wind instruments.

⟦ ILLUSTRATION XXXIII ⟧

UNIVERSITY OF ILLINOIS CONCERT BAND

Mark H. Hindsley, Conductor

PROGRAM

March 19 and 20, 1953

EUGENE D'ALBERT	*Overture to "The Improvisator"*
JOHANN SEBASTIAN BACH	*Toccata and Fugue in D minor*
RICHARD STRAUSS	*Finale to the symphonic poem "Ein Heldenleben"*
ROBERT RUSSELL BENNETT	*Suite of Old American Dances*

INTERMISSION

RICHARD WAGNER	*Prelude to Act III of "Lohengrin"*
ERNO VON DOHNANYI	*Andante and Rondo from "Symphonic Suite," Op. 19*
CHARLES CARTER	*Sinfonia*
GEORGES ENESCO	*Roumanian Rhapsody No. 1*
JOHN PHILIP SOUSA	*Manhattan Beach*
EDWIN FRANKO GOLDMAN	*Illinois*

⟦ ILLUSTRATION XXXIV ⟧

The Department of Music, Lehigh University
presents the

WINTER CONCERT
of the
LEHIGH UNIVERSITY CONCERT BAND
JONATHAN ELKUS, *Conductor*
SATURDAY, FEBRUARY 6, 1960 — 8:15 P.M.
GRACE HALL, LEHIGH UNIVERSITY

PROGRAM

A Jubilant Fanfare, for military band   Sir Arthur Bliss (b. 1891)

Overture to *The Light Cavalry*   Franz von Suppé (1819-1895)
Transcribed by Henry Fillmore

Theme and Variations, Op. 43a, for band   Arnold Schoenberg (1874-1951)
     Theme: *poco allegro*
     Variation I: *(the same)*
     Variation II: *allegro molto*
     Variation III: *poco adagio*
     Variation IV: *tempo di valzer*
     Variation V: *molto moderato*
     Variation VI: *allegro*
     Variation VII: *moderato*
     Finale: *moderato - allegro - tempo primo - adagio*

Overture to *Susanna's Secret*   Ermanno Wolf-Ferrari (1876-1948)
Transcribed by Capt. J. F. Dean, A.R.C.M.

INTERMISSION

SEVEN MARCHES:

Olympia Hippodrome   Russell Alexander (d. 1916[?])
    Mr. Robert Barnhouse, publisher of *Olympia Hippodrome*, has been generous in pro-
viding the following note:
    "Of all the composers in our catalog I would say we know the least about this man
than any. Russell Alexander was an old vaudville performer with the act 'The Ex-
positon Four'. The act was made up of Newton and Woodruff Alexander (his brothers)
and a man named Brady. One of the members of this group played two cornets at one
time, playing a duet on those two instruments simultaneously.
    "Mr. Alexander toured Europe with the Barnum and Bailey Circus playing Baritone
during the years 1898-1902. This was information obtained from Henry Fillmore."

Trojan March from *The Capture of Troy*   Hector Berlioz (1803-1869)
Transcribed by Erik Leidzén

Siegfried's Funeral March from
     The Twilight of the Gods   Richard Wagner (1813-1883)
Transcribed by Jonathan Elkus

President Washington's Quick Step
    Melody from *Beck's Flute Book* (*ca.* 1790)
Freely adapted by Richard Franko Goldman

The People's Choice! A March for Election Eve, for band
    Douglas Moore (b. 1893)
    Dr. Moore, MacDowell Professor of Music and Head of the Department at Columbia
University, has based the March on a theme from his recent opera *The Ballad of Baby
Doe*. It intends to evoke the atmosphere of an election celebration during a campaign in
which William Jennings Bryan ran for the Presidency and to catch the spirit of Bryan's
"silver tongued" orations and the less dignified voice of the typical election-rally crowd.
The March was first performed on June 18, 1959, by the Goldman Band, which commissioned the work in memory of its founder, Edwin Franko Goldman.

Triumphal March from *Peter and the Wolf*, Op. 67
    Serge Prokofieff (1891-1953)
Transcribed by Richard Franko Goldman

Semper Fidelis   John Philip Sousa (1854-1932)

〖 CONTEMPORARY BANDS 〗

playing in bands, and its recreational, social and cultural value, is forcefully emphasized by these figures.

The same situation on a larger scale is found at Purdue University where over *400* students are enrolled in the band program under its director, Al G. Wright. There is no Music Department at this University. The band students come from all of the schools on campus: engineering, agriculture, home economics, pharmacy, science, education, and humanities, industrial management and veterinary science and medicine. The Symphonic Band, which of course consists of the best players, numbers *117*.

THE BAND IN THE HIGH SCHOOL

1956 statistics of the United States Office of Education indicated a total of approximately *21,000* public high schools in the United States. This number is fairly close to actuality for the *1960*'s, since consolidation of smaller schools into larger "comprehensive" schools will probably compensate at least to some degree for the great increase in numbers of students. In any case, completely accurate figures are not absolutely necessary for the purposes of this study. We know that over *80%* of the public high schools have bands, and can arrive at a probable figure of somewhere between *16,000* and *18,000* bands in the public high schools alone. Add to this figure a large number of bands in parochial schools, and a very small number in other private schools, and one can take roughly *20,000* as a safe working total. This is exclusive of bands in separately administered junior high schools and grade schools, for which usable figures are not available.

Approximate figures are enough to indicate the truly impressive growth of the band program in the schools, and to give some idea of the number of students and teachers involved. (On the other hand, the reader is cautioned against readily accepting a variety of slipshod figures that have been circulated on occasion. Thus, one fairly recent book declares that *9,000,000* high school students are in bands. If there are about

⟦ CONTEMPORARY BANDS ⟧

20,000 bands, this would mean about *450* players in each band! The figure of *35,000* high school bands has also been cited, which is interesting in view of the *1956* estimate of the total number of high schools. It would probably be safe to guess that over the twenty years from *1940* to *1960,* over *10,000,000* Americans *have* played in high school bands. This figure seems rather staggering, but cannot be far off the mark.)

The beginnings of the high school band movement have been described above, and we can now see the rapidity and extent of its growth. It is obvious that the band is an extremely popular activity among high school students, and that it has the support of parents and school boards. It hardly needs to be pointed out that the size and proficiency of the bands themselves vary enormously. Throughout the country there are dozens of high school bands, of all sizes, that play expertly; these are the ones that are shown off at conventions and on special occasions. At the other extreme are school bands whose playing taxes parental love to the utmost. But the youngsters in these bands are striving toward something, and are perhaps having as much fun, and deriving as much benefit from their efforts, as the youngsters in much better bands. At any rate, it must be assumed that the achievement must be measured in pedagogic rather than in absolute musical terms.

The variation in size and quality depends on many factors: size of school, ability of the band director, support of school and community (moral as well as financial support!), enthusiasm of parents, and many imponderables. A very small school in a small community sometimes produces a fine school band. There seems to be little correlation between type of school and quality of band. One of the best high school bands I have ever heard came from a highly-rated "academic" school in which the band was decidedly not given pampered treatment. On the other hand, some poor bands come from schools in which all the factors would appear to favor the development of outstanding groups.

The high school band is basically an agency of music education, and its aims are, or should be, governed by the general educational aims of its school and environment. It exists for the instruction of students in disciplines that, in generalized form, are accepted as beneficial and as

⟦ CONTEMPORARY BANDS ⟧

properly belonging in a balanced curriculum. The nature and quality of this instruction naturally vary a great deal, and improvement is constantly sought. Trained instrumental instructors, and better-trained ones, are being graduated each year from the universities and from schools of education. The relation of the college or university band and the high school band is thus a constant one.

In essence, the high school band performs on a more limited scale a function similar to that of the college band. The high school band entertains at football and other games, spends a lot of time working out formations and drills, and rehearses to improve the quality of its musical performance at both athletic events and occasional concerts. The best high school bands, as has been noted before, are astonishingly proficient in all of these areas. One wonders, indeed, when one both hears and sees them, how much time must have been spent in preparation, and whether the students can possibly have any time at all left for other subjects in the curriculum. But this is beside the point. Most high school bands do not tempt one to this kind of wonder; and it would not be proper that they should. For the high school band properly exists *for its players,* and not for the admiration of a wide general audience, except on rare occasions.

In the larger school systems, and in many smaller ones as well, instrumental instruction starts in the junior high school or even earlier, so that the players in high school bands are not usually beginners. "Pre-instrumental" classroom instruction is started as early as kindergarten in many instances. One finds therefore, along with many students of average ability, a surprising number of advanced and genuinely talented players in high school bands. Anyone who has heard or adjudicated solo contests at the high school level can bear witness to this.

The instrumental supervisor or band director in the high school must be highly qualified in many diverse ways. The job is a hard one, for he must not only be a conductor, but he must teach most of the instruments, figure out and supervise marching procedures, be a master diplomat with parents and the community at large, be responsible for thousands of dollars' worth of equipment, and must also do a good many

〖 CONTEMPORARY BANDS 〗

extra-curricular jobs as well. He must be a musician first and foremost, but he also has to be partly an animal-trainer and partly a promoter. It is extraordinary to observe what some of these supervisors and directors are able to accomplish, and most of them deserve the greatest praise and admiration.

The incentives for the high school musician are many and diverse. Some youngsters join the band because of the uniforms, or the social activity, or the trips that some bands make; some join simply because friends have joined; some are pushed in by parents (a few are also kept out by parents); and some join because it is a musical activity. The band director has to fuse this diversity into a unit that is harmonious in every sense of the word. To be successful at this requires personal as well as musical qualifications of a very special kind.

Among the incentives for the students are the many festivals and special events that take place during the school year. The national contests were abandoned many years ago, when they became unwieldy. They were replaced by regional contests, but these too were abandoned when the competitive aspects, originally considered to be good for morale and incentive, produced questionable results (especially among non-winners). Finally the idea of festivals replaced the idea of competitions. Ratings by division (first, second, third, etc.) are still in use at these festivals, and provide adequate reward while avoiding the less amiable aspects of direct competition.

No one who has attended a high school music festival can have any doubts about how exciting and rewarding it is to the students participating, nor how seriously the events are taken. The large festivals often include not only band competitions, but solo and ensemble divisions as well, and the striving for First Division (top) rating is intense. One of the best-known and largest of these high school festivals is the Tri-State Music Festival held annually in Enid, Oklahoma, under the joint sponsorship of Phillips University and the citizens of the city. In *1960*, the twenty-eighth annual Tri-State Festival attracted *114* bands from twenty-one states, as well as an impressive number of school orchestras and choral groups. Over *10,000* students in all took part in the

〖 CONTEMPORARY BANDS 〗

various events. A festival of this scope must be seen to be believed. The services of approximately fifty adjudicators are required, working all day long and well into the evening for three days. From the standpoint of logistics alone, the Festival is a phenomenon; over *10,000* students, accompanied by several hundred teachers, are lodged and fed for three days in a city of about *43,000* population. The arrangements for a festival of this sort take infinite planning; and the Tri-State is a year-round job for its efficient organizer and director, Dr. Milburn Carey.

For competition purposes, ensembles and soloists are classified according to the size of the school from which they come. These classifications vary slightly from region to region, but the Tri-State division is representative:

	Organizations from High Schools of:
Class AA	more than 1000 enrollment
Class A	751-1000 enrollment
Class BB	401-750 enrollment
Class B	251-400 enrollment
Class CCC	176-250 enrollment
Class CC	101-175 enrollment
Class C	86-100 enrollment
Class D	less than 86 enrollment (grades 9-12)

Most festivals do not sub-divide as thoroughly as the above. The general rule holds that a school may enter a higher class, but of course not a lower one.

Festivals of this sort usually wind up with a gala concert, featuring a massed band made up of several hundred selected players from participating bands. The massed band is musically perhaps not the most satisfying thing in the world, but it provides color and excitement, and has a certain appropriateness for these occasions. It carries us back to Gilmore and a time-honored idea of festivity; Gilmore himself would have loved the whole idea.

⟦ CONTEMPORARY BANDS ⟧

The high school band movement is highly organized in state, regional and national associations. Many states feature annual selection of an all-state band; the larger ones precede this with meetings of all-regional bands, from which the all-state selections are made. The assembling of the all-state band, and its rehearsal and performance, generally coincide with a meeting of the state band or music educators association. Even more than with the college all-state or regional bands, these occasions give an opportunity to the students to perform programs of greater scope and difficulty than most of them could do with their own school bands.

A typical regional high school festival includes regional (or sectional) orchestras and choruses as well as bands, and is generally climaxed by a concert in which all these groups take part. A typical affair of this sort is the White Plains (N.Y.) Sectional All-State Concert of January, *1960*. The band of about *120* players, selected from twenty-eight high schools in a single county, performed the following selections:

Charles Simon Catel: OVERTURE IN C
Darius Milhaud: SUITE FRANÇAISE
Percy Grainger: IRISH TUNE
Cyril Scott: PASSACAGLIA
Edwin Franko Goldman: ON THE MALL

This concert was sponsored by the Westchester County Music Association, and presented by the New York State School Music Association. One sees in this way how the organization of high school music proceeds from the local level up through state, regional and finally national organizations. The Music Educators National Conference (MENC), a unit of the National Education Association (NEA) is the general co-ordinating and supervisory agency. Many states or regions have autonomous organizations, and some are confined to bands, or to vocal music. There are also a number of more or less autonomous organiza-

[CONTEMPORARY BANDS]

tions on a national scale, and new ones are still being formed from time to time.

The program above is interesting because this region, just outside of New York City, has never been nationally famous for its outstanding high school bands. On the other hand, the region is such, economically and socially, that many of the students are able to take private instrumental lessons with top-notch specialized teachers. The selected group of players is therefore quite remarkable, and the *1960* band was able to give a very good performance of a work of the difficulty of the Milhaud *Suite Française,* surely a feat that none of the high school bands by itself could have accomplished.

One further feature of high school band activity should be mentioned: the extent to which summer music schools and camps supplement the regular instruction and band work of the school year. The National Music Camp at Interlochen, Michigan, founded in *1928* by Joseph Maddy, is of course the most famous of these summer institutions, but there are now dozens of schools, camps and workshops in all parts of the country offering high school students instruction and vacations combined. Many are held on the campuses of colleges and universities; others are in attractive resort areas. Some receive aid from educational systems or organizations; others are privately owned and operated. The summer music camp appears to be growing steadily in popularity and scope.

Since we are concerned with what bands perform, it will be interesting to reproduce some typical high school band programs from various parts of the country, representing schools of different sizes (pages *129-133*.) Instrumentation used by these bands is given below:

Greensboro (N.C.) Senior High School Concert Band
Herbert Hazelman, Director

Instrumentation (*1960*): *14* flutes (piccolo, E♭ flute, alto flute, *3* oboes (English horn), *1* E♭ clarinet, *18* B♭ clarinets, *4* alto clarinets, *4* bass clarinets, *3* BB♭ contra-bass clarinets, *2* bassoons, *2* alto saxophones, *2* tenor saxophones, *1* baritone saxophone, *8* French horns, *8* cornets, *2* trumpets, *4* euphoniums, *6* trombones, *4* tubas, *6* percussion players (Total: *92* players)

Grand Junction (Colorado) Concert Band
Marion L. Jacobs, Director

Instrumentation (*1960*): *17* flutes, *2* oboes, *3* bassoons, *21* B♭ clarinets, *1* E♭ clarinet, *2* contra-bass clarinets, *6* alto saxophones, *4* tenor saxophones, *1* baritone saxophone, *7* bass clarinets, *18* cornets, *4* trumpets, *6* French horns, *5* trombones, *6* baritones, *4* tubas, *1* double bass, *10* percussion players (Total: *118* players)

The Senior Concert Band, South High School,
Valley Stream (N.Y.)
Robert Leist, Director

Instrumentation (*1960*): *14* flutes, *1* oboe, *23* clarinets, *4* bass clarinets, *1* bassoon, *2* alto saxophones, *2* tenor saxophones, *1* baritone saxophone, *10* cornets, *7* French horns, *4* trombones, *3* baritones, *4* basses, *1* double bass, *11* percussion players (Total: *88* players)

Joliet (Illinois) Township High School Concert Band
Bruce H. Houseknecht, Conductor

Instrumentation (*1960*): *11* flutes and piccolos, *2* oboes and English horns, *2* bassoons, *16* B♭ clarinets, *4* alto clarinets, *5* bass clarinets, *2* contra-bass clarinets, *2* tenor saxophones, *2* baritone saxophones, *1* bass saxophone, *4* trumpets, *8* cornets, *1* baritone, *6* French horns, *7* trombones, *5* basses, *15* percussion players (Total: *93* players)

129

[[ILLUSTRATION XXXV]]

GREENSBORO SENIOR HIGH SCHOOL
CONCERT BAND

Herbert Hazelman, Director

January 14   PROGRAM   *1960*

O Jesu Blest from the "Saint Matthew Passion"   JOHANN SEBASTIAN BACH

Euryanthe Overture   CARL MARIA VON WEBER

Trauersinfonie   RICHARD WAGNER

Good Friday Spell from "Parsifal"   RICHARD WAGNER

Conducted by the arranger, Earl A. Slocum

INTERMISSION

Dramatic Essay for Trumpet and Band   CLIFTON WILLIAMS

Carnival of Venice   HERBERT L. CLARKE

Ode for Trumpet   ALFRED REED

Emerson Head, guest trumpet soloist

Selections for concert band from "Gigi"   FREDERICK LOEWE

(Senior High School Auditorium, Greensboro, N. C.)

⟦ **ILLUSTRATION XXXVI** ⟧

GRAND JUNCTION CONCERT BAND

Marion L. Jacobs, Director

PROGRAM

EDWIN FRANKO GOLDMAN   *Franklin Field March*

VINCENT PERSICHETTI   *Pageant*

KALINNIKOV-BAINUM   *Finale, G minor Symphony*

(*Note: this program was shared with the High School Symphony Orchestra, the High School A Cappella Choir and the High School Combined Choruses.*)

131

⟦ ILLUSTRATION XXXVII ⟧

SOUTH HIGH SCHOOL, VALLEY STREAM

THE SENIOR CONCERT BAND

Robert Leist, Director

February 27   P R O G R A M   *1960*

EDVARD GRIEG   *Solemn Procession*

JOHN P. DALBY   *Tarantella*

JANET AKERS, FLUTE SOLOIST

FRANK ERICKSON   *Second Symphony for Band (1st Movement)*

MAURICE C. WHITNEY   *Rumba*

FRANK MCPARTLAND, SAXOPHONE SOLOIST

JOHN J. MORRISSEY   *Nightfall*

ROBERT GROSSMAN, CLARINET SOLOIST

ROBERT LEIST   *Parade of the Rusty Muskets*

GEORGE WILSON, WILLIAM GOUGH AND NED KOPPLESON, TROMBONISTS

ERNESTO LECUONA   *San Francisco El Grande*

JOHN PHILIP SOUSA   *Hands Across the Sea*

JANET AKERS, STUDENT DIRECTOR

132

⟦ ILLUSTRATION XXXVIII ⟧

JOLIET TOWNSHIP HIGH SCHOOL CONCERT BAND

Bruce H. Houseknecht, Conductor

April 10   PROGRAM   *1960*

Heroic Procession (Huldigungsmarsch)	RICHARD WAGNER
Toccata	GIROLAMO FRESCOBALDI
West Point Symphony: Finale	ROBERT J. DVORAK
March: Band Pioneer	ERNEST O. CANEVA

DIRECTED BY SENIOR STUDENT CONDUCTOR TERRY GUIDETTI

I   *March: Totem Pole*   ERIC OSTERLING

DIRECTED BY SENIOR STUDENT CONDUCTOR NOBLE ALLAN

Vltava (The Moldau), Symphonic Poem	BEDRICH SMETANA
Introduction and Scherzo	MAURICE WEED
William Tell Overture	GIACCOMO ROSSINI

INTERMISSION

II   *Selections by the high school male chorus, The Singing Steelmen*

Procession of Nobles	NICOLAI RIMSKY-KORSAKOV
La Rougette	DAVID BENNETT

HARP SOLOIST, MISS PENNY HOWK

III   *Concertino for Percussion and Band*   CLIFTON WILLIAMS

MARSHALL ERICKSON, DIRECTOR OF CADET BAND, CONDUCTING

The School Musician, Concert March   WILLIAM BEEBE AND CHRISTOPHER PAUL

133

[ILLUSTRATION XXXIX]

NATIONAL MUSIC CAMP HIGH SCHOOL
SYMPHONIC BAND

Kresge Assembly Hall, Interlochen, Michigan

George C. Wilson, Conductor

July 9   P R O G R A M   *1960*

Vanity Fair Overture
FLETCHER

Suite for Concert Band
KECHLEY

Fugue with Chorale
LEIDZEN

Concertino for Percussion and Band
CLIFTON WILLIAMS

March—Inglesina
DELLE-CASE

Reverie
DEBUSSY-JOHNSON

Little Suite, from "Comedy on the Bridge"
MARTINU-JARMAN

Selections from "Flower Drum Song"
RODGERS-LANG

March—Jubilee
GOLDMAN

⟦ CONTEMPORARY BANDS ⟧

COMMUNITY AND MUNICIPAL BANDS

There is today a decided upsurge in the field of community bands, and many long-established municipal bands are again becoming more active. These bands, in many, if not most cases, have received a boost because of the desire of instrumentalists to continue playing in bands after graduation from school or college. Most of these bands are mixed professional and amateur groups, and their modes of operation vary so greatly that it is impossible to generalize. They are supported in almost every imaginable way. Municipal bands, properly so called, receive financial support from the cities in which they operate. The amounts allotted are extremely variable, but they are not as a rule very large, and the bands are therefore usually small. The number of concerts offered in a given season is also a budgetary matter. Few manage to give a large number of concerts, but it seems quite possible that in the future more support will be available in many communities, and that there will be more permanently established municipal bands giving more extended series of concerts.

The idea of community bands is spreading rapidly, and it is no longer possible to keep up with the number of new ventures in this field. Most of these bands include adult players and students, and the majority of them are directed by bandmasters in the local or nearby schools. The proficiency of these groups must, by their nature, vary a great deal, as does their size and instrumental constituency. The support of these bands is also subject to any number of local variations. Some receive funds, in limited amounts, from the community; others are "membership" groups with dues; others depend on good-will and voluntary contributions. Often business firms or private citizens undertake part or all of the support. One of the pioneers in the field of the community band, especially designed to give opportunity to high school players after graduation, was Arthur H. Brandenburg, of Elizabeth, New Jersey, whose organization in that community was for many years a model.

It is sometimes difficult to draw the line today between the mu-

[CONTEMPORARY BANDS]

nicipal and the community band, and it is not impossible that the two types, originally somewhat distinct, will tend to merge in the not distant future. The community band (and also the municipal band insofar as it is tending to become indistinguishable from the community band) exists for two main reasons: to provide entertainment in the traditional way of bands, and also to provide a social and musical activity for the players. These functions are equally important and useful.

It is very probable that, with the increasing number of players who are anxious to join a post-school group, and the renewed popularity of local band concerts, these bands will grow in size and receive additional financial support. The growth of these bands certainly is a healthy and encouraging sign of life in the world of band music, and one that all bandsmen must wish to see continuing and developing.

INDUSTRIAL BANDS AND OTHERS

The industrial band, that is, the band maintained by a business concern for the enjoyment and entertainment of its employees, has much in common with the community band. Like the community band, it is often composed of both amateur and professional players (the latter being employed to give "body" to the band, and being given jobs in the factory or business); sometimes a full-time professional is hired as leader, and sometimes a member of the company's staff does additional duty as bandmaster. The purpose of this type of band is primarily that of a recreational facility for employees, but it also advertises the business and provides entertainment. One of the most noted of these bands was the Armco Band of Cincinnati, directed for many years by Frank Simon. This band concertized extensively, and was a good professional outfit in every respect. The Philco Company of Philadelphia maintains one of the best of these bands today, under the direction of Herbert N. Johnston, an engineer by profession but a fine cornetist and bandsman. The present instrumentation (*1960*) of the Philco Band is as follows: [1]

[1] (Note: The Band's personnel also includes the conductor and a librarian, bringing the total to 60.)

⟦ CONTEMPORARY BANDS ⟧

4 flutes and piccolos	1 baritone saxophone
2 oboes	6 cornets
1 E♭ clarinet	2 trumpets
14 B♭ clarinets	4 French horns
1 alto clarinet	2 baritones
1 bass clarinet	6 trombones
2 bassoons	3 tubas
2 alto saxophones	2 string basses
1 tenor saxophone	4 percussion players

Total: 58 players

A typical program by the Philco Band, given April *29, 1960,* at the Lower Moreland High School in Huntingdon Valley, Pa., for the benefit of the scholarship fund is shown on page *140.*

There are many other types of bands flourishing in the United States: American Legion Bands of all sizes; fraternal bands, circus bands, and miscellaneous professional bands organized and hired for single engagements or specific occasions. All are interesting, and all contribute to the liveliness of the musical scene, but they do not involve us in any new considerations of organization, repertoire or activity. Circus bands play circus music, although even circus music produces a new wrinkle from time to time, as when Stravinsky was commissioned to do his *Circus Polka* for the Barnum and Bailey elephants. Circus bands are, as a matter of fact, among the oldest types of bands in the United States. One of the first circus bands in the country was led by Thomas Coates; subsequent leaders of circus bands have included some of America's most popular bandsmen, among them Karl King and Merle Evans. The first circus band was active in about *1840,* and they have been going ever since, despite the changing nature of the circus itself. It will be a sad day when we have a circus without a band!

[ILLUSTRATION XL]

THE PHILCO CORPORATION BAND

Herbert N. Johnston, Conductor

April 29, 1960

PROGRAM

Charles Camille Saint-Saens	March "Occident et Orient" *
Antonio Carlos Gomez	Overture "Il Guarany"
Jules Massenet	"Meditation" (from "Thais")
Victor Herbert	"Indian Summer"
Nicholas Rimsky-Korsakov	"The Flight of the Bumble-Bee" (from the "Tsar Saltan")
John Philip Sousa	"By the Light of the Polar Star" * (from "Looking Upward" Suite)

INTERMISSION

Richard Franko Goldman	"A Curtain Raiser and Country Dance" *
Herbert N. Johnston, arr.	Fantasie "Minka"

CORNET SOLO—HERBERT N. JOHNSTON

Herbert N. Johnston	March "Pastorius Pageant" *
Edwin Franko Goldman	March "The Golden Rule" *
Jean Sibelius	Tone Poem "Finlandia"

* Original band works

⟦ CONTEMPORARY BANDS ⟧

THE SYMPHONIC WIND ENSEMBLE

The new trend toward the so-called "Symphonic Wind Ensemble" is best exemplified by the Eastman Symphonic Wind Ensemble, organized in *1952* by Frederick Fennell, its active and gifted conductor. Mr. Fennell's thoughts about this type of ensemble, which he very firmly does not consider a "band" in the old sense, are best given in his description which forms the program note to a concert given on March *20, 1960*.

Our decision to establish this new group was made after twenty years of careful study and performance by the Eastman School Symphony Band of the significant musical literature for the wind band, both original and transcribed. In establishing the Wind Ensemble as an adjunct to the Symphony Band, it has been our desire to strike out in new directions which would begin from the premise that we could make music with the minimum rather than with the maximum number of players, that we would confine our rehearsals and performances to the study of the original music written for the massed wind medium, and that we should embark upon a most active program to stimulate the composition of music for the Wind Ensemble by contemporary composers everywhere.

We do not call our group a band simply because we do not believe that it is a band. To qualify for that distinguished classification a group should be uniformed in the tradition of the band, should be able to march and perform in the open air in the tradition of that band, should perform the traditional musical literature of the band, and maintain those time-honored traditions and associations to which the public and its institutions have become so rightfully accustomed.

With the full knowledge of what has gone before in the history of composition and performance, and with due respect for the existence of the symphony orchestra, military band, and concert band, there is validity in the premise that their contributions to the arts of public performance, composition, and musical education may be supplemented by an ensemble which combines the appropriate features of those three established mediums of musical art.

The instrumentation of the Ensemble is as follows:

3 flutes (piccolo)
3 oboes (English horn)
1 E♭ clarinet
8 B♭ clarinets
1 alto clarinet
1 bass clarinet
1 contrabass clarinet
2 bassoons
1 contrabassoon
2 alto saxophones

1 tenor saxophone
1 baritone saxophone
5 French horns
6 trumpets
4 trombones
2 euphoniums
2 tubas
6 percussion players
1 contrabass (string)
1 harp

Total: 52 players

There can be little doubt that all of the original band music, which this group plays to the exclusion of arrangements and transcriptions, can be perfectly performed by this group of players who are of professional calibre even though they are still students. It is here again that the question of band instrumentation must be considered in relation to the ability of the performers. The abstract idea of a "standard" or "perfect" instrumentation is at the mercy of the kind of performers one has available, and no amount of schematic planning will help if a part is not played well. Fennell's group is in considerable contrast to the tendency of most bands to strive for *size*. Its critics seem to feel that, excellent as its performances are, they lack the massiveness of a good band sound. This kind of sound is not, however, what Fennell seeks, and the criticism seems pointless in many ways. If, as Fennell claims, the wind ensemble is a *different* type of performing group, there should be no comparisons at all. But the question does remain: how different is it?

A typical program of the Eastman Wind Ensemble is this one:

140

[**ILLUSTRATION XLI**]

*P*rogram

LINCOLNSHIRE POSY . . . . . *Percy Aldridge Grainger*
"Lisbon Bay'
"Horkstow Grange"
"Rufford Park Poachers"
"The Brisk Young Sailor"
"Lord Melbourne"
"The Lost Lady Found"

SERENADE NO. 10 IN B FLAT (K. V. 361)
. . . . *Wolfgang Amadeus Mozart*
Movement VI: Theme with variations

SUITE NO. 1 IN E FLAT, OPUS 28a . . . . *Gustav Holst*
Chaconne
Intermezzo
March

SYMPHONIES OF WIND INSTRUMENTS . . *Igor Stravinsky*

CHORALE AND ALLELUIA . . . . . . *Howard Hanson*

THREE MARCHES
MARCH, OPUS 99 . . . . *Sergei Prokofiev*
INGLESINA . . . . *D. Delle Cese*
NATIONAL EMBLEM . . . . . . *Edwin E. Bagley*

⟦ CONTEMPORARY BANDS ⟧

The points of similarity between the "band" and the "wind ensemble" are, I should think, just about as numerous as the points of difference. First of all, there is the central question of repertory. The ensemble, it is true, reaches into areas that are not band music—at least not band music for an outfit of *80* to *120* players!—such as the Mozart Serenades, and the *Symphonies of Wind Instruments* of Stravinsky. It can easily become a chamber ensemble for works conceived on a smaller scale than that of the modern band, or it can play works, such as the Stravinsky, conceived essentially for the wind section of the orchestra. This flexibility is musically advantageous and admirable, and might well encourage other bandmasters to modify their groups for specific works where appropriate. But the fact remains that most of Fennell's repertoire is standard band literature, including, as one will note, standard military marches, and the performance of his ensemble must therefore challenge that of the normally constituted band on its own ground. The Holst Suites, for example, were written for conventional British military bands. It is thus rather amusing to note that *almost no one* in this country is really playing them as written! Most bands are *over*-instrumented: in fact, for an American market, the publishers had to *add* instruments to Holst's original scoring. But this is, of course, another problem, to which we shall return later.

The advantages of the wind ensemble are in the extension of repertoire that is made possible by the ensemble's flexibility, and in the clarity of sound and execution resulting from the elimination of excess "fat" in the usual band sound. A group that performs *only* music written for winds needs no other musical justification, and indeed it fills a very valuable role in the general performance picture. An ensemble of this sort carries on very logically the development of the wind band from its origin as a military or marching unit through the era of popular concert-giving, based on transcriptions of light standard repertoire, to the best concert band practice of our time. It becomes, in effect, the realization of what a concert band aims for in its most musically serious moments, and its appeal should be very great for those who feel that the age of miscellaneous transcriptions is over, and that the wind band can exist on a somewhat more sophisticated level than is commonly attained.

Whether the wind ensemble should do transcriptions at all may be a moot point. It would be inconsistent to attempt the argument that what bands do, wind ensembles automatically should not do. Yet here again, if the wind ensemble is to be distinguished from the band in terms of its functions and repertoire, as well as of its size and instrumentation, there is perhaps also an inconsistency on this side. Fennell has in the past few years begun to play some conventional band arrangements, Walton's *Crown Imperial*, for instance, originally written for orchestra.

It is probable that the ultimate utility and place in the musical scene of the wind ensemble, like that of the band, the orchestra, the string quartet or any other performance medium, will be determined by the repertoire historically at its disposal, and the contributions to that repertoire that composers will make in the future.

part two

Technical
Problems
of the
B · A · N · D

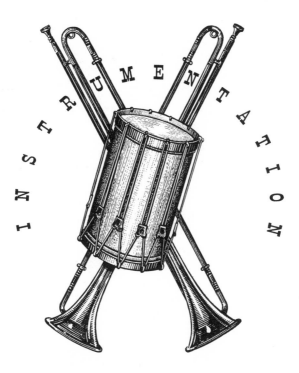

INSTRUMENTATION

⟦ INSTRUMENTATION ⟧

There are available a great number of excellent descriptive treatises on the wind and percussion instruments, and it would be superfluous in this volume to attempt another account of these instruments one by one. What concerns us here is their use in bands, past, present, and even more important, future.

The wind instruments divide basically into woodwind and brass, and the proportion of woodwind to brass in the band has always been one of the first major problems. England has always shown a predilection for all-brass bands and, as we have seen, bands of this type were also dominant in the United States until just before the Civil War. All-reed bands, on the other hand, have never been considered seriously, since they would provide no outstandingly useful musical resource. The brasses of course traditionally combine the advantages of portability, robustness and brilliance, as well as a certain homogeneity of sound that makes the ensemble unified and pleasing.

We have seen that the instrumentation of the band developed in an irregular manner, and that its make-up was determined by a great variety of factors. Local traditions exerted some influence, but the most important determining elements were first, the functions which the bands filled and second, the mechanical development of the instruments themselves. Without the inventors and perfecters of valve and piston systems, without the work of Sax, Boehm, Klose and others, there would be no modern wind instruments. Our present instruments are the result of a kind of evolutionary survival of the fittest. Yet it should not be altogether forgotten that some valuable assets may have been lost in the process of elimination, and that even modern instruments do not represent the whole gamut of possible wind instrument timbres—and much less, in fact, do those instruments commonly serving as the basic body of the American band. They do, however, represent what has been found to be most consistently useful, satisfactory and practical.

At one time or another, almost every instrument into which breath can be blown to produce sound has been employed in a band. Also, at one time or another, the instruments which have survived, and with which we are now familiar, have been built in an indescribable variety

⟦ INSTRUMENTATION ⟧

of keys. The C clarinet, for example, held sway long before the B♭ became standard. One further point should be remembered: although in many cases nomenclature has not changed, the instrument itself has changed considerably. Thus, the cornet of *1960* (as generally manufactured in the United States) is not quite the same as the cornet played in *1900*. Today's oboe differs somewhat in sound from the nineteenth century oboe. Other instruments continue to evolve; the changes are slow, but none the less real.

Today, as a rule, we use representative members of families that were originally used more or less completely. We have seen that at one time the prevailing group was the family of related instruments. Oboes, for example (or shawms), were constructed in all sizes from soprano to bass. We have today in common use only the oboe and its alto, the English horn. (The bassoon descends from another family; when the "quartet of double-reeds" comes up in present-day discussions, it might be well to remember this!) Until recently, one found bands in which only the B♭ clarinet was used, with occasionally a bass clarinet. As a rule only the B♭ trumpet or cornet is found, although it can be maintained that these have relatively close family connections in trombones, baritones, and possibly altos, tenor horns and tubas.

There is today, as every bandsman knows, a growing tendency to reinstate full family representation in a good number of the instrumental sections of the band. This is especially true of the clarinets. Although the E♭ sopranino still meets with resistance, the E♭ alto and the B♭ bass are now used much more than formerly, and there is much sentiment in favor of both E♭ and BB♭ contrabass instruments. The saxophone family is also returning, as Sax wished. Many nineteenth century bands used only alto and tenor; today we invariably have a quartet of two altos, tenor and baritone, and many bandsmen would like to add the bass. Curiously enough, few seem interested in the soprano. There is no such interest at the moment in bass oboes or flutes, although both these instruments exist. There are some expressions of interest in higher cornets and lower trumpets, as well as in the great assortment of saxhorns (the brass family devised by Sax). And there are other instruments, such as sarrusophones, in which little interest has been expressed by American bandsmen.

All this is sufficient to indicate that the instrumentation of the band is largely a matter of choice among an endless number of possibilities. The band has no stabilizing influence in the shape of a classical repertoire written for its specific and exclusive use. The available published repertoire of arrangements and original works, as it exists in *1961*, rests on generally accepted conventions that have not until recently been seriously challenged. These conventions, so far as band music in the United States is concerned, stem from the ideas of British band instrumentation as evolved in the nineteenth century, and as transplanted to this country by Gilmore and Sousa. *The band today could, if it wished, scrap its entire existing repertoire and start all over again.* All that would be seriously missed would be a handful of original band compositions written in recent years. These would, if the band changed, have to be re-scored. But since the rest of the repertoire consists of arrangements, all that would be involved would be the making of new arrangements. All one can say is that they would sound either better or worse than the old ones, with a fifty-fifty chance either way. The certain outcome is that they would sound *different*.

I trust that this presentation of the basic truth about the band and what it plays is sufficiently startling to bring it home emphatically to all readers. If a bandmaster or a manufacturer or an arranger should decide tomorrow that the modern wind band should consist of *16* English horns, *16* saxophones, *8* flügelhorns, *8* piccolos and *8* string basses, with no clarinets or cornets or trombones, there would be no reason to stop him from trying it. He would simply have to have some quite special arrangements made of anything he wanted to play, or else start out fresh with a brand-new repertoire written with this new combination in mind. Such an experimenter would have to justify his procedure by the assumption that the *sound* of the new combination would be so exciting in itself, and present so many possibilities, that it would be worth revolutionizing previous concepts of the band; or he would have to take the position that anything he wanted to play (from the old repertoire)

⟦ INSTRUMENTATION ⟧

would sound better played by his new combination. He would, of course, have to decide how a Sousa march, for example, would sound unless, of course (and this would be his privilege), Sousa marches were among the things he no longer wished to play.

I have exaggerated a little here (although really not as much as one might think) in order to emphasize this problem, which does not usually receive the attention it warrants in a serious discussion of the wind band's instrumentation and the problems stemming from it. The artistic life of the orchestra depends on its *existing* repertoire; there is no question of this repertoire being arranged to fit a conductor's idea of what combination of instruments might make it sound better. Also, a tradition of orchestration exists on an international basis; but it has been made international by the universal appeal of the masterpieces created within this tradition as it has developed, as well as by an assumption of artistic responsibility by performers (including, above all, conductors) to the repertoire. The artistic truth is that the performer exists for the repertoire—not vice versa.

In previous chapters we have presented typical band instrumentations of the past and present. European bands of the present offer still further variations.[1] The possibilities of combination are indeed many, both as regards variety and numbers. Below is a list of wind and percussion instruments from which one might choose in making up a band:

Flutes:

piccolo in C
piccolo in D♭
flutes in C, D♭ or E♭

Single Reeds:

Clarinets:
    sopranino in A♭
    soprano in E♭

---

[1] See *The Concert Band;* also many studies in American periodicals.

⟦ INSTRUMENTATION ⟧

fifes in B♭
alto flute in F
bass flute

Double Reeds:

oboe
English horn
heckelphone
bass oboe
bassoon
contrabassoon
sarrusophones:
   sopranino in E♭ to
   contrabass in E♭

Brasses:

trumpet in E♭ (high)
trumpet in B♭
trumpet in E♭ (low)
alto trombone
trombone in B♭ (tenor)
trombone in B♭, G, F or E♭ (bass)
cornet in E♭ (high)
cornet in B♭
French horn in F or B♭
Saxhorns:
   fluegelhorn in E♭ (high)
   fluegelhorn in B♭
   alto horn in E♭
   mellophone
   tenor horn in B♭
   baritone in B♭
   euphonium in B♭
   tubas in B♭, C, F, E♭ and BB♭

clarinet in B♭
alto in E♭
bass in B♭
contrabass in E♭ or BB♭
Saxophones:
   soprano in B♭
   alto in E♭
   tenor in B♭
   baritone in E♭
   bass in B♭

Percussion:

timpani
bass drum
tenor drum
snare drum
cymbals
chimes
xylophone
vibraphone
triangle
tambourine
wood block
celesta
gongs
castanets, etc.

〖 INSTRUMENTATION 〗

The reader might set himself the problem of making up an "ideal" instrumentation from this assortment of instruments. Certain problems would immediately suggest themselves, aside from those connected with repertoire. First, some of the instruments are less effective in masses than others. For example, a large body of saxophones would possess a heavier, less flexible sound than a comparable body of clarinets. For that reason, one would probably hesitate to make a saxophone choir the basic choir of a band. Second, there is the matter of range. *No wind instrument* can compete in extent of useful range with the violin, viola or 'cello. For a melodic leading instrument, the extent of range is an important consideration. Among the woodwinds, the clarinets have the greatest useful range, although the top register should not be over-taxed, especially when clarinets are playing as a section. Oboes and saxophones have comparatively limited ranges. Flutes have, in theory, three octaves, but in wind instrument combinations the low notes are apt to be lost.

One can continue a consideration of these theoretical problems before getting down to specific questions. Most of the instruments have distinctive sounds. How many distinctive sounds does one want? Does one want every possible variation of solo color, to be used specifically as color? How will all of the various distinctive timbres blend with one another? What kind of a *tutti* sound do we want? Under certain circumstances it might be delightful to have at one's disposal a representation of everything. Yet even on a limited scale, it can be observed in practice that not all of the instruments in the list above blend happily with other instruments. Others have timbres of which one tires easily if they are used too steadily. (This again, is an advantage of strings; one does not get tired of the quality of a string orchestra.) Still another consideration is weight and volume. Wieprecht once attempted a band structure based on classifications of soft, medium and loud instruments. Euphonium and flute, as a duet combination, are not the same in any respect as violin and 'cello. There are relations in different voices of the band that must be considered.

What emerges from even a brief consideration of the problems just suggested is that, by and large, the "average" present-day band is a

⟦ INSTRUMENTATION ⟧

fairly good compromise. It depends on instruments such as the clarinet, the cornet, the trombone, baritone and tuba, which blend pleasantly, which have timbres sufficiently "neutral" and agreeable to enable one to hear them steadily over long periods, and which have sufficient flexibility to meet characteristic melodic demands in their various ranges. These instruments, with French horns, seem to give a satisfactory foundation to band sound, as well as a reasonable extent of compositional possibilities. One must remark, however, the greatest deficiency of the combination: its weakness in the extreme top and bottom registers, and the grouping of maximum strength (as to quality and tone) in the middle.

The band has never been built, as has the orchestra, around a basic choir of homogeneous timbre and complete extent of range. The strings of course provide this in the orchestra, and to the basic string orchestra other instruments have been added by degrees. The twentieth century orchestra has at times tended to assume other, less orthodox forms (as in many works of Stravinsky), but most orchestral works are still written in a way that is traditional, no matter how "developed" the wind writing may seem. The argument has been advanced that the band should imitate the orchestra by instituting a choir of clarinets, from top to bottom ranges, comparable to the orchestra's string choir. There is much discussion of this possibility, but little agreement. My own view is that such a choir would, for many reasons, not achieve its purpose, and that the best effect of band music will probably not be achieved by attempting to model its part-writing style on that of the orchestra. The idea of the complete choir might be useful and effective if an antiphonal style of writing were to be employed almost exclusively, so that each family of instruments might exhibit its special qualities, but the *tutti* of a band so constructed would, because of the duplication of heavy timbres, be of an extremely unpleasant thickness and lack of flexibility.

The woodwind section of the band as now conventionally constituted, consists of an assortment of instruments that must be handled with considerable care by the composer or arranger. We have flutes, oboes, clarinets, saxophones and bassoons. There is much duplication in the middle and middle-low registers, and insufficient strength on top and in the very low range. With B♭ clarinets, alto and tenor saxophones, alto and bass clarinets and bassoons available, there is bound to be much doubling, and not all of it is satisfactory in sound. Many bands use a large number of flutes in an attempt to give some body to the top register, but the flute does not have the same value, against other winds, that it has against strings, or even in the woodwind choir of the orchestra. The E♭ clarinet and the piccolo are often de-emphasized, but if attention were given to developing good players, their usefulness would surely be apparent. At the bottom, the contrabass clarinets are most useful, and so is, unquestionably, the contrabassoon. Here too, it is players of great skill who must be found.

The brasses of the band are a more homogeneous group, even though they are of different families: trumpets, sax-horns and various hybrids. The French horns, of course, do double duty, as in the orchestra, functioning with both woodwind and brass sections. The brass is again fundamentally a middle register group, with no high soprano and with much duplication in alto and tenor. The only real bass is the tuba, a marvelous instrument in the hands of a truly expert player, but far from perfect in the hands of an average one. It is the general acceptance of the weakness of the wind-instrument bass that has led to the inclusion (with very little opposition) of the string bass as a standard and indispensable member of the modern wind band. As to the top, there is now much sentiment in favor of the E♭ cornet. This would appear to be an excellent idea (I have used this instrument, on and off, since *1939* in the Goldman Band), but it actually offers more of a difference in timbre than a great upward extension of range.

Even with its limitations, the brass choir forms a solid and admirably blending group. It is really, when all is said and done, still the backbone of the band, and the all-brass band still demonstrates to us the versatility and satisfactory quality of brasses as an ensemble. The arranger and composer today has no such problems or difficulties in writing for this section as he has in writing well and effectively for the woodwinds.

〚 INSTRUMENTATION 〛

The matter of proportion of woodwind to brass has engaged the attention of bandsmen ever since the modern band came into being. A small reed section gives the impression that the band is fundamentally a brass choir with added woodwinds; a very large woodwind section often tends to rob the band of the brilliance that can be one of its most attractive features. A few representative bands may be cited as indications of what various bandmasters have thought on this point. In the following table, percussion and stringed instruments are not counted. French horns are tabulated with brass.

	Woodwind	*Brass*
Wieprecht, 1867	39	40
Gilmore, 1878	35	27
Sousa, 1893	27	19
Sousa, 1900	48	24
Goldman, E. F., 1930	32	24
Col. Howard, U.S.A.F., 1945	35	32
Revelli, Michigan, 1956	63	33

All of these bands are, or were, excellent bands, and it is interesting to note the startling differences in the proportions tabulated above. What must be stressed is that each of these excellent bands has, or had, *its own special sound quality.* A judgment as to which is best must obviously be a subjective one.

An equally interesting tabulation is the proportion of B♭ clarinets to total woodwind strength. See the table on page *156*.

The recent great growth of woodwind strength in both practice and theory is shown clearly by two "ideal" band instrumentations set forth in papers presented at the Tenth National Conference of the C.B.D.N.A. in *1958*. The first, suggested by L. Bruce Jones of Louisiana State University, has fifty-nine woodwinds to thirty-three brass; the sec-

⟦ INSTRUMENTATION ⟧

	B♭ *Clarinets*	*Total Woodwinds*
Wieprecht	16	39
Gilmore	16	35
Sousa, 1893	14	27
Sousa, 1900	26	48
Goldman, E. F., 1930	19	32
Howard	14	35
Revelli	26	63

ond, submitted by Mark Hindsley of the University of Illinois, requires fifty-three woodwind and thirty brass. In both, the proportion of B♭ clarinets to total woodwind strength is smaller than has usually obtained up to now, because of the addition of more flutes and lower clarinets.

There is much current discussion in organizations such as the C.B.D.N.A. and the American Bandmasters Association about the two closely allied topics of an "ideal" band instrumentation and its consequent, a "standard" instrumentation. It is clear that the weakness of the band at top and bottom has at last been generally recognized, and that much earnest thought is being devoted to remedial measures.

The general tendency over the past few years has been toward the enlargement of the band, and the increase of its woodwind component. So far as size is concerned, it is easy to find a number of excellent reasons for the increase. The band today is characteristically amateur, that is, made up of students who do not have to be paid. Size is therefore no longer, as it was with the professional band, a matter of economics. The ample budgets enjoyed by most school and college bands provide plenty of instruments, uniforms and other equipment. And the prevailing "philosophy" of education welcomes the participation of as many as possible in a given activity. The size of bands in educational institutions is thus not altogether determined by considerations of musical effectiveness. However, it is also possible to argue that the larger band provides greater musical resources, and this is the only argument that we can be concerned with here.

⟦ INSTRUMENTATION ⟧

There *are* good musical arguments in favor of large bands. First, there is the argument that a larger variety of tone color may be possible. This is true, of course, only if the instruments are used with discretion, and depends in the long run much more on the composer and arranger than on the organizer of the band. For example, a large band more or less constantly used in full force would be simply the equivalent of an organ with more stops and couplers used, and would not necessarily be more pleasing or more effective. But a large band, with the maximum of instrumental resource, could surely, if intelligently employed, give a wide variety of color and contrast. Second, it is acoustically true, as Berlioz well knew, that a large ensemble is capable of a more beautiful *pianissimo* than a medium-sized one. Its entire dynamic range can be more tellingly handled and projected. Third, a large band, if well-proportioned, can add strength at top and bottom without sacrifice of body in the middle registers.

The generally recommended instrumentations, whether they originate with organizations of bandmasters or elsewhere, almost all have points in their favor. It is hard to see how any reinforcement of the top and bottom registers of the band can do harm; on the other hand, it seems that the addition of more instruments in the middle registers is more difficult to justify. The most reasonable plans for "ideal" or "standard" instrumentation are those that allow either for optional instruments or for practical doubling. Thus, the alto clarinet, which seldom has a part of any individuality, is never missed in most present band scores. On the other hand, it is perfectly sensible to allow for the possibility that some day someone will write a good part for the alto clarinet. In that case, it is of course proper to have this instrument available! It is further possible that once this usage of the alto clarinet is generally established, it will then be decided that the basset-horn in F is more desirable.

We can speak with certainty only of the present situation in instrumentation, which is inextricably connected with the present repretoire, both of original compositions and arrangements. Addition of instruments, or radical changing of balances can, with respect to the music now available, have no very salutary effect on the way this music will

⟦ INSTRUMENTATION ⟧

sound. And I think that with all of the proper concern shown for *improvement*, most bandmasters would agree that there is sufficient material of value in the present repertoire to make it inadvisable to think of scrapping it *in toto*. (All would, on the other hand, probably agree that a good deal of it could disappear without serious loss.)

The present "standardization" of band instrumentation, insofar as it is standard at all, is the result, as I have stated above, of practical compromises and the experience of several generations of outstanding bandmasters. It is also to some extent the result of works like Sousa's marches, *which sound best with a band resembling his own,* which is, after all, what he had in mind when he wrote them. These marches have a wonderful sound when played by what today would be called a small or "basic" band, without oboes, bassoons, alto, bass or contrabass clarinets; even without saxophones. What is more, the sound is not improved by the addition of these instruments! On the contrary. What a Sousa march needs is lots of piccolo, lots of tuba and trombone, good percussion and of course cornets, clarinets, horns and baritone. Everything else is superfluous. I cite Sousa marches because they do not represent an extreme case. Not only are they a real staple of the repertoire (heaven forbid that we should see the day that they are abandoned in favor of arrangements of *Verklaerte Nacht,* or original band works modeled after Webern!), but they represent a kind of band sound that is primary, and unfailingly attractive. This basic band sound is the fundamental assumption of much band scoring right up to the present. Oboes, flutes, bassoons and other instruments have proven indispensable for concert music; they have added color and range, but they have not basically altered the conception of the band. Most of the original band music that has been written still follows this general conception, as indeed for many reasons it has been forced to do.

The addition of instruments, or the changing of balances in the band of the present or future poses other problems than those of adaptation of repertoire. As I have pointed out, but must re-emphasize, there will probably never be agreement among bandmasters as to what constitutes the "best" band sound. Bandmaster W likes a crisp sound; Band-

⟦ INSTRUMENTATION ⟧

master X a rich, organ-like one; Bandmaster Y can't stand piccolos; Bandmaster Z detests saxophones. Bandmaster A likes a clear sound, with minimum vibrato; Bandmaster B likes a large and massive sound. Bandmaster M wishes to have a complete, orchestrally-proportioned choir of clarinets; Bandmaster N would rather have more double-reeds. The arguments can be endless.

The discussion about "color" instruments in the band is also an interesting one. It is perfectly true that many instruments not commonly used are quite beautiful in sound. It is also true that one may draw the subtlest distinctions as to timbre, volume, action and so on. William Russo, the well-known jazz composer and arranger, for example, used both slide *and* valve trombones in his experimental twenty-two-piece orchestra at New York's Birdland in *1960*. Could concert bands perhaps also add something by doing the same? And why not insist on real alto trombones? In all of the discussions I have seen, this is one potentially useful instrument that is never mentioned!

The cornet and trumpet discussion is still another which gives rise to a variety of opinions. In many cases, the differences between these two instruments is almost as slight as that between valve and slide trombones. Is there a real distinction today? If there is, how many bandsmen exploit it? Most bandsmen believe in using *both* instruments. My father, for one, was very firm on this subject, but insisted, as most good bandsmen do, that they be used properly. In my father's playing days, roughly *1895-1910*, there was, however, a much greater difference between the two instruments. The difference, in today's instruments, has been somewhat minimized, but it nevertheless still exists. The difference between players is, however, more important still. What is hard to explain is the practice in some school bands of giving the trumpet parts to the weakest cornet players.

This last consideration brings us to specific problems of instrumentation as they concern amateur bands. It is absolutely true that in such bands (not only high school bands, but in many college bands that I have heard) the matter of *number* of players does not prove to be conclusive as to balance. I have heard, as an instance, bands numbering

〖 INSTRUMENTATION 〗

twelve or more flute players, all charming young girls, looking lovely, but practically inaudible. A single robust performer would produce more sound. The school band must, of course, deal with a turn-over of performers, and its strength in the several sections may vary considerably from year to year. A band may have fine oboes one year, and poor ones the next. That is the year the band should go easy on music with important oboe parts!

There is one other important problem of instrumentation that affects the balance of most school bands, and even of many college bands: the number of players in relation to the number of written parts. It is not unusual, for example, to see in a school band four youngsters playing a single tenor saxophone part, while the horn, oboe and bassoon parts are barely covered, or covered by weak players. This obviously will throw the entire ensemble out of balance, and destroy the effect of the music, no matter how well it is arranged. This problem will be discussed more thoroughly in the next chapter, as it bears on arranging as well as instrumentation. But it is a characteristic and major problem of band performance, and cannot be overlooked here. Once again, one is forced to make an unfavorable comparison with orchestral usage (even with *amateur* orchestral usage!), for no orchestra or orchestral conductor would tolerate doubling, much less tripling or quadrupling, of parts meant to be played by single instruments. The only exception would be for some kind of massive performance in which *all instruments were doubled or augmented in proportion.* But we would shudder at the idea of an orchestra in which the two written clarinet parts were each played by three clarinetists, while the flute and oboe parts were played as usual by single performers.

No discussion of the band's instrumentation would be complete without a consideration of the percussion section, including the melodic percussion (xylophone, vibraphone and others), and also of the now commonly added instruments such as the harp or the piano. The percussion is, as everyone knows, a basic constituent of band and orchestra

Victor Herbert in uniform as leader of the Band of the Twenty-Second Regiment of New York. Courtesy, The Library of Congress

[[PLATE II]]

John Philip Sousa with his celebrated Marine Corps Band at the St. Louis Exposition. Courtesy, The Bettmann Archive

[[PLATE III]]

With the flourish of the 'nineties, Nahan Franko and his band at Manhattan Beach (1894). From the author's collection

*The author with his father, the late Edwin Franko Goldman,
founder of the Goldman Band. Courtesy "The New York Times"*

*John Philip Sousa and Edwin Franko Goldman enjoying a mo-
ment of relaxation together in 1928. From the author's collection*

[[PLATE v]]

Rehearsing for summer concerts, The Goldman Band with its conductor, Richard Franko Goldman. Photo by Impact

[[**PLATE VI**]]

The author, the Goldman Band, and Percy Grainger recording "Over the Hills and Far Away." Photo by Burnet Cross

The Philco Corporation Band under Herbert N. Johnston, conductor.

Courtesy, The Philco Corporation Band

[[PLATE VIII]]

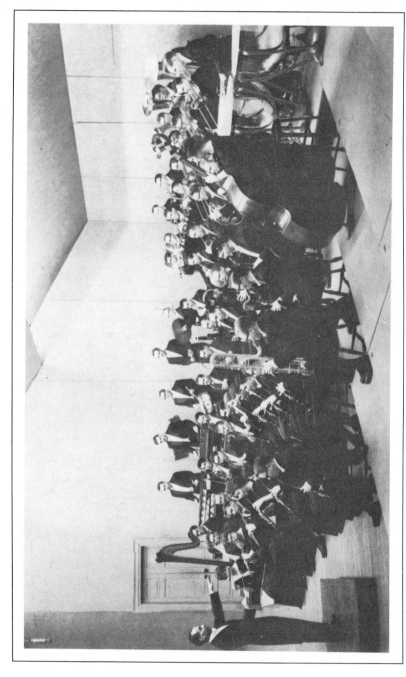

Organized in 1952, The Eastman Symphonic Wind Ensemble, with its conductor, Frederick Fennell. Photo by Louis Ouzer

[PLATE IX]

Richard W. Bowles, the University of Florida Symphonic Band, and trumpet trio. Courtesy, The University of Florida

[[PLATE X]]

Organized in 1942, the United States Air Force Band under the baton of Colonel George S. Howard. U.S. Air Force photo

[[PLATE XI]]

The United States Army Field Band performing in front of the Capitol, August, 1956; at left, Lt. Colonel Chester E. Whiting, the Band's first conductor; at right, Major Robert L. Bierly. U.S. Army photograph

[[PLATE XII]]

The University of Illinois Concert Band and its conductor, Mark Hindsley. Courtesy, The University of Illinois

[PLATE XIII]

The Purdue University Symphonic Band performing in 1960 under conductor, Al G. Wright. Courtesy, Purdue University

[**PLATE XIV**]

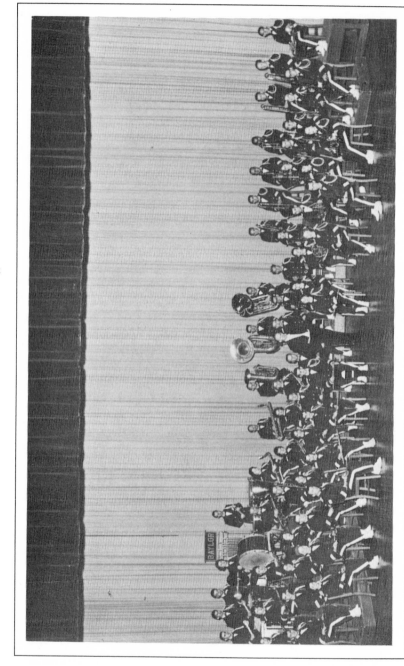

The Baylor University Concert Band conducted by Donald I. Moore, Director (1960). Photo by The Windy Drum Studio

[[PLATE XV]]

Conductor Leonard Falcone and the Michigan State University Concert Band. Courtesy, Michigan State University

[PLATE XVI]

Under the baton of Herbert Hazelman, the Greensboro, North Carolina, High School Band. Photo by Martin's Studio

⟦ INSTRUMENTATION ⟧

equally. Its use in such forms as the march is determined by tradition and in concert music by the wishes of the composer. In band music, the great danger is its over-employment. William Schaefer, in his paper on band instrumentation presented at the C.B.D.N.A. in *1958*, wrote: ". . . An evening of contemporary band music tends to sound like an evening of percussion concerti. I sometimes wonder if we will look back on this period in band writing as the period in which percussion was discovered, and the rest of the band lost. . . ." Mr. Schaefer need not have limited his observations to contemporary band music. I recall my father's reactions many many years ago, when school bands were relatively in their infancy. He had been asked to conduct an arrangement of the *Tannhaüser* Overture. Much to his not very happy surprise, the entire percussion section, including xylophone, kept hammering away all through the piece. When he stopped to ask about this, the school bandmaster explained that "the youngsters like to be playing all the time; otherwise they lose interest. Also, they have difficulty counting rests. . . ." Now this anecdote unquestionably represents an extreme case, but it does point up a problem that exists, especially with amateur players. The problem involves the conception of band instruments and their functions, but it can be more properly discussed as a problem of arranging in the next chapter.

The harp and the piano are, by and large, matters of taste so far as the band is concerned. As with the string bass, their use simply poses the question: why stop here? Sousa took the position that if one had the string bass one might as well have the 'cello and violas too. And, in fact, a few bands, notably the U.S.A.F. Band under Colonel George S. Howard, *do* use 'cellos as a normal part of their make-up. Two or three violins would certainly make all of the difference in the world so far as the top register of the band is concerned, but to my knowledge the idea of using violins has not yet been seriously entertained by bandmasters. The harp is used mostly for two effects, a *pizzicato* to reinforce a woodwind *staccato* where percussion is not employed, and the usual *glissando* so generally beloved and overworked. Many bandmasters today seem to feel that the piano will do better anything customarily assigned to the harp

⟦ INSTRUMENTATION ⟧

in band scoring; the piano can, of course, also be a valuable percussion instrument. However, all of these instruments are, at the present time, probably best classified as "extras" and not part of the indispensable complement of the wind band.

Parts written for such instruments as harp and piano in today's band scores are usually optional; they may add some effectiveness if used, but their absence will not normally be damaging. But this brings us back, for a final summary, to the question of the normal or "standard" band instrumentation. The argument today in favor of attempting to standardize the band is usually based on the desirability of letting composers and arrangers (and even music publishers) know exactly what they are writing for: what instruments, and in approximately what proportions, they may expect to find present in any good band. This seems both realistic and reasonable—much more so than the approach to standardization based on any ideas of "best" sound, on which agreement seems extremely unlikely. But standardization must be accompanied by a liberalizing of many current band practices as well. It must, for example, treat many additional instruments as "optional" and allow many possibilities of variation. It will be of inestimable advantage to the composer or arranger to know that he can count on having, let us say, a contrabass clarinet or an E♭ cornet; but he must also have the right to leave them out of his score if he wishes. If better composition and arranging is to result, the composer or arranger must also have the right to put down as few notes as he pleases for any given instrument; in other words, he should not have to write notes merely to keep the player busy. A second alto saxophone might just possibly have to play three notes in a ten-minute piece. These three notes might be useful and effective, far more so than the constant doubling of some other part which is so frequent, for many practical reasons, in much of today's scoring.

With a standard instrumentation, the composer should also have the right to call for any additional instrument that he likes, for special purposes. If a composer desperately feels the need for writing a four-bar

⟦ INSTRUMENTATION ⟧

heckelphone solo, let him write it! It can be cross-cued, as usual; but a few bands, intent on completely literal and perfect execution, will manage to find a heckelphone player. Here, at least, the band *can,* in the pursuit of higher musical ambitions, take a lesson from the orchestra. Symphony orchestras do not normally carry a saxophone player on the regular payroll. But if the conductor programs a piece which has saxophone in the score, then a saxophone player is engaged for that concert. There is also this: the symphony orchestra personnel does normally include a tuba player. He performs in works by late nineteenth century and some contemporary composers, but he stays in the dressing room for Mozart and Beethoven. He gets paid just as much as the other musicians, and is just as essential. But the conductor does not have him sit in and play along in every piece, *just because he is there.*

This is even more pointedly true of the use of percussion. As a rule, percussion players have less to do in Schubert than in works by Morton Gould. Should the Schubert be re-arranged so that the percussion section can be kept busy? The amateur player must be persuaded that, just as in athletics, the player who sits on the bench is also valuable; when he comes out on the field for one minute to kick a point after touchdown, he has proven his value to the team, the game, and to the audience as well.

These points may seem to some readers to be too obvious to bother emphasizing. But I have often been told that what may hold good in professional practice does not and can not apply in amateur music, especially with young players. I do not feel that this must or should be so; we are dealing with musical performance as well as with group activity, and musical considerations should come first. It is the *musical* attitude of the bandmaster that will count, and his transference of this attitude to the players whose education is his responsibility.

Among our forward-looking bandmasters all this is widely recognized, and provides the most encouraging promise for the musical future of bands. The papers submitted at the Tenth National Conference (*1958*) of the C.B.D.N.A., so often cited above, all stress the elasticity and musicianship that will be needed to implement any recom-

⟦ INSTRUMENTATION ⟧

mendations on the instrumental make-up of the future band, and on the responsibilities of bandmasters in these respects. William Schaefer writes:

We should offer composers and arrangers the option of writing for such of the instruments of the band as he wishes: omitting instruments as he pleases, as the orchestral composer is free to do. We should not insist that every player have a part—resulting in fictitious E♭ clarinet, piccolo and percussion parts sometimes super-imposed by publishers or ghost arrangers on the original score. . . .

L. Bruce Jones writes:

Instrumentation is so irrevocably tied in with composing, scoring, publishing, and distribution that I very often feel that the best answer to the question of what instruments to include in the band roster is simply, 'Offer the composer the richest possible tonal palette and leave the choice of instruments and the amount of divisi, in fact, all problems of scoring entirely in his hands without guidance!'

The great composers of the past have always "broken the rules" and pioneered in "new sounds." However it is important that the composer know what is available, and what we think is a standard instrumentation. But in being perhaps too insistent on what we want rather than on what we have to offer, and particularly in asking the composer to share our "practical problems" we may stifle expression that would mean so much to our literature. . . .

Mark Hindsley writes:

The conception of the wind band as a concert organization has gone through several periods of evolution. It may go through more such

⟦ INSTRUMENTATION ⟧

periods. Sometime, however, the concert band should reach a reasonable state of stability comparable to the reasonable state of stability of the symphony orchestra. Whether or not there has been enough evolution and experience to attempt to stabilize the band instrumentation at the present time remains to be seen. There are still various points of disagreement among band conductors. Nevertheless, there must be efforts toward stabilization, and it is in this spirit that I am prompted to write my own views. . . .

I have mentioned a "stable" rather than a "standard" instrumentation. If the latter term is used, it should only indicate the instruments and players a composer or arranger can depend on having available in various size organizations, with a normal number and division of parts. More specifically, a standard instrumentation should refer to "fulltime" instrumentalists and their natural and common "doubling" instruments. The composer or arranger need not use all of these instruments merely to conform to a standard instrumentation, neither should he be restricted to these instruments. He deserves to know, however, what he can generally expect in a band, and weigh the chances of his music being played in the manner he intends.

It is my feeling that to a great extent we can be both idealistic and realistic in our approach to instrumentation. This is to say that a composer or arranger should be unfettered in his scoring, using whatever combination he desires from an idealistic standpoint, yet through the use of alternate cues make the composition playable by a standard group if he wishes to be realistic. Some will not wish to do this, and it is their privilege. Every encouragement should be given to freedom of expression on the part of the creator, and every effort should be made to re-create the music as he has set it down. There should be room within our framework for all compositions specializing in the wind and percussion instruments. It remains, however, that before there can be a "departure" there must be a point of departure. A standard instrumentation is desirable both for its own value and to provide this point of departure. . . .

⟦ INSTRUMENTATION ⟧

Statements such as these surely indicate the kind of constructive thought that is being applied to the complex subject of band instrumentation, and are an excellent augury for the future development of America band music.

The planning and thinking of these leaders in the field of college bands and band music crystallized in a report submitted to the Eleventh National Conference of the C.B.D.N.A. in December, *1960*. This Report was drafted as the result of a conference on the band's repertoire, instrumentation and nomenclature called by James Neilson, of Oklahoma City University, then President of the C.B.D.N.A., in June, *1960*. Those invited to the conference, in addition to members of the C.B.D.N.A., included prominent composers, arrangers and publishers. The C.B.D.N.A. was represented by Dr. Neilson, Dr. William D. Revelli and Dr. R. Bernard Fitzgerald. Composers and arrangers present were Paul Creston, Vittorio Giannini, Morton Gould, Philip J. Lang and Vincent Persichetti. Publishers who attended were Benjamin V. Grasso, Ralph Satz, and Alfred Reed, representing their respective firms.

This group's report is, I believe, of unusual interest. The recommendations as to instrumentation may or may not be universally, or even generally, adopted, but they show clearly the direction in which present-day thinking on the subject is proceeding. The recommendations of individual members of the group varied only slightly, and the collective construction of an "ideal" band is shown on page *167*.

Several things are noteworthy in this "ideal" instrumentation. First of all, the concensus arrived at a band of medium proportions (seventy-two players). This may indicate the beginning of a tendency to avoid the band of excessive size, although it is possible that the *pattern* indicated above may lend itself to proportional doubling and strengthening of sections. Second, it is interesting to note the strong feeling (mentioned in the text of the Report) for the use of the soprano saxophone, the E♭ clarinet and the E♭ cornet. The use of these instruments has in previous plans of band instrumentation usually been considered without

⟦ INSTRUMENTATION ⟧

Instrument	Players	Comments
Piccolo (c)		One part for piccolo
Flute	6	Two or three parts
Oboe	2	First and second parts
English horn	1	Possibly an oboe player doubling
Bassoon	2	First and second parts
E♭ clarinet	1	
B♭ clarinets	18	First and second parts
E♭ alto clarinet	6	
B♭ bass clarinet	3	
E♭ contrabass clarinet	2	
B♭ soprano saxophone	1	Straight soprano
E♭ alto saxophone	1	
B♭ tenor saxophone	1	
E♭ baritone saxophone	1	
B♭ bass saxophone	1	
E♭ cornet	1	
B♭ cornet	3	Two parts, three voices
B♭ trumpet	3	Two parts, three voices
French horn	4	Four parts
Trombone	3	Two parts, three voices
Bass trombone	1	
Euphonium	3	One or more voices
BB♭ tuba	3	One part
Percussion	5	Two parts
Total:	72	

enthusiasm. This change can only be welcomed, as the inclusion of these soprano instruments may well help the band at its weakest point. Third, the recommendations as to distribution of parts is unusual in that it recommends the division of B♭ clarinets into two, rather than the cus-

⟦ INSTRUMENTATION ⟧

tomary three, parts. The third part would in the above instrumentation probably be assigned to the alto clarinets. In any case, the evolution toward a choir of clarinets is notable here.

Other points to be noted are the preference expressed for the $E\flat$ contrabass clarinet, as opposed to the $BB\flat$, and the exclusion of tubas other than the $BB\flat$. The committee also expressed a favorable opinion on the inclusion of the bass saxophone, establishing a quintet rather than a quartet of these instruments, but with a caution against needless doubling. No specification was made as to the distribution of the recommended five percussion players.

The suggested instrumentation recommended in this Report will no doubt be subject to considerable discussion and possible modification in practice. It does nevertheless represent what is to date one of the most serious and responsible plans submitted for the consideration of American bandsmen. If a good number of college bands eventually conform to the instrumentation suggested, the problems facing arrangers and composers in the band field will in many respects be simplified, if not altogether solved. The ultimate utility of the projected "ideal" band will, as in all instances in the history of music, be determined by the composers whose interest may be further stimulated by the possibilities of the ensemble, and whose collective efforts may eventually result in a repertoire of still greater interest than that now available.

BAND

arranging

AND

SCORING

⟦ BAND ARRANGING AND SCORING ⟧

Many of the considerations touched on in previous chapters will have given the reader indications of the basic problems of scoring or arranging music for band. We have discussed the variability of the band's instrumentation, the variety of functions the band is supposed to fulfill, the uncertainty as to its size and balance, and other factors which make band arranging in practice much more difficult than it would seem to be in theory.

The question of scoring and arranging overlaps the areas of both instrumentation and repertoire. The composer, starting fresh, must think of the instrumental combination for which he is writing, and of the players and audience for whom his composition is designed. The arranger must do the same, but must also justify his act of arranging or transcribing as a useful musical employment. There is no question at present, until a literature of original band music assumes much larger proportions, that arrangements and transcriptions are still needed. But what sort of music should be arranged, and for what reasons?

The question of *what* is transcribed for band, and perhaps what should or should not be transcribed, may be left for our discussion of repertoire. But *how* music is or should be transcribed is a question that is relevant here. There are many opinions concerning what a band arrangement should try to achieve. One school of thought holds that a band arrangement should strive for maximum fidelity to the original source; another advocates re-casting the work in terms of band sonorities and potentialities. The first opinion was widely held in the past, but is yielding to the second. One no longer hears very often the comment that the clarinets "sounded like violins," because today no one really wants them to. It is usually a happier experience when they sound like clarinets. The wisest arranger is the one who takes advantage of the characteristics of each instrument and does not try to make one substitute for another. The practical problem is how to accomplish this while preserving somehow the character of the music one is arranging or transcribing.

There are many textbooks on band arranging, from slender ones involving hints and general notions, to exhaustive treatises exploring minute details of technique. The student will find some of these useful,

〚 BAND ARRANGING AND SCORING 〛

but none are as useful as direct experience with instruments themselves and constant attentive listening to instruments in combination. Arranging or scoring for band is not difficult provided one knows more or less exactly what instrumental combination one has available, and what kind of players. It is the choice of what to transcribe that is infinitely more difficult. My experience with young musicians and students is that they can easily turn out a perfectly sound band arrangement, provided that they have not chosen an absurd piece to transcribe—one that is so dependent on specifically orchestral or pianistic effects that *no* band arrangement will turn out well. Has anyone ever heard, for instance, an effective band arrangment of anything by Chopin? I think that poses—and answers—the question.

Arguments about the merits of transcriptions or arrangements *in principle* can be waged endlessly. There are a few purists who object to the procedure of transcribing any music from one performance medium to another. It is perfectly possible to maintain this position with honesty and consistency, although to do so one must overlook the fact that many composers, from the great to the near-great, have sanctioned the practice, and many of them, from Bach to Ravel, Schoenberg and Stravinsky, have applied it to their own works as well as to works of other composers. It is perfectly true, however, that the bulk of the classical repertoire, for orchestra, chamber combinations or piano solo, never at any time depended on transcribed material. With the band, we are faced with the very simple fact that the "serious" concert repertoire has, on the other hand, depended almost entirely on transcriptions, and we are thus forced to deal with fact rather than with theory or preference. For some time to come, it is obvious that transcriptions or arrangements will continue to be a factor, and indeed I think it altogether safe to surmise that there will always be some place for them as a special characteristic of the band's literature.

When a composer sets out to write a woodwind quintet, a piano piece or a string quartet, he knows, by definition, exactly what instruments he is writing for, what their capacities are, what is idiomatic for them and, within certain limitations, exactly how his work ought to sound. Up to a point, this is also true when he writes for orchestra. He may use as much or as little of the orchestra as he pleases, but he knows that he can depend on any standard orchestra having roughly the expected proportion of winds to strings and having all of the conventional instruments in conventional numbers. If the conductor wants to play a given work calling for additional or unusual instruments, he may even hire extra players for the occasion.

The composer or arranger writing a work for band is not quite as fortunate. He knows in general what instruments are available in most bands, and what instruments are likely to be found in only a few bands. What he does not know, even with the basic and dependable instruments, is how many of each there may be. Unfortunately, our present conventions of writing for band do not give the composer or arranger the right to specify *precisely* what he wants. If he writes a part to be played by *one* alto saxophone, as against perhaps one oboe, he may find to his distress that the passage is being played by *three* alto saxophones against one muted trumpet substituting for a missing oboe.

At the present time (*1961*) a general convention is in force for the instrumentation of American bands so far as published (or publishable) arrangements and compositions are concerned. This convention has remained relatively unchanged for a period of twenty years or more. It was originally evolved as the result of recommendations made by the American Bandmasters Association, the National High School Band Association and representatives of music publishing houses. (It should be borne in mind that new "standard" instrumentations are constantly being proposed. See Chapter 5.) The practice in band arranging and publication has been to provide parts for a *maximum* instrumentation (usually known as "symphonic band"), but to ensure that the work is also playable by one or two smaller combinations (known as "full band," "standard band" or "concert band.") It is evident that this kind of necessity, if necessity it is, imposes the most serious handicap on the composer. In essence it means that he writes for the *minimum* band almost invariably, doubling or adding unnecessary parts to fill out to the maximum. Erik Leidzen, in his *An Invitation to Band Arranging*, put the situation succinctly when he wrote:

. . . with few exceptions it has been the conductors, *singly or grouped in various associations, who have determined what instruments were to be included; and this means not only what instruments* might *be used, but what* must *be used. Inasmuch as this has been applied uniformly to all band scores, the writer for band must now use a stereotyped instrumentation, for he cannot—without risking every chance of reaching publication—leave out any instrument, nor can he add anything, however much he would like to do so, for he is—at the present time, at least—ringed by two impenetrable walls, namely, (1) a standard instrumentation imposed on all band-publications and (2) a certain unchangeable set of band instruments, which must all be supplied with a part.*

The fact that a certain instrumentation is being widely used does not necessarily mean that it cannot be improved upon, and it must not be inferred that the majority of the writers for band are anxious to make the existing band score still larger. Most of us would, no doubt, favor fewer parts and a somewhat different distribution of the instruments. . . .

The so called standard, concert, and symphonic versions on the market are not three different arrangements, but the parts of one single score distributed in such a way that even the smallest group (the so called "standard") is able to "cover" the music. It must logically follow that if the music played by the small combination is complete, then the parts added for the larger groups cannot contain much of importance. The composer and arranger must therefore sacrifice much of the characteristic treatment he would like to give certain instruments if he were sure they would always be present.

It is really no wonder that some of us are in favor of a somewhat smaller band instrumentation, for it is downright humiliating to have to write parts which add little or nothing to the general effect. One solution would be completely separate instrumentations for small and large bands, but this could only be brought about by a unified demand from all the smaller organizations to have their particular needs considered of equal importance with those of the larger groups. Too often the leaders of the small bands are too busy imitating what is done by larger groups—in the firm belief that they represent perfection—to find out what the real needs of their own bands actually are; and the leaders of large bands too often put their trust in mere size and bulk. Meanwhile it is quite clear to most of the writers *that as things are now, neither the small nor the large combinations get the best possible scoring.*

Most band works are now issued in two rather than three sizes, and it must be remembered that there are minor variations in the editions issued by different publishers. Sometimes the instrumentations vary slightly according to the character of the work. Basically, however, the "full band" edition will have a small number of all the essential parts. 2nd oboe and 2nd bassoon, bass saxophone, contrabass clarinet and similar parts may sometimes not be included in the "full band" set, but will of course be included in the "symphonic band," which will also include additional extra parts for most of the instruments likely to be found in large numbers.

The same arrangement obviously must do duty for bands of different sizes, for bands having but one oboe or one bassoon, for bands lacking contrabass clarinet—in fact, for all bands, no matter how widely they may vary from the "normal" complement and distribution of instruments. The arranger can be nothing if not cautious. He must avoid writing anything essential for second oboe or second bassoon, and must not take chances on several other instruments. In addition to the presence or absence of instruments, and their unpredictable quantities, there are several other limitations which he knows from experience. For example, he is aware that many school bands assign trumpet parts to the weakest cornet players. Hence, he must write parts of no great difficulty for trumpets, and must avoid writing solo passages for them. Similarly, it

is not uncommon for a school bandmaster to put all of his good clarinetists on the first clarinet part; consequently, the second and third parts
must be considerably easier. Still weaker players may be found on alto
and bass clarinet parts, and the music must be written accordingly.

One additional major problem faces the arranger. He may have
to indicate "cues" for instruments that are lacking. A bassoon solo, for
example, may be alternately given to a saxophone or to the baritone to
cover the possibility that the band will either not have a bassoon at all,
or else that no player will be able to play the solo passage well enough.
Oboe solos may have to be cued in clarinet or possibly alto saxophone
or muted trumpet. A passage for E♭ clarinet almost certainly has to be
cued, since this instrument is often absent, and more often poorly played.

There are still other limitations imposed by performance practices
in school bands. We have previously mentioned the general preference
for having all the players play as much as possible. The arranger has to
be, as a rule, chary of writing too many rests. He thus has to manufacture
extra notes, usually doublings, in order to keep the players busy. What
is remarkable, with all this, is not that so many band arrangements sound
poorly as that so many of them work fairly well. The all-purpose band
arrangement survives some hard use, and often when a bandmaster or an
audience feels that an arrangement is bad it is not the arrangement that
is at fault, but the band itself.

The question, very simply, with band arrangements is: should the
band fit the arrangement, or the arrangement fit the band? The best
sound is produced when an arrangement is made specifically for a given
organization, by an arranger who knows the group. Gilmore, Sousa and
Goldman all had large numbers of arrangements made for their own
bands. They sounded well because the arrangers knew exactly what they
could expect, not only in numbers and proportions, but in quality of
performance. It is only in this way that results, in terms of tone quality
and balance, can be calculated with any degree of effectiveness by the
arranger. There can be no question but that an arrangement made for
a specific band of sixty players will sound very different when played

⟦ BAND ARRANGING AND SCORING ⟧

by a much larger band in which the distribution of instruments may be quite dissimilar. It may be equally interesting, but it will certainly not be the same.

At any rate, the fundamental fact about arrangements is that they are made to fit a preconceived general idea of what instruments are supposed to be present, and in approximately what proportions. Further, everything that is arranged for band is supposed, as present practice has it, to be written for the same combination of instruments. In other words, the band plays a Sousa march, a Bach fugue, a Verdi overture, an excerpt from Wagner, and selections from the latest Broadway show all with the same instrumentation. Whether or not this is artistically or musically appropriate may be argued, but it is none-the-less the fact in the world of band performance. The practice in writing for band is not only that such and such instruments are available, but that *they all must be used*. This includes the percussion of course. I do not know how many copies of Bach arrangements have been returned to the publishers because they did not have snare drum parts!

Were separate arrangements of standard repertoire generally available for college and professional bands, as distinct from high school and junior high school bands, most of these problems would not be of great importance. However, the band arrangement published today attempts to satisfy the needs and desires of all types of bands. The publisher is properly interested in selling copies of band works, and his market is much larger in the high school field than in the college field. He therefore is also concerned with the *difficulty* of the arrangement, which includes not only the technical difficulties of individual parts, but the demands put upon the band as an ensemble. Thus it happens today that the best bands are occasionally required to perform arrangements (and, unfortunately, original compositions as well) that were made with less proficient bands in mind. This has become increasingly true in recent years, as the margin of profit in music publication has diminished, and the business risk of publishing an artistic work of more than moderate difficulty has become much greater.

[BAND ARRANGING AND SCORING]

One obvious result of the tendency to make works more easily playable by large numbers of bands is the almost universal practice of writing band music in flat keys. Thus an orchestral piece in D major will as a rule be played in E♭ by a band; a piece in A may go to either A♭ or B♭. This does not disturb most people, unless they know the original keys and have absolute pitch, but it does occasionally produce curious alterations of the original. More unfortunate than transposition is the practice often found of "simplifying" the orchestral originals. This practice is so widespread that it is probably a permanent fixture in so-called "educational" repertoire. I can say only that I think it should be avoided, but I am aware that mine is a minority voice in the matter.

The problem here is again one to which reference has previously been made. Years ago, the level of musical culture among band audiences was lower than it is today. A bandmaster playing even so familiar a chestnut as the *William Tell* Overture could probably assume that hardly anyone in his audience had ever heard it as written by Rossini. If the band arrangement was in a different key, if it was abbreviated or simplified, who would know? But this is hardly true today; almost everyone must have heard this piece at one time or another played by an orchestra, and if not live, then via radio or phonograph. Even if most listeners may not remember the original very accurately, the band is still offering its arrangement as a more or less competitive experience. And the more intelligent players, if the arrangement is bad enough, may feel that they are somehow being cheated, as indeed they are.

I believe that we must inevitably come to the realization that there should be two sorts of band music made available. There should be compositions and arrangements written from a standpoint of nothing but musical effectiveness, to be performed by college and professional bands and some of the best high school bands, willing and able to play them *exactly* as written; and on the other hand there should be (as there is at present) an adequate repertoire of compositions and arrangements written specifically with the average school band and its problems in mind. No other solution to the present problems would be as satis-factory.

To a certain extent, this solution is already effective in practice. It has, however, not been carried through completely, and in some circles it is not even considered decent to talk about it. In general, the more difficult works published for band exhibit a greater artistic freedom than the easier ones of wider circulation. However, even those of the greatest artistic integrity show the effects of the standardization that produces unwelcome compromise. In part this problem is tied up with the commercial aspects of music publishing. It is obvious that publishers will not publish many works of which only a limited number can be sold; the publisher, as has been said before, is interested in the widest possible market. But the practice of having works available on a rental basis, as is usual with orchestral material, is now gaining acceptance in the band field, and this practice will go far to help solve the problem of the artistically interesting but commercially impractical band arrange-ment or original composition. It is encouraging to note that recently, with a few of the more serious original compositions for band, the publisher is issuing only *one* set of band parts: a "complete" set, dis-tributed according to the composer's intention, and with no attempt at making the publication do service for "small," "full" or "symphonic" bands. This has taken courage to do, and deserves mention and com-mendation.

The best band sound and the best artistic effect are, as I have pointed out, obtained when the composer or arranger knows exactly what he is working with. Here the suggestions of an organization such as the C.B.D.N.A., *if they are carried through conscientiously,* may make a great difference. If the composer or arranger can depend on having certain instruments, and neither too few nor too many of them, with the privilege of using only those he wishes, we will have arrived almost at Utopia. Frederick Fennell now enjoys an advantage of this sort with his symphonic wind ensemble. He can invite composers to write *for this group, or any part of it,* with a firm understanding that the composer's

⟦ BAND ARRANGING AND SCORING ⟧

wishes will be respected. This is a return to the old professional practice of having arrangements made specifically for the use of a given group, the practice that has produced—from the days of Gilmore and Daniel Godfrey—some of the best band music we have had. With this situation, the imagination of the composer or arranger is the only limiting factor.

For the all-round practical band arrangement, many problems will always remain. A glance at the instrumentations of various bands given in Chapter *4* will illustrate the variety of combinations and numbers for which a given band arrangement or composition is supposed to serve. What happens, in effect, is that the arranger or composer must rely on the basic elements of the band: clarinets, cornets, trombones and tuba, plus saxophones, which cover all of the possible deficiencies in horns and double-reeds. Everything else in these arrangements is simply super-imposed, and in most cases need hardly even be played. The basic five instruments listed above give the fundamental band sound. Flutes and baritones are also present in almost all bands, but they are not as a rule as well played, especially in high school bands, as the other basic instruments. There are exceptions, of course, but I should say that in the thirty years I have been listening to high school bands I have heard very few really good flute or baritone players—certainly no number nearly comparable to the excellent players of cornet, clarinet or trombone, even proportionally. I think it also worth mentioning that although saxophones are always plentiful, one hears very little good saxophone playing. For some reason, bandmasters seem to have developed a tolerance for poor saxophone playing which does not apply to other sections of their bands. Perhaps a certain amount of despair enters into the tolerance; in any case, I can only note what I have observed to be the general situation.

Often, with amateur bands of any size, age or proficiency, one comes across oddities and special instances. It is not uncommon, for example, to come across a relatively mediocre band that has one or two brilliant performers, perhaps an outstanding oboe player, or a great tuba player. Conversely, one can find a really fine band in which the only weak spot may be the baritone. The first band obviously should choose arrangements in which the good oboe player can be used to advantage; the second band should avoid works with important baritone solo passages. As things stand, this is the only practical way of making the best of circumstances and utilizing available all-purpose arrangements intelligently.

With clarinets, cornets, saxophones, trombones and tubas as a basis, the arranger of "commercial" (i.e., publishable and saleable) band music will add parts for all of the other instruments listed as presumably, potentially or desirably present. He will in any case add flute parts because they are essential to the high register, and he will simply hope that they will be well and audibly played. He will throw the oboe into all the *tuttis,* knowing that its presence or absence will make no difference; if, as often happens, he wishes to write a solo passage for oboe, he will cue it in the clarinet, saxophone or muted trumpet. He will write bassoon parts which generally double either saxophones, baritones, trombones, clarinets or perhaps all of them. As with oboe, any solo passage must be carefully cued. The baritone part is written as an essential one, even though the arranger is aware that he must use caution. Horn parts will generally be sustaining harmony parts or afterbeats, backed up or protected by saxophones or trombones. Horn solos also must usually be cued. E♭ soprano and E♭ alto clarinets are problematical. Except in rare arrangements today, parts for these instruments are simply thrown in to make the score larger, and they may be left out *ad libitum.*

This is taking the situation as it exists, and not considering ideal plans for the future. Whatever plans may receive general approval, there will still be some variations and discrepancies in high school band practices, and probably in college band practices as well. The composer or arranger seeking to find the widest market will still have to provide for most of these contingencies. In terms of band *sound,* his major problems will continue to be:

1) balancing top, middle and bottom registers in the woodwinds.
2) avoiding a consistently mixed *tutti* sound with the great variety of overlapping instruments.

⟦ BAND ARRANGING AND SCORING ⟧

3) exploiting solo instruments (requiring cues) against backgrounds of various mixtures that cannot be accurately planned.
4) providing contrast of choirs and sections.
5) staying within a pre-determined grade of difficulty in *all* the parts.

BAND SCORES

A composer usually, but not invariably, writes out a full score, which he makes from his preliminary sketches. An experienced arranger often does the same thing when he is transcribing an already existing piece. But he may, since he knows his trade very well, simply copy out band parts without making a new score, or he may make a short or condensed score as a guide. He can do this because the distribution of parts in a conventional band work is governed to a great extent by both tradition and the limitation of possibilities. The scoring of a march, for example, is not expected to be novel or "different." (No one would like it if it were!) Everyone with the slightest experience of band music knows that in general the clarinets and cornets take the melody, the horns the afterbeats, the trombones the counter-melody and so on. In much band music, aside from marches, the same conventions are usually observed.

With music of this sort a score is hardly necessary. The conductor can use a "lead" sheet, often a solo cornet or clarinet part, with important counter-melodies or other features sketchily indicated. This is all that conductors usually had in the old days. It goes without saying that a piano score is somewhat better; it at least gives a more or less complete harmonic sketch of the work, and any instrumental solos or unusual distributions can be indicated by printed directions. Such two-line scores were in use for a considerable time and are still sometimes seen. If the music is of no great complexity, they are still fairly serviceable.

Originally, whether the composer or arranger made a full score or not, the full scores of band works were never published. Either a simple "lead sheet" or a condensed score was made available. The reasons for this were entirely practical. In the first place, since most band concerts formerly took place in the open air, a full score posed a page-turning problem. (Anyone who has conducted an outdoor concert on a windy day can appreciate this!) Second, most band music did not abound in subtleties of instrumentation that required the most scrupulously exact notation for the conductor. Third, the economics of the publishing business did not permit the luxury of large scores that were not demanded, and would probably not have been used even if made available. Fourth, most of the "standard" transcribed literature was presumably already familiar to the conductor, and he could be expected to guess which instrument would be playing what notes in the band arrangement. Also, most "new" band music would follow a formula that would contain no surprises for the experienced conductor.

Today bandmasters have come to demand something more elaborate in the way of scores. The reasons for this are obvious: the increasing of the band's instrumentation and repertoire, the new seriousness with which band music is being taken, and the still new and developing function of the band as a medium of artistic, as well as popular, concert activity. It is now taken for granted, or at least strongly desired, that any band work of any seriousness should be published with full score. The advantages of the full score for study purposes surely do not have to be stressed. The full score enables the conductor to know the parts, and the sum of the parts, *exactly*. With such knowledge, not only can he give a better performance, but he can also save immense amounts of time in rehearsal; he does not, for example, have to stop to ask who has the B♭ in measure *13*, as one often must when working from an inadequate condensed score.

The full score for band is a large affair and often, with its twenty-five to thirty staves and many transpositions, is difficult to read accurately with any speed. Its layout is not completely standardized, although it proceeds in an orderly fashion from high woodwinds at the top to low brass and percussion at the bottom. Placement of bassoons, horns and a few other instruments is subject to some variation. A typical full score for modern band is shown in Illustration *42*.

For many works, a full score is either unnecessary or economically impractical. In many instances, the present three- or four-line "condensed" conductor score is perfectly adequate. The merit and usefulness of a condensed score depend on the care which arranger, editor and publisher bring to its make-up. Many of them are for all practical purposes complete; a few leave a great deal to be desired. An example of a typical well-made condensed four-line score is given in Illustration *43*.

In recent years, composers, arrangers and publishers have begun experimenting with different types of "compressed" or "compact" scores of from five to eight lines, or on occasion of as many as fourteen lines. These scores are less unwieldy than the conventional full score, and the best ones simply take the practice of placing several similar instruments on the same staff, and continue the practice logically. In some cases the "compact" scores are notated in concert pitch, similar to the piano or three-line condensed score. This obviates the necessity of transposition, and simplifies matters in some ways for the less experienced conductor. An example of a typical "compact" score is given in Illustration *44*.

There are a few works written for band in recent years for which full scores are indispensable. These are works, such as the Schoenberg Theme and Variations, Opus *43A*, in which the movement and distribution of parts are both unorthodox and complex, and in which the performance depends on the most delicately exact observance of instrumentation, dynamics, phrasing and nuance. It would be impossible to present this music in a "condensed" version, and the composer and publisher wisely decided not to make the attempt. There are other works in the present repertoire which for similar reasons must be studied and performed from full score. Although condensed scores have been made available for some of these, they represent makeshifts which are not really satisfactory. The preparation of a *good* condensed score, it should be noted for the record, requires a great deal of skill, and every bandmaster or student must have noticed, and probably commented on, how

⟦ ILLUSTRATION XLII ⟧

First two pages of the conductor's full score of Robert Ward's "Prairie Overture."

⟦ ILLUSTRATION XLII ⟧

⟦ **ILLUSTRATION XLIII** ⟧

First page of the conductor's condensed score of Beethoven's March from "Egmont."

⟦ ILLUSTRATION XLIV ⟧

A page from the conductor's compact score in concert key of Russo's "Brookville."

[BAND ARRANGING AND SCORING]

very much these scores differ in successfully fulfilling their purposes. In many cases, it is impossible to reduce all of the notes to a three-line score, and one has to shift to four or five lines; conversely, there are passages that may easily and clearly be placed on two lines. The problems are many and various: how consistently to indicate percussion; how carefully to indicate the part distribution in a *tutti* passage; should one indicate, and if so in what manner, when instruments stop playing, as well as when they enter? These are just a few examples of the considerations involved.

As a practical exercise for the student arranger or conductor, I should like to suggest the assignment of making several condensed scores from full scores of varying degrees of complexity, starting of course with simpler ones. This is one aspect of practical work that is usually overlooked in courses in both arranging and conducting, and I can assure the student that it is of inestimable benefit for many reasons. It is helpful toward understanding the score, as well as the inherent problem in arranging; it gives practice in transposition, draws attention to voicing and voice-leading, focusses attention on problems of balance, and lastly, gives the conductor an immediate and profound grasp of the performance problems. It is, in fact, an almost ideal way both to begin and to terminate a course in band arranging.

part three

THE

r·e·p·e·r·t·o·i·r·e

of

the

BAND

7

Repertoire

AND

its

development

⟦ REPERTOIRE AND ITS DEVELOPMENT ⟧

Today, more than at any other time in its history, the central problem of the band is its repertoire. We have surveyed various aspects of the repertoire in previous chapters, noting the changes in the musical and social functions of bands and band music, and by reproducing a variety of typical programs we have already presented a cross-section of actual repertoire material in use at different times and under varying circumstances. But the band today is at a cross-road with respect to repertoire; there is a wide-spread realization that the band, in a musical sense, must develop along new lines suited to its new function as an arm of education. It can no longer function as a poor man's orchestra, or purely as a medium for very light entertainment, at least in schools and colleges. And since the future of band music will be determined almost entirely by the schools and colleges, the question of future repertoire becomes paramount.

The professional bands, and the service and community bands as well, can continue, as agencies of entertainment, to perform any kind of music that their audiences find enjoyable. Any education that results from their activities can be considered as welcome, but necessarily secondary to the bands' primary purposes. These bands are directed outward; that is, they perform for audiences rather than for their own pleasure or instruction. It is true that some of the bands in schools and colleges seem to assume that they, too, are engaged in professional concert-giving; but while the bands may be of quite professional proficiency, this is a thorough distortion of the purposes of education. The school or college band should have its attention directed inward: to the instruction and profit of its members, and to the "educational" experiences that they may derive from participation. The audience of the school or college band is also, in most cases, a school or college audience whose interest, properly speaking, should not be of the same nature as that of a mixed public. It is therefore not only appropriate, but actually necessary, that the choice of repertoire be guided by suitable considerations in the many different situations that arise.

It has already been suggested that the major change in the band's status took place in the *1920*'s, with the advent of new forms of popular

⟦ **REPERTOIRE AND ITS DEVELOPMENT** ⟧

entertainment and the development of new media of mass communication and concomitant changes in social patterns. It was at about this time, also, that serious bandmasters began coming to grips with the problem of repertoire, and that the developments in school and college music began to promise the arrival of an entirely new orientation for the band. For all practical purposes, we can divide the history and discussion of repertoire at about this point in time.

The function of the old popular band was manifold, as we have seen. But at a certain period of its development the band became primarily a medium of light popular entertainment. It continued to be a utilitarian body for parades and outdoor ceremonies, for which, in general, marches and patriotic music were its only required repertoire. But bands like Sousa's, for example, never marched in parades, nor did most of the other popular concert bands, except on the rarest occasions. They concentrated entirely on concert-giving activities, for which a characteristic concert repertoire was developed.

One of the most interesting points about the repertoire of these bands up until the present time was their sameness. I mean not only the sameness of programming one finds among the many bands, but also the similarity of the programs given under different circumstances. These bands, by and large, played the same type of music at a county fair, or a world exposition, in a "formal" concert hall, or at a popular resort or amusement park. They expected, and drew, essentially the same type of audience at any of these places.

This audience was, with hardly any exception, unsophisticated and uncritical. It had not been made self-conscious about "music appreciation," nor had it had the opportunity to hear many of the world's orchestral or operatic masterpieces in anything resembling their original form. It was an audience that knew what it liked rather than what it was supposed to like, and what it liked was mostly what it knew. (In this respect audiences have not changed very much.) The basis of the band's repertoire was therefore what had become familiar through repetition, plus new pieces which reminded the audience in some way of those they already knew. Here again, the problem of the band's repertoire was not

⟦ REPERTOIRE AND ITS DEVELOPMENT ⟧

essentially different from that of other performing bodies. New material is always added gradually, and accepted gradually by the public; moreover, a great deal of what is listed as "new" is new in name only, but not in style or sound.

One should hasten to add that there is nothing wrong in all this; on the contrary, it is entirely proper and fitting. The field of entertainment is defined by precisely such limitations, and always will be. There is room in the field for the startlingly new, the unexpected, the different, but only as an exceptional departure designed to attract attention or to provide variety when it is appropriate and effective. This is as true in the theater as it is in musical ventures, insofar as the theater is considered as a medium of entertainment rather than as a high art form. And it is certainly true in the contemporary media of mass entertainment such as radio, television and motion pictures.

The determination of repertoire by function is clearly demonstrated by the rapid disappearance of the original band repertoire created at the time of the French Revolution. These pieces were conceived with a kind of artistic idealism that did not fit at all the practical uses of bands. The pieces by Gossec, Catel, Méhul, Jadin and their contemporaries, which will be discussed more fully in Chapter *8*, were patterned after the high art music of the period. They consisted of symphonies and overtures more or less in classic sonata form, without programmatic trimmings, and were in all respects "serious" music for which the band public was not ready. I believe that the same holds true for the *100*-year-long neglect of the Berlioz Symphony for Band, and the few other nineteenth century works written for band with serious intent by major composers. That these, on the other hand, can be revived and played today, shows again how very greatly the function of the band and its relation to its audience have changed.

In any case, a discussion of the general band repertoire until recent times does not have to concern itself with serious original band music, for it was not in any way a factor in band programs. The original band music that was performed in the nineteenth century was mostly music of passing interest, composed by bandmasters—the kind of music

⟦ REPERTOIRE AND ITS DEVELOPMENT ⟧

known universally as *Kapellmeistermusik*. Aside from marches, very little of this survives from one generation to the next; it follows ephemeral fashions and serves well for a season. A glance at old programs shows its extent and variety. A good portion of it might be described as outdoor salon music; dance pieces of the prevailing fashion account for another sizable amount; and patriotic pieces for various occasions account for most of the rest. These types of music we still have with us; the names of the pieces have changed, and the rhythms of the dance music, but they are in all essentials the same. They are, it should be added, quite necessary for the balanced repertoire of any all-purpose band.

So far as the general concert repertoire of the nineteenth century band is concerned, a sampling has been offered the reader in the programs cited in Chapters *3* and *4*. "Serious" music, as has been noted, is represented on these programs by operatic overtures and potpourris, a few standard non-operatic concert overtures, occasional movements of symphonies, and lighter orchestral "classics," especially suites and descriptive pieces. In the early nineteenth century, Rossini was by far the most popular of all great composers found on band programs; by the middle of the century he was rivalled in popularity only by Verdi and Meyerbeer. The efforts of the most educationally minded bandmasters, such as Wieprecht, to add Mozart and Beethoven symphonies to the band repertoire, do not seem to have met with very great success; perhaps this lack of success reflects a sort of musical justice. Gilmore occasionally played a movement of a Beethoven symphony, but this was as far as he dared or cared to go. Perhaps the most important thing to note about his programming was that whenever he played a "heavy" number (such as a symphonic excerpt) he followed it immediately with a piece calculated to get the audience tapping its feet or being otherwise thoroughly diverted. This practice has generally been true of all band programming until recent times, and is again a reflection of the nature of the band concert and of the band audience, and their interaction.

In point of fact, this heterogeneous nature of the band concert is possibly one of its greatest charms. No other medium offers the audience such curiously diversified musical fare, with such startling juxtaposi-

[REPERTOIRE AND ITS DEVELOPMENT]

tions. Gilmore, the reader may remember, sandwiched the Andante of the Beethoven Fifth Symphony between a piccolo solo and a cornet solo; and one would not have to seek far in modern band programs to find other samples of programming every bit as startling. But this is done at band concerts with an ingenuousness, and ordinarily with a lack of pretentiousness, that makes it acceptable and even, at times, agreeable. The proof is, in any case, that programming of this kind has "worked" in the area of popular entertainment, and nothing indicates, if one watches television programs, that popular taste has vastly changed.

With respect to the present average band repertoire, the old one demonstrates that there has been little change in nature or content except for the presence today of a growing body of original band music, and the extension of the transcribed repertoire both backward in musical history and forward into the realm of contemporary music. (But it must be remembered that when the bands in Paris in *1867* played Wagner and Meyerbeer they were performing works of contemporary composers. In some respects, the best bands of the mid-nineteenth century were more audacious than the famous American business bands of the end of the century.) If one looks at old programs, one realizes that most of the standard fare is still very much alive in the band programs of today. Wagner and Tschaikowsky long ago joined Suppé and Rossini among the ranks of the band's most popular composers. But the point made previously in the discussion of arrangements is again brought home by this. We have each year new arrangements of Verdi and Rossini overtures, the same ones played by The American Band in the *1840*'s and '50's, or by Gilmore in the '60's and '70's. What has changed is only the concept of the band's instrumentation. And, as has been pointed out, this means only that the old *arrangements* are discarded and replaced. The band can reconstruct its library every generation or so without in the least altering its repertoire!

It may be interesting, while on this subject, to note the sort of band music requested by audiences at the Goldman Band concerts. By

[REPERTOIRE AND ITS DEVELOPMENT]

far the largest number of requests is for nineteenth century warhorses such as *Les Préludes* of Liszt, the Finale of the Tschaikowsky Fourth Symphony, the *1812* Overture, excerpts from the most familiar operas of Verdi, and various operetta or musical comedy selections. Oddly enough, there seems to be very little difference in the musical tastes of young and old in this respect. Youngsters who have played in bands request the same sort of thing as their elders; and of course it is true that many bands in the schools still play a good bit of this material. Older people do ask for certain pieces remembered from their youth, usually something that they heard Sousa play at Willow Grove sixty years ago, but the name of which they cannot remember. (One always has to be patient and polite when a fan asks to hear a number that goes "um-tiddly-um etc.," without getting near any recognizable tune.)

Requests for the newer pieces in the original band repertoire usually come from bandmasters or students who have played these works or who have an understandable curiosity about them. The original band works requested by the public are generally the older and simpler ones, often the ones based on folk tunes, such as the Holst Second Suite. This is not meant to imply that average audiences dislike the newer music. It is simply a matter for the record (as all performers know) that most audiences prefer the accessible and the familiar.

How the conductor should deal with this is a matter for each one to decide for himself. But here again I must emphasize the difference between the situation of the professional conductor, playing for the *entertainment* of what he hopes will be a large audience, and that of the school or college bandmaster, performing under the auspices of an educational institution. Perhaps this difference is not always as sharply marked as it should be, but it is to be hoped that the distinction will be noted. The high school band in particular should not be primarily audience-oriented. There is an ample literature of honest music, both original and transcribed, that can be used for the advancement of music and of education, without resorting to either pretentious imitation music or to novelties that belong in the category of vaudeville. It is of course true that the bandmaster's own taste and judgment should be at least one step

⟦ REPERTOIRE AND ITS DEVELOPMENT ⟧

ahead of that of the average audience, in both professional and school concert activity. But the ultimate selection of programs and program material will depend on what the bandmaster conceives to be the function of his band.

To return for a moment to the activity of the Goldman Band, which is typical enough in this respect, I am often asked by letter-writers or members of the audience why I don't play such-and-such a piece. One must be careful not to offend members of the audience, of course, and it is unwise to state that I don't play such-and-such because I don't like it, or that I think it is cheap, or that we have played it so much that the Band is tired of it. But these are nevertheless good reasons. As to works such as *Les Préludes* and the Finale of the Tschaikowsky Fourth, my reason for not playing them is simply that I do not think that any band can play them as well as the Boston Symphony, the Philadelphia Orchestra or for that matter any lesser orchestras. And furthermore, these pieces are played *quite often enough* by orchestras in concert and on the radio to eliminate any real need for the band's playing them. On technical grounds, no band *can* actually play the Finale to the Fourth at the proper orchestral tempo. I have tried it, taken very close to the proper speed, much to the amusement and exhaustion of the players. There are a good number of other pieces of this kind, in which the band arrangements for one reason or another simply do not come off, and these pieces I avoid as much as possible.

At any rate, these are some of my own observations and practices with respect to repertoire, it being always remembered that I am speaking of concerts in public parks, attracting people of all sorts. I do still play some of the orchestral overtures and other "standard" works that seem to me to have entered the band world, and to be more at home there now than they are in their original habitats. There are a good many pieces in this category: pieces no longer often played by orchestras in the concert hall, or pieces such as the *Light Cavalry* Overture which have become band pieces by tradition. Pieces such as these are probably more familiar as band pieces than they are as orchestra pieces; moreover, they sound every bit as effective, sometimes even more so, in good band arrangements, since the originals never depended on subtleties of orchestration or intensity of expression. Works such as these—at least many of them—also have traditionally been "arranged" in every form from café trio to brass band, so that their original status is somewhat obscured. Most of them are distinctly on the lighter side of the repertoire, and many of them are from the area of theater music, and are thus in no sense to be considered as "symphonic."

The question of distortion does not enter into the performance of music of this type when it is transcribed for band. The question does, however, arise with many other types of music in band arrangements. The performance of a Mozart overture, conceived for an orchestra of perhaps thirty players, and on a scale of sound that is calculated with extreme delicacy, seems to me to be a musical outrage for a wind band of a hundred players. This is not only because of the texture and scale of the music, but also because this is *serious* music, in a way that Suppé or Rossini overtures are not. I do not, for instance, have the same feelings about a transcription of a "popular" piano piece, such as "the" Chopin Polonaise, as I might have about the transcription of such a piano work as the Beethoven Opus *110*. Both are written for the piano, and are perhaps equally "transcribable" in technical terms, but musically they are worlds apart, and the question of artistic as well as simple technical distortion must be considered.

Most musicians are perfectly aware of this, and I might cite as a convincing instance the fact that while Sibelius himself suggested that I transcribe his *Karelia Suite* for band, he did not suggest that I transcribe his Fourth Symphony. Technically speaking, the Fourth Symphony might have been easier; *Karelia,* in fact, posed a good many difficult technical problems. But artistically or musically speaking, there is far less of what I have termed "distortion" in transcribing a light, popular work such as *Karelia,* however good or bad the arrangement, than there would be in transcribing the Symphony, no matter how excellent the arrangement might be.

Aside from technical and artistic considerations, there remains the question of the band's audience. A transcription of the Sibelius Fourth

⟦ REPERTOIRE AND ITS DEVELOPMENT ⟧

Symphony (to continue using this as an example would be insufferably "high-brow" from every standpoint. It may certainly be safely assumed that any members of a band audience who would enjoy listening to the Sibelius Fourth would prefer hearing an orchestral performance; they would, in fact, be the *first* members of the band audience to walk out. A number of the less sophisticated listeners might consider that they were being "educated," and might feel proud of themselves for listening to an arrangement of a real symphony (which possibly confers a higher "status" than listening to a mere overture or potpourri) but this is a high price to pay, and a lot of effort to make, for pseudo-culture. As a matter of fact, performances of this type take the band out of its proper role as an honest expression of popular culture, and place it in the false position of a manifestation of fake culture.

The band is not "high-brow" and should not try to be. The highbrowism one occasionally finds in band circles not only leads to a dead end, but is culturally regressive. We suffer from some confusion on this point today in all fields. (Putting Shakespeare in comic books is an example: people who read Shakespeare do not normally read comic books, and people who habitually read comics should leave Shakespeare alone!) The band, however, as a medium of *popular* culture, does have a responsibility in that area: it can contribute significantly to *improving the quality* of the popular culture in which it thrives. But this is not, as a rule, effectively done by transcriptions of symphonic masterpieces which are quite readily available in first-class recorded or live orchestral performances.

The allusion to Shakespeare and comic books, which may seem rather harsh to some readers, brings us to one other phenomenon of current band literature: the "simplified" arrangement of a "great" work, made for school bands that are not very advanced. This has always seemed to me, and to many other bandsmen as well, an indefensible practice. It contributes nothing to the education of student or audience; on the contrary, it provides a false, and in many instances, a lasting impression that hinders rather than helps the development of musical taste or knowledge. One might cite here the famous dictum of G. H. Lewes in

〚 REPERTOIRE AND ITS DEVELOPMENT 〛

his classic biography of Goethe: "One must grow up to the masterpiece; *it will not descend to us*." But that is exactly what the "simplified" arrangement and the comic-book Shakespeare try to do. And this is neither education nor anything else that is conceivably useful.

In addition to the variety of "simplified" arrangements, there is of course today a tremendous repertoire of easy band music specifically composed or transcribed for young players. This is quite clearly a practical necessity, and there is little to be said on this subject except that there is a great variation in quality here, as there is in more ambitious band music. Some of the "educational" material that is offered is of excellent quality, and some of it is sheer garbage. The responsibility of the educator in selecting from the huge mass of published material is, needless to say, a very serious one.

Bandmasters on all levels have to some degree this problem of selection in dealing with the published repertoire of arrangements, even when their bands have the technical skill to play anything that is written. There is, to begin with, an incredibly large amount of published band music from which to choose. In addition to this, the bandmaster will often find several arrangements of the same work. A great many of the standard overtures, for example, are available in at least three or four editions. They are not by any means all equally good. But some of them are clearly superior to others in musical terms, while a few are of such poor quality that they should not be used by anyone. Nevertheless one continues to hear quite a few inexcusably poor arrangements in common use. It becomes an additional responsibility of the bandmaster to compare the available arrangements of any work he wishes to perform, and to select the one that appears to him the best, both in general musical terms and in terms of practicality.

The question of arrangements, or of comparative editions, does not enter into the consideration of works originally composed for band, since there is (as long as the copyright is valid) only one version of each. As the repertoire of original band music grows—and I include good

⟦ REPERTOIRE AND ITS DEVELOPMENT ⟧

original band music written for very young bands as well as that written for the best concert bands—it is possible that there will be much less reliance on arrangements and transcriptions in the band's repertoire. But this will be a gradual evolution. Meanwhile, it is certain that original band music is what a band is best employed in playing, and that the future of concert band music depends on it. What is important at this stage is the *quality* of original band music. Because a work is written directly for band does not, alas, make it good. Everyone who reads this book has, I am sure, listened to some fairly dreary original band music. The time has come to be discriminating in this field as well as in the field of transcriptions and arrangements. One should not play second-rate original band music just because it is "original." The band will be better off continuing to play *Poet and Peasant,* and the audience would rather hear that. And the bandmaster should remember that a good march is worth more than a bad "symphonic poem."

The band concert, always remembering the band's various publics, and the functions of the band in both education and entertainment, should be a lively miscellany. I believe firmly, as I wrote many years ago, that the future importance of bands as concert or educational organizations depends on the cultivation of a special repertoire, embracing the few traditional forms that belong to the band, such as the march, and the new original literature that is so auspiciously growing. It is these two parts of the repertoire that can give musical meaning to the band's performing activity, and that justify its existence as a branch of education. So far as the public is concerned, one can add to this as much of the old standard band repertoire as the public still wants to hear, provided that one can justify, from one or another viewpoint, its appropriate inclusion on band programs. But by and large, the time has come to drop the standard orchestral pieces from band programs, and to concentrate on doing what best suits the band in all of the phases of its activity.

8

ORIGINAL

B · A · N · D

1760 ~ MUSIC ~ 1960

⟦ ORIGINAL BAND MUSIC, 1760-1960 ⟧

There is extant no music composed for winds prior to *1760* that can properly be termed band music, unless one excepts the original score of Handel's *Music for the Royal Fireworks,* written in *1749* for three trumpets, three horns, twenty-four oboes and twelve bassoons. Even this cannot be considered a "band," or certainly not a normal one, although it represents an outsize wind combination. We have already seen that the military and municipal bands until the latter part of the eighteenth century were small groups, irregular in instrumentation, and with nothing approaching a repertoire of distinction or interest.

Any wind instrument music of interest before this time must today be considered wind ensemble music, and of this there is a great deal, mostly for the brasses. All students of band music should be familiar with this large and interesting literature. It provides variety and additional interest in band programs, and is invaluable for the musical training of band players, all of whom should have the benefit of experience in smaller ensembles.

The great treasury of brass ensemble music begins with Andrea and Giovanni Gabrieli at the very end of the sixteenth century. The *canzone* and *sonate* of the Gabrielis and their contemporaries are magnificent in sound, and represent a high point of instrumental composition in their period. Many of these works, written for performance at the Cathedral of San Marco in Venice, or for other situations with appropriate acoustical properties, involve antiphonal choirs of instruments. Giovanni Gabrieli (*1557-1612*) generally divided his instrumental forces into two choirs, each of four or five voices; but one of his Sonatas calls for as many as twenty-two voices, divided into five choirs. Giovanni Gabrieli is also one of the first composers to make use of "echo" effects, and to specify contrasts of *forte* and *piano*. These works are far better known today than they were in *1938,* when I first called the attention of American bandsmen to them, and a large number of them are available in excellent modern performance editions. The best and most complete American source for these is the catalog of Music for Brass, 7 Canton Street, North Easton, Massachusetts. One should also consult the catalogs of Musica Rara (London) and other publishers.

⟦ ORIGINAL BAND MUSIC, 1760-1960 ⟧

As has been noted previously, the Venetian School did not continue to produce instrumental music of this type. The concerted music for wind instruments produced during the remainder of the seventeenth century is scattered, although there are a few pieces of real interest. The so-called *Tower Sonatas* of Johann Pezel (*1639-1694*) have been mentioned. In detail, Pezel's works (all for cornetts and trombones) are as follows:

Hora Decima Musicorum Lipsiensium-zum Abblasen um 10 Uhr Vormittage in Leipzig ("Ten O'Clock in the Music of Leipzig— To Be Played at Ten O'Clock in the Morning in Leipzig.")
    Containing Sonatas, etc., for Cornetts and Trombones.
    Published at Leipzig, *1670.*
Intraten a 4, nehmlich mit einem Cornett und 3 Trombonen ("4-Part Intradas for *1* Cornett and *3* Trombones.")
    Published in *1683.*
Fünfstimmige Blasende Musik ("Five-part Music for Winds.")
    Frankfort, *1685.*

Many of these are available in modern editions. The reader is again referred to the catalog of Music for Brass, as well as to that of Musica Rara and the German editions of Breitkopf and Härtel and others.

Rather similar to the Pezel is the collection published at Leipzig in *1696* by J. G. Reiche (*1667-1734*), entitled *24 Neue Quatricinia— vornehmlich auff den Rathhäusern oder Thürmen mit Fleiss gestellet* ("Twenty-Four New Four-Part Pieces Specifically to be Played from Municipal Buildings and Towers." Tower-Sonatas for *1* Cornett and *3* Trombones. Original Volume published at Leipzig in *1696*.) These "tower sonatas" are musically agreeable and make fine brass ensemble material. The works of Reiche and Pezel have served as models for

[ORIGINAL BAND MUSIC, 1760-1960]

Hindemith's contemporary *Morgenmusik* for four-part brass choir, and for other works by twentieth century composers.

Among other seventeenth century works for brass, one might cite the *Funeral Music for Queen Mary* of Purcell, the *Music for the Coronation of Charles II* of Matthew Locke (*Musick for the King's Sagbutts and Cornetts, 1661*), and occasional pieces by Johann Schein, Samuel Scheidt, André Philidor and others. One of the Philidor pieces, for three trumpets and timpani, is published by Music Press, and there are examples of other brass music of this period in the catalogs of Musica Rara, Musica Antiqua (Schott & Sons), as well as of Music for Brass and other American catalogs.

The woodwind music of this period is considerably less interesting. The marches of Lully, for example, while historically of interest, are negligible musically. One may be found in the catalog of Musica Rara, and three were edited by L. Chomel for the publishing house of Buffet-Crampon (Paris). The other woodwind "divertissements" and occasional pieces, by Mouret, Rosiers, Pez and any number of others are in general not of a character to warrant revival, even for the sake of antiquarianism.

The latter part of the eighteenth century saw the establishment of a more or less "standard" wind ensemble or band, as described in Chapter 2. The regimental band of Frederick the Great, imitated throughout Europe, consisted of two oboes, two clarinets, two horns and two bassoons. This combination was used not only for military music and marches, but also attracted the interest of most of the composers of the period, from Haydn to Schubert. Many of the Serenades, Divertimenti, Sonatas and other works composed for these eight-piece "bands" are of outstanding musical interest, and should be familiar to all bandsmen and wind instrument players. Nearly all are available in good modern performing editions, as well as in the complete collected editions of the works of the various composers. Among them should be mentioned several beautiful Divertimenti of Josef Haydn, the two famous Serenades of Mozart, the *Rondino* and the Octet, Opus *103* of Beethoven and a Menuet and Finale from an Octet of Schubert. Both Haydn and Mozart wrote many works for other combinations of wind instruments, both smaller and larger. There are many divertimenti and other pieces for the sextet of two oboes, two horns and two bassoons by Haydn and others, and on a somewhat larger scale, the *Serenade* (K. *361*) of Mozart, for two oboes, two clarinets, two basset-horns, four French horns, two bassoons and contra-bassoon. There is also the little-known *Eine Kleine Trauermusik* in E♭ minor of Schubert, for two clarinets, 2 bassoons, contra-bassoon, two French horns and two trombones, published as No. *23* in the Breitkopf and Härtel *Kammermusik-Bibliothek*.

Among other works which should be mentioned are several marches by Johann Christian Bach, two for two clarinets, two horns and two bassoons, and four for the standard octet. Of Karl Philip Emmanuel Bach, there are six sonatas for two flutes, two clarinets, two horns and one bassoon; of Karl Ditters von Dittersdorf there is a *Parthia* for two oboes, two horns and bassoon. (The K. P. E. Bach and the Dittersdorf are published in modern editions by Musica Rara.) There are also a *Serenade* by Pleyel (*1757-1831*), two by Gyrowetz (*1763-1850*) and one by Franz Anton Rossetti (*1744-1792*), not yet available (as far as I know at this writing) in modern editions. In addition, the reader may already be familiar with the woodwind quintets of Franz Danzi (*1763-1826*) and those of Anton Reicha (*1770-1834*). These are apparently the earliest works written for what has become the stardard woodwind quintet of flute, oboe, clarinet, horn and bassoon. The Mozart *Quintet* in E♭ (K. *452*) for piano, oboe, clarinet, horn and bassoon, of course should not be forgotten, nor the Beethoven Opus *16*, also in E♭, for the same combination. (This combination was also used by Spohr and many others during the early nineteenth century and has continued to our own times.)

The above sketch of wind ensemble music is sufficient to give the student an idea of the interesting repertoire created between roughly *1760* and *1820*. A great deal of it is readily available in good editions (which was not true twenty years ago) and more is constantly being rediscovered, re-edited and published by responsible musicologists and publishers. The bandsman and student are urged to investigate this literature, for obvious reasons. At the same time, the user of this music is cautioned against irresponsible reconstructions and slipshod editions

⟦ ORIGINAL BAND MUSIC, 1760-1960 ⟧

of these works, and of attributions which are not carefully documented by authoritative scholars and musicians. Here again, unfortunately, we must be chary of "simplified" or questionable editions produced for supposedly educational purposes. Good editions are easy to obtain, and there should be no excuse for not using them.

From this preliminary sketch of wind ensemble music, we may turn to the development of what we may more properly classify as band music. Most of the works in this category, prior to the French Revolution and for some time after are, as we might expect, marches. The majority of these are of slight interest, except as historical curiosities, but there are many still worth playing. Here again, works in this category are available as they were not a few years ago. The early collections, made by J. Kosleck for Breitkopf and Härtel, and by L. Chomel for Buffet-Crampon, are unfortunately no longer in print, although isolated numbers from the Chomel group can be found. Among those edited by Chomel are a march by Lesueur (*1760-1837*) and one by Paisiello (*1741-1816*), the latter composed for Napoleon in *1803*. This is a slight piece, though of obvious historical interest, and completely characteristic of the marches of that period.

Among isolated military marches, we may cite one by Frederick the Great (*1712-1786*), published by Schlesinger, Berlin, but no longer available; a March and Allegro by J. N. A. Witassek (*1771-1839*), published by Musica Rara; and a charming *Turkish March* by Michael Haydn (*1737-1806*), available from Mercury Music Corporation. There are also several marches by Cherubini and Spontini, as well as dozens of others by minor composers. The greatest number are not at this time available.

With the collaboration of Mr. Douglas Townsend, American composer and musicologist, I have been working for some time on the restoration of a series of the most interesting of the early marches, to be published through Mercury Music Corporation. At the present time (*1961*) the following are available or are in preparation:

⟦ ORIGINAL BAND MUSIC, 1760-1960 ⟧

Ferdinand Paër (1771-1839):
> *Four Grand Military Marches* (Composed for the wedding of Napoleon I and Marie-Louise of Austria, April 2, 1810.)

Johann Nepomuk Hummel (1778-1837):
> *Three Grand Military Marches* (C major, E♭ major, C minor. Composed about 1820 for the Grand Duke Nicholas of Russia.)

Gioacchino Rossini (1792-1868):
> *Three Marches* (Composed for the marriage of the Duke of Orleans.)
> *March* (Composed for the Sultan Abdul Medjid.)

This series will eventually include marches by Charles Dibdin (*1745-1814*), Samuel Wesley (*1763-1837*), Francis Xavier Süssmayer (*1766-1803*), Sigismond Neukomm (*1778-1858*), Luigi Cherubini (*1760-1842*) and Sir Henry R. Bishop (*1766-1855*).

Rossini, Cherubini and Hummel are, of course, well-known composers. All of the others were celebrated in their day, and are still interesting in many ways. Paër was famous as an opera composer, and some of his works were performed in France until fairly recently. He was Maître-de-Chapelle to Napoleon I, and later became a conductor of the Opéra Comique. Dibdin was perhaps the most popular English composer of his time, famous especially for his songs and stage entertainments. Samuel Wesley was the son of Charles Wesley and the nephew of the founder of Methodism. He was the greatest English musician of his time; his anthems and motets are still widely admired, although his instrumental music is inadequately known. Süssmayer was the collaborator of Mozart who completed the unfinished *Requiem*. Neukomm was an immensely popular and most interesting Austrian composer and virtuoso, who travelled widely and spent considerable time in Brazil (where he composed one of his works for military band). He is one of the most interesting minor figures of the early nineteenth century. Sir

241

⟦ ORIGINAL BAND MUSIC, 1760-1960 ⟧

Henry Bishop is, of course, remembered as the composer of *Home Sweet Home.*

    The military music (marches) and the serenades, divertimenti and *Parthien* of Europe were reproduced on this side of the Atlantic during the late eighteenth and early nineteenth centuries. There are preserved, for example, several *Parthien* and an interesting "water-music" for wind instruments by the American Moravian, David Moritz Michael (*1741-1827*). The *Parthien* were scored for two clarinets, two horns and one or two bassoons. A few call for additional flute or trumpet. His water music of *1808* and *1809* (the latter entitled *Bestimmt zu einer Wasserfahrt auf der Lecha*—"Intended for a water ride on the Lehigh") was scored for a similar small combination. The first performances of actual military music in the Moravian settlement of Bethlehem were organized in *1809,* and there was undoubtedly a great deal of music written in this genre and still reposing in the Moravian archives.

    In Chapter *3*, I have given a brief account of other military music composed in America between *1760* and *1850*. With the assistance of Mr. Roger Smith and Mr. Robert Leist, I have undertaken a project of restoring and reviving many of the most interesting marches and other pieces associated with historical events. The series so far completed or in progress includes:

    The Battle of Trenton (1792): James Hewitt
* *The Wood Up Quickstep* (1835): John Holloway
    March of the First Alabama Volunteer Regiment (1837): John
        Holloway
    The Hero's Quickstep (1836): Henry Schmidt
    The Lion Quickstep (1834): James Hooton
    Jefferson's March (1804): Alexandre Reinagle
    Tippecanoe Quickstep (1840): Henry Schmidt

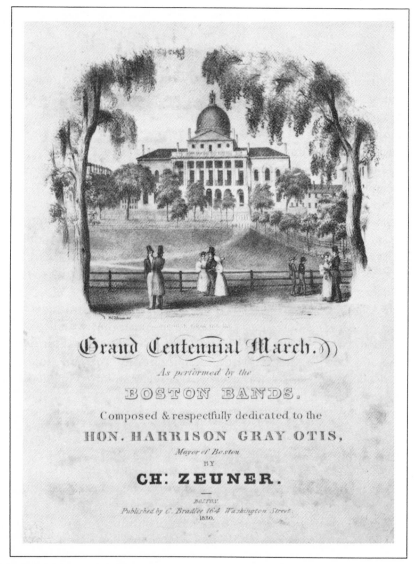

Typical of the military music popular in America during the 1830's is this march performed by the Boston Bands. The cover is shown here. From the author's collection

⟦ ORIGINAL BAND MUSIC, 1760-1960 ⟧

President Harrison Funeral March (1841): J. H. Seipp
* *The New York Light Guards* (1839): Francis H. Brown
Grand Centennial March (1830): Charles Zeuner
Bangor March (1807): Oliver Shaw
Grey's Quickstep (1839): B. A. Burditt
* *Santa Ana's Retreat from Buena Vista* (1848): Stephen Foster
   (asterisks indicate pieces recorded by the Goldman Band)

It has already been noted that the single most important development in the history of bands and band music took place as a concomitant of the French Revolution. This is equally true of the band's repertoire and the band's instrumental development. The works composed for band at this time are the first truly serious and developed music in the band repertoire. Until quite recently, these works were known only to musical scholars, and no attempt had been made to revive and perform them. I have suggested the reasons for this neglect of these works in the preceding chapter. However, since my first revival of the *Classic Overture* in C of Gossec in *1948* (followed by those of the *Military Symphony* in F of Gossec and the Overture in F of Méhul and the Overture in C of Catel), it is apparent that the band and the band's public are once again receptive to music of this type and have welcomed their restoration to the current repertoire. They are certainly of musical, as well as historical, interest.

François Joseph Gossec (*1734-1829*) was the leading symphonic composer of France during the latter part of the eighteenth century, and was a musician of considerable importance and influence. He wrote twenty-six orchestral symphonies, many operas and oratorios, and during the period of the Revolution gave his best talents to the composition of works for wind band and for chorus. Among these works are the two mentioned above, and several others that appear to be lost. He also composed a *Hymn to the Goddess of Reason* and a *Hymn to the Supreme Being,* for band with chorus, as well as a Funeral March and several miscellaneous small pieces. The *Classic Overture* in C, written in *1795,*

⟦ ORIGINAL BAND MUSIC, 1760-1960 ⟧

appears to be the first movement of an incomplete or lost symphony. It is in straightforward sonata form, non-programmatic, and in style somewhat recalls Gluck. A modern edition, prepared by Roger Smith and myself, has been available for some time, and the work has been widely played, a testimony to its acceptance as a repertoire piece and as a landmark in the original band literature.

The little *Military Symphony* in F, composed in *1793* or *1794,* is a slighter work, but possesses considerable charm. It is hardly a symphony in the developed sense of the term, but it also does not fall into the category of divertimento or serenade. Its three brief movements (Allegro, Larghetto and Allegro) are effectively contrasted; each is a simple two-part form without development. This work also has been available for some years, in an edition prepared by Robert Leist and myself, and has been performed frequently.

The *Overture* in F of Etienne Méhul (*1763-1817*), available in an edition by Mr. Smith and myself, is among the most important and interesting of the band compositions of this period, although it has more elements of string conception in it than the works of Gossec or Catel. The Méhul Overture is a well-developed classical piece of ample proportion and elegant design. Méhul, of course, was one of the renowned composers of his time, highly esteemed by his contemporaries. Several of his orchestral overtures are still occasionally heard, and his opera, *Joseph,* was a fixture in the repertoire for over a century.

The *Overture* in C by Charles Simon Catel (*1773-1830*), composed as was the Méhul, in *1795,* is perhaps the most satisfactory of the works of this period. Catel, though less famous as a composer than either Gossec or Méhul, was nevertheless a musician of distinction who made a substantial contribution to the musical life of his time. He became assistant to Gossec as director of the Band of the National Guard, and was one of the important professors of the Conservatory. His harmony textbook was for many years the standard one used in France. With Gossec, Méhul, Cherubini and others, he engaged in important public activities on behalf of music. His compositions include operas, symphonies and chamber music, as well as the works he wrote for wind instruments. The

⟦ ORIGINAL BAND MUSIC, 1760-1960 ⟧

Overture in C, in its elegance and clarity, is characteristic of the perfection of late eighteenth century style. It is in conventional sonata form, with a slow introduction, and is delightful both melodically and harmonically. The development is ample and interesting, and the influence of Mozart (especially in the second theme) is clearly discernible. It is clearly and neatly conceived from the standpoint of wind instruments, and serves as an example of the best achievements in serious music of composers for wind band in the period. This Overture too is available in a modern edition by Mr. Smith and myself.

There is also an *Overture* in F by Catel, of almost equal interest and appeal, and several works by the brothers Louis (*1768-1853*) and Hyacinthe (*1759-1800*) Jadin, which are worthy of notice and revival. Louis Jadin composed a *Military Symphony,* two Overtures and several Suites for band. His Overture in C is especially striking. Among the works of Hyacinthe Jadin, there is a splendid Overture in F, which would certainly be a welcome addition to current band repertoire. None of these works is available in any form at the present time.

Many other composers, less known to us, but conspicuous in their day, also wrote for band between *1795* and *1810.* They include Etienne Ozi (*1754-1813*), a celebrated bassoon virtuoso, Etienne Solère (*1753-1817*), an equally celebrated clarinetist, and others whose names are no longer at all familiar.

The original scoring of the Méhul Overture, as an example of the format of these works in their time, included the following: two piccolos, first and second clarinets, two horns in F, two trumpets, two bassoons, bass trombone, serpent and timpani. One sees here quite clearly the nucleus of the modern band, and is surprised only by the absence of oboes. The saxophone and the saxhorns (cornet, baritone, etc.) one must remember, had not yet been invented.

These works are, or should be, to the band repertoire very much what the earliest symphonies of Haydn are to the orchestral repertoire: the first completely realized and still interesting works in the medium. And with the new status of the band today, as a serious medium of musical expression, many of these works, having been re-discovered and made available, have assumed their proper places as the prototypes of all serious composition for wind band. Musically and stylistically, they are on a high level, and provide a musical background in which modern bandsmen may take considerable pride.

COMPOSITION FOR BAND IN THE NINETEENTH CENTURY

The work of Gossec, Catel, Méhul and their contemporaries was not continued in the next generation. The impulses that had brought forth this music had lost their force, and the democratization of the arts proceeded along other lines. But the tradition of noble wind music for great ceremonial occasions was revived by Hector Berlioz (*1803-1869*) in his *Grande Symphonie Funèbre et Triomphale,* Opus *15,* composed in *1840* for the Tenth Anniversary of the Revolution of July *1830,* and for the dedication of the Bastille Column.

It seems odd that this noble and imposing work, surely the most important ever conceived for wind band, should have had to wait *107* years for its American premiere! But until my performance of it with The Goldman Band on June *23, 1947,* it had never been heard in America and, as a matter of fact, had rarely been played in Europe since the death of Berlioz. The Symphony was written for a huge band, of *208* players, with the option of adding a chorus toward the end of the last movement. At a later date, Berlioz also added optional strings, but he himself usually performed the Symphony (in France, Germany and Russia) without them.

The Symphony is in three movements, and, as with all symphonic works of Berlioz, is of a programmatic character. The first movement— Moderato, un poco lento, 4/4—is subtitled "Funeral March," although it is cast in symphonic rather than march form. It is a movement of great breadth and nobility, rich in harmonic texture and pure melodic inven-

〖 ORIGINAL BAND MUSIC, 1760-1960 〗

tion. Contrasting sections bring the solemn and moving main themes into effective relief. The second movement—Adagio, non tanto, 4/4—Andantino, 3/4—Andantino poco lento e sostenuto, 4/4—is the "Recitative and Prayer," and was intended by Berlioz to portray in music the thought of a "discourse or farewell addressed to the illustrious dead." In this movement a trombone solo represents the voice of the orator, intoning his address in a voice of simplicity and dignity. No sorrow marks the discourse; the melodic line is a cantilena of a calm but growing expressiveness. This movement is particularly interesting as one of the very rare examples of a solo for the trombone written by one of the great masters.

The final movement, the "Apotheosis"—Allegro non troppo, e pomposo, 4/4—is in brilliant contrast to the two preceding. Here Berlioz presents a stirring martial sound, bright and forthright, on the programmatic theme of Glory and Triumph. A fanfare of brasses opens the movement and leads directly to the statement of the principal theme, an eight-bar melody of brisk and militant character. Toward the end of the movement occurs the choral hymn, based on this theme, which may be used *ad libitum* with the band. The string orchestra parts, added later, are also for *ad libitum* use. The entire movement is dramatic and suggestive of the stage, as is much of Berlioz' best and most effective music.

The Symphony is among the least known of Berlioz' works; a few critics have felt that it is not among his best. Richard Wagner, however, a man not known for his generosity toward his fellow-composers, called it "great and noble from the first note to the last," and wrote that it convinced him of the genius of Berlioz. More recent musicians and critics, among them Jacques Barzun, author of the classic study, *Berlioz and the Romantic Century,* have also given it high rank among the composer's works. Barzun writes that, in this work, ". . . he [Berlioz] fully achieved his goal of blending grandeur with nobility and simplicity with elevation . . ." Another of our leading composers and critics, Virgil Thomson, writing in the New York *Herald Tribune* on the occasion of the Symphony's American premier, had the following to say:

⟦ ORIGINAL BAND MUSIC, 1760-1960 ⟧

The sound of the thing is Berlioz at his best. No other composer has ever made a band sound so dark, so rich, so nobly somber. That sound is not only a beautiful and wondrous thing in itself; it is also part of the work's expressivity. It is everything that could possibly be meant by the adjectives funereal and triumphal. The tunes are noble, too; not one is lacking in sobriety. The whole composition is at once simple, serious and utterly sumptuous. It is as impersonal as a public building and at the same time deeply touching.

The touching quality does not come from any private emotional assertion of the composer and still less from any calculated attempt on his part to provoke our tears. It comes, believe it or not, from the perfect taste of his stylistic conception . . . the military combined with a memorial subject calls forth a richness of utterance and an impeccability of tone that make his "Grande Symphonie Funèbre et Triomphale" one of the great ceremonial pieces of all time.

There is no other comparable work for band written during the nineteenth century, or, for that matter, in our own time. The nineteenth century was, in the band field, precisely what I have described earlier: a period of popularization through transcriptions of easily assimilated orchestral music, and of mountainous quantities of *Kapellmeistermusik*. Nevertheless, a few works of interest were composed, each under special circumstances. This is a fact that also must be remembered, for there was no general demand for a literature or a repertoire, and the few works we have were all prompted by particular occasions, or composed for specific local groups.

Chronologically, the first of the interesting nineteenth century works is the *Nocturne* in C, Opus *34*, by Louis Spohr, composed in *1815* for Wind Band and Turkish Music (i.e., percussion). This is an uneven work, in six movements of moderate length, scored for a band of medium size, disposed as follows:

⟦ ORIGINAL BAND MUSIC, 1760-1960 ⟧

2 flutes in E♭ (both alternating with piccolo)
2 oboes
2 clarinets
2 bassoons
contrabassoon
2 French horns
2 trumpets
post horn
trombone
bass horn
bass drum, cymbal, triangle

The six movements are a March, Menuet, Air and Variations, Polacca, Adagio and Finale (Waltz). Of these, the March, Adagio and Polacca are decidedly the most interesting, the Adagio being in fact one of the most charming examples of Spohr's elegant Romanticism. The scoring and texture are lovely, and the music gives one an idea of why Spohr was so very highly regarded in his time. Richard Strauss particularly admired this work, and performed it occasionally in Europe. But like the Berlioz, it had never been performed in America until I presented three movements of it in *1959,* on the *100th* anniversary of the death of the composer.

The *Three Grand Military Marches* of Hummel have already been mentioned. These were composed in about *1820,* for a somewhat larger band, and they are without question among the very finest examples of concert marches in the entire repertoire, whether for band or for orchestra. The three marches, which of course may be performed separately, are delightfully contrasted, and when played as a group, make an effective suite. The original scoring calls for:

flauti 1, 2, 3
flauto 4, and piccolo

[**ORIGINAL BAND MUSIC, 1760-1960**]

oboes
piccolo clarinet in F
clarinets in C
corni di bassetto
fagotti
contrefagott
corni in C
trombe in C
tromboni (3)
basshorni
percussion

Hummel is once again being recognized for the fine composer that he was, and the discovery and editing of the marches in *1960* by Douglas Townsend is a piece of great good fortune for bandsmen.

From *1824*, we have the well-known *Military Overture, Opus 24,* of Felix Mendelssohn. When I say "well-known," I am conscious again of a certain irony, for this work too had to wait for its American premier until my father performed it in *1945!* Mendelssohn composed this entirely characteristic work (at the age of fifteen) for the band at the resort of Dobberan, on the Baltic Sea, where he occasionally spent vacations with his family. While the *Overture* is not on a level with the Octet or the music for *A Midsummer Night's Dream,* I cannot agree with those who find it trivial or unrepresentative. And if one compares it with the bulk of the nineteenth century music still performed by bands, its merits must become obvious. The tendency to under-rate Mendelssohn is wide-spread, and affects even his greatest works. The *Military Overture* is good, solid band music, the more interesting because we have so few examples of the sort from the pens of the great composers.

Mendelssohn composed, in about *1826*, another work for band, an *Andante and Allegro* written, according to Sir George Grove, for the wind band of a beer garden which he used to pass on his way to bathe. Sir George evidently had seen the manuscript of the piece, for he states that it was "interesting-looking," but diligent research has failed to discover any extant copy.

There are a few insignificant works by Carl Maria von Weber, a few marches by Boieldieu, some pieces by Ponchielli and a Funeral March by Donizetti, all composed for various versions of the wind band, but these need not detain us. Composition for band was indeed at a low ebb during this period. The *1840*'s, however, saw at least one other work of consequence in addition to the Berlioz Symphony. This is the *Trauersymphonie zur Besetzung C. M. von Webers* ("Weber Funeral Symphony") of Richard Wagner, composed in *1844* for the ceremonies attendant on the transfer of Weber's remains to his native Germany. The "symphony," scored by Wagner for a band of seventy-five pieces plus six muffled side drums, was based on two themes from Weber's *Euryanthe,* and thus represented a musical homage to the older composer. The score remained unpublished until *1926*. It is one of the most satisfying of all works composed for wind band, noble in sonority and effective in performance. Frederick Fennell describes it as "solemn and deeply moving," and adds that "no apology need be made for this music." Herbert Peyser, well-known New York critic wrote, after the first American performance in *1927,* that the effect of the music was "magnificent and heart-shaking."

The *Huldigungsmarsch* of Wagner was also composed for band, but no score of the original appears to be available. The versions performed today follow the orchestral transcription made by Joachim Raff. The *Kaisermarsch,* frequently performed by bands, was originally composed for orchestra.

One is amazed that neither Verdi nor Meyerbeer wrote extensively for wind band. Meyerbeer was known to have expressed interest in bands, and Verdi had extensive experience with them during his youth. Meyerbeer did compose three *Torch Dances* for various ceremonial occasions, in *1846, 1850* and *1853*. These polonaise-like dances are theatrical and effective; the first is the best known and most frequently performed.

There is no major work of Verdi for band, but Mr. Roger Smith has pointed out to me that there are many numbers in the operas that are straightforward band pieces, and intended as such. Most of these pieces, for performance by the stage bands, were not scored by Verdi, but written simply in a piano score, with the understanding that they would be performed by whatever wind players the opera house happened to have available. An excellent example of this type of band music is "King Duncan's March" in the opera *Macbeth* (1847). This may legitimately be considered as "original" band music, for it is obviously a real band piece, and a charming one.

For the remainder of the century there are not many works other than marches of various types, but a few of these are of extraordinary interest. In about *1865*, Anton Bruckner, the great Austrian symphonist, wrote three marches for the band of a regiment stationed near his home. These marches were never published in Bruckner's lifetime, but manuscripts of two of them were discovered through searches instituted by my father. The third is apparently lost forever. The two surviving marches, one entitled *Apollo March* and the other simply March in E♭, are totally unexpected pieces to come from the pen of Bruckner. They are gay and lively, possessed of a typical Viennese charm that might well remind one of Johann Strauss. They are amusing trifles, but genuine and delightful souvenirs of an era.

Of an entirely different character is the dark and eloquent *Trauermarsch* composed in *1866* by Edvard Grieg on the occasion of the death of his friend and compatriot, the poet Richard Nordraak. Grieg first wrote the march (in the key of A minor) for piano; shortly after, upon his return to Norway, he scored the work for full band, transposing it to G minor. The full score was published by Peters in Leipzig, and is one of the first published full scores for band. (The Berlioz Symphony was published earlier in full score by Schlesinger in Paris.) The Grieg Funeral March is, in my opinion, one of the grandest works composed for band. It has a great intensity, marvelous color and immense pathos. The work is more in the nature of a rhapsodic lament than a march; its effect depends in large measure on a performance of sweep and breadth.

⟦ ORIGINAL BAND MUSIC, 1760-1960 ⟧

It is among the most difficult of all nineteenth century band works to perform successfully, but it amply repays the effort.

There are quite a few marches and march-like pieces by secondary French composers of the period. The only one by a front-rank composer is the march *Orient et Occident* of Saint-Saëns, composed in *1869*. This is a rather elaborate, and not wholly effective number, of a programmatic nature as the title suggests. The contrast between oriental and occidental motifs is on the conventional side, and somewhat overstrained. The piece nevertheless is colorful and has a certain appeal which makes it at least worth noting.

The last remaining nineteenth century piece of any interest is the *Marche Militaire* of Tschaikowsky, composed in *1892* for the band of the Russian *98th* Infantry Regiment, of which A. P. Tschaikowsky was Colonel. This is a serviceable march, of no extraordinary distinction, but worth retaining in the repertory as a sample of straightforward writing of an effective kind. The march is rather pompous, with fanfare passages, and has an agreeable trio.

There are doubtless many other minor works by nineteenth century composers, greater and lesser, but it may seriously be doubted that any will be "re-discovered" that will prove to be of interest. The field has by now been gone over fairly thoroughly; certainly there are no works in larger forms, unless one allows for the faint possibility of there being a scattering of works by nineteenth century Russian composers which are now inaccessible. There is, of course, the Concerto for Clarinet and Band of Rimsky-Korsakov, and other works of this kind are said to exist. Even allowing for this possibility, the likelihood of any startling "re-discoveries" is rather small. We are left with a handful of works which are of some interest, both historically and musically, and these should certainly be known to every bandsman, in the same way that the historical orchestral literature is known to every orchestral conductor.

For the convenient reference of bandsmen who have urged me to compile such a listing, I give below in tabular form a summary of the nineteenth century works of chief interest, arranged chronologically:

Year	Composer	Title	Editor	Publisher
1810	Beethoven	*Ecossaise* / *Polonaise*	Erik Leidzen	Associated
1815	Spohr	*Nocturne* in C, Op. 34 (3 movements)	Richard Franko Goldman	Mercury
1816	Beethoven	*Military March*	Felix Greissle	Schirmer
c. 1820	Hummel	*Three Grand Military Marches*	Douglas Townsend	Mercury
1824	Mendelssohn	*Military Overture in C*, Op. 24	Felix Greissle	Schirmer
1836	Mendelssohn	*Funeral March*, Op. 103	Erik Leidzen	Associated
1840	Berlioz	*Grande Symphonie Funèbre et Triomphale*, Op. 15	Richard Franko Goldman	Mercury
1844	Wagner	*Trauersymphonie*	Erik Leidzen	Associated
1846	Meyerbeer	*Torch Dance* (No. 1)	M. L. Lake	Presser
1865	Bruckner	*Apollo March* / *March in E♭*	Erik Leidzen	Presser
1866	Grieg	*Trauermarsch* (title changed)	Maurice Whitney	Bourne
1869	Saint-Saëns	*Orient et Occident*		Durand (Paris)
1892	Tschaikowsky	*Marche Militaire*	Edwin Franko Goldman	Mills

〚 ORIGINAL BAND MUSIC, 1760-1960 〛

COMPOSITION FOR BAND
IN THE TWENTIETH CENTURY (TO 1940)

Although the first "major" band work of the twentieth century is generally considered to be the First Suite for Band, in E♭, of Gustav Holst (*1879-1934*), composed in *1909*, a stirring of interest was evident in wind music some years earlier. Grainger's *Hill-Songs*, the march, *Lads of Wamphray,* and parts of his *Lincolnshire Posy* had, for example, been sketched or completed by *1905*. The *First Hill-Song* was actually completed in *1902,* and *Lads of Wamphray* was performed soon after *1905* by the Band of the Coldstream Guards. These works were not published, however, until much later, and the credit for being the first available and universally recognized original band work of the century must unquestionably go to Holst's Suite. This credit belongs to the work for reasons other than simply priority of time. For this work of Holst, together with his Second Suite, in F major, of *1911*, established an altogether new style of idiomatic band writing and, one might say with all justice, a new conception of band sound and of the kind of forthright music most suited to the performing medium. These Suites have survived splendidly the test of a half century of use, and have served as models for uncounted others. It would be no exaggeration to say that no more effective pieces have been written for band.

In her biography of her father, Imogen Holst tells us this about the First Suite:

The lessons he had learnt in writing for children and amateurs proved helpful in his works for military band. Here his players were highly skilled experts as far as their instruments were concerned, but the music they played had to be simple and economical. The First Suite *in E♭ was an experiment in form, each movement being founded on a fragment of the opening Chaconne. He was in his second apprenticeship: having learned that symphonic development and leitmotif were equally hopeless for his sort of tune, he was trying to find a form that would satisfy his own needs, and the Chaconne proves how far he had travelled since the first years of the folk-song influence. The whole suite is superbly written for military band, especially the scherzando variation in the Intermezzo which exactly suits the brittle texture of the woodwind. It must have been a startling change from the usual operatic selections, and there are bandsmen who still remember the excitement of the first rehearsal in 1909. In spite of its original approach, the Suite never breaks away from the essential traditions of the band, and the March is the sort of music that is beloved of bombardons and euphoniums. It was not for nothing that Holst had played trombone on the pier in his student days: when he opens out into an inevitable* meno mosso, *it is with the assurance of an experienced bandsman who knows exactly what the other players are going to enjoy.*

The Suites were originally published in the standard British military band instrumentation, with two-line condensed scores. It was not until very much later that the demand of the American market prompted the issuance of a full score, with added instruments, of the First Suite.

Holst wrote one other work for band later in his life. This is the *Prelude and Scherzo,* "Hammersmith," Opus 52. This work remained in manuscript for many years, and was not published until *1956.* It is a work of more ambitious musical character than the Suites, but is perhaps not as completely realized in the band version as it is in the orchestral arrangement which was made later by the composer.

Percy Grainger's *(1882-1961)* unique and enormous contribution to band music has by now been universally recognized. As a young man, he spent much time in England, where he heard many of the famous British bands, and where he also became friendly with Holst and others interested in the study of British folk music. His early ventures in writing for large wind combinations have already been mentioned, but these remained unknown for many years. In the meantime, Grainger had established, and was extending, his reputation as one of the foremost pianists of his time, introducing his celebrated settings of folk tunes in a

〖 ORIGINAL BAND MUSIC, 1760-1960 〗

variety of versions, and composing for conventional and unconventional groups of instruments. Grainger came to the United States in *1915*, to settle permanently, and was an Assistant Instructor at the Army Band School on Governor's Island during World War I. It was at this time that his interest in band music revived, and the earliest of his published band works date from this period. They include the beautiful settings of *Shepherd's Hey, Molly on the Shore,* the *Irish Tune from County Derry,* and many original works including the *Children's March, Over the Hills and Far Away,* the *Gumsucker's March* (both of these for band with piano) and the *Colonial Song.* All of these date from the years *1917-1919,* and thus represent the first interesting body of new work for band after the Holst Suites.

All of Grainger's works for band are characterized by the most imaginative exploitation of band sonorities. With the exception of a very few scores composed in recent years, I think that there are no works in the entire band literature that compare with Grainger's in sheer beauty of band sound. Grainger's originality and resourcefulness as a composer and virtuoso manipulator of instruments is only now beginning to be truly appreciated. But even so simple a piece as his setting of the *Irish Tune* speaks for itself.

Grainger's band works are all written purely and simply as music; they are not specially designed for amateur bands, standard instrumentations or limited levels of ability. All of them use a full complement of normal band instruments, and several of them require relatively uncommon instruments such as soprano saxophone or contra-bassoon. Cues, where possible, are usually provided for these, but no cues can replace the important parts often assigned to such instruments as the French horns, E♭ clarinet, bassoons, piccolo and others whose particular timbre is desired for those parts. These parts are on occasion of considerable difficulty, although always idiomatically written, and indeed beautifully conceived for the instruments. But of course they must be played, and the ensemble must be in balance.

Two scores of Grainger are of special beauty and interest, and may serve as the most characteristic examples of his style. They are the

⟦ ORIGINAL BAND MUSIC, 1760-1960 ⟧

Children's March, Over the Hills and Far Away, written in *1918,* and the suite, *Lincolnshire Posy,* completed in *1937.* Both of these works may be heard in recordings that the composer himself considered nearly perfect: the first by the Goldman Band with Grainger himself at the piano; the second by Frederick Fennell and the Eastman Wind Ensemble. The *Children's March* is probably the first original composition using piano as an integral part of a band score. It also is the first band score which represents an entirely new type of band sound, making a liberal and highly effective use of low reeds such as the bassoon, English horn, bass clarinet, contra-bassoon and low saxophones, contrasting with brighter sounds of brass, and with a notably fresh and vigorous use of percussion. The *Lincolnshire Posy* is a masterpiece of band sonority, in which all of Grainger's accumulated skill in writing for wind instruments is fully exploited. This work, unlike the *Children's March,* which is entirely original in melodic material, is based on folk tunes, but set in an inimitably imaginative and distinguished manner, full of fresh invention and inspiration.

Grainger's other works for band include a setting of the American folk tune *Spoon River, The Immovable Do (1941),* the vigorous and brilliant march *Lads of Wamphray* (revised in *1937-38* and published subsequently), the *Marching Song of Democracy (1948)* and a very large work for band with organ, *The Power of Rome and the Christian Heart,* which was commissioned by The League of Composers for the concert honoring the seventieth birthday of Edwin Franko Goldman, in *1948.* All these works of Grainger exhibit those characteristics of his style that have made his music so widely popular and at the same time so greatly appealing to musicians. The total of Grainger's contribution to the band repertoire still remains the greatest made by any single composer of any time.

Grainger served, with Victor Herbert, as judge of the competition for the prize offered in November *1919,* by Edwin Franko Goldman, for the best new original composition for band. This prize was won by the distinguished Danish-born composer, Dr. Carl Busch (*1862-1943*), who at the time was conductor of the Kansas City Symphony Orchestra. Dr. Busch's work, the Symphonic Episode, *A Chant from the Great Plains,* was performed during the *1920* season of the Goldman Band and was published by Carl Fischer. The principal motive of the composition is an idealized version of a theme taken from Alice C. Fletcher's *A Study of Omaha Indian Music*. Subsequently Dr. Busch wrote several other works for band, all characterized by a high degree of professional skill and by a thorough understanding of the problems of band scoring.

The contributions of Percy Grainger and Carl Busch to the advancement of original band music were recognized by the American Bandmasters Association soon after its formation, when both composers were made Honorary Life Members.

The *1920*'s saw a small but steady increase in the number of compositions written for band. Most of these have not remained established in the repertoire. The notable exceptions are the two works composed by Ralph Vaughan Williams (*1872-1958*), the *English Folksong Suite* and the *Toccata Marziale*, both written in *1924*. These works are familiar to all bandsmen, as they deserve to be. The *English Folksong Suite* is a model of its kind, and indeed it has been imitated countless times. It is a straightforward, admirably scored selection of attractive tunes, set with taste and skill, and happily lacking in pretentiousness. The Suite was transcribed for orchestra at a later date by Gordon Jacob, and is also well known in that form. The *Toccata Marziale* is a very brilliant and effective short piece and one of the most distinguished contributions to band repertoire of its period. Vaughan Williams also composed a march, *Sea Songs*, based on chanteys and other folk material, and in style much resembling one of the movements of the *Folksong Suite*.

One other noteworthy work of the *1920*'s is the *Dionysiaques* of Florent Schmitt (*1870-1958*), composed in *1925* for the band of the Garde Républicaine. This is an ambitious and elaborate work, strikingly scored (for the specific instrumentation of the Garde Républicaine), and in a rather conservative late romantic style. Another large work by a French composer is the Symphony in B♭ by Paul Fauchet (*1858-19??*). This work, although called a symphony, is more in the nature of a concert suite. It was first performed by the Band of the Garde Républicaine in *1926*.

⟦ ORIGINAL BAND MUSIC, 1760-1960 ⟧

In the late *1920*'s and the early *1930*'s, a number of works began to come from the pens of American composers. Henry Hadley (*1874-1937*), Clarence Cameron White (*1880-1960*), Daniel Gregory Mason (*1873-1953*), James R. Gillette (b. *1886*), Burnet Tuthill (b. *1888*) and others of their generation wrote works of varying interest. The 'Thirties also saw a variety of pieces by well-known Europeans. There is an early *Concert Music* by Paul Hindemith, a *Spiel for Wind Band* by Ernst Toch, the *Divertimento* of Boris Blacher (b. *1903*) and three Marches by Ernst Krenek, all published in Germany or Austria. Respighi (*1879-1936*) wrote his *Huntingtower Ballad* in *1932* at the request of my father, for whom Albert Roussel (*1869-1937*) wrote his *A Glorious Day* in the following year. All of these works are worth noting, although none can be considered a landmark of band literature.

Three excellent works from *1937* remain comparatively little known in the United States. These were written by Roussel, Arthur Honegger (*1892-1956*) and Georges Auric (b. *1899*) for *Le Quatorze Juillet,* an early pageant by Romain Rolland, revived in connection with the Paris Exposition of *1937*. The composition of the incidental music was commissioned by the French Government and apportioned among a number of France's most distinguished composers, including the three above-named. Rolland's pageant dramatized incidents of the French Revolution, and it was therefore most appropriate that the music commissioned was written for band. Roussel's contribution was a Prelude (to the Second Act). This is a work of far greater interest than his earlier *A Glorious Day*. The Prelude is sombre and expressive, full of interesting ideas and color. It opens with an andante containing highly chromatic motives, leading to a short allegretto; the andante returns and is succeeded by an allegro moderato, and the work finally returns to the mood of the opening. The scoring is not "practical" for most American bands. Six horns, contrabassoon, a large saxophone choir and few clarinets are indicated. But the work is definitely worth knowing, and worth performing by any bands able and willing to follow the exact instrumentation indicated.

The same is certainly true of Honegger's contribution, "The

⟦ ORIGINAL BAND MUSIC, 1760-1960 ⟧

March on the Bastille," written for the most dramatic moment of the pageant. This is, in my opinion, one of the great band pieces, highly dramatic and superbly scored, with great forward thrust and power. It has been recorded by The Goldman Band in its exact original instrumentation. The Auric contribution is a slighter piece, entitled "Le Palais Royal," but it has a great deal of liveliness and charm, and evokes in a witty way the music of an earlier period. None of these works is available in printed form, but they may be obtained in the United States on a rental basis from Leeds Music Corporation.

During this same period, there was a revival of interest in band composition in Russia. The first of Prokofiev's two jolly marches for band, the *Athletic Festival March* (the other is the better-known Opus *99*), dates from *1937*. Compositions by Glière (*Dramatic Overture*), Shostakovich and others appeared in the years immediately following. The most substantial and significant work is the Symphony for Band (Symphony No. *19*) In E♭, Opus *46*, of Nicholas Miaskovsky (*1881-1950*), composed in *1939*. This four-movement work is the first important symphony composed for band since the one by Berlioz, almost *100* years before, and it is an altogether satisfactory work that should be a permanent fixture in international band repertoire. It is quite conservative in style, in the forthright Russian tradition of Tschaikowsky, full of melodic and harmonic interest, pleasantly proportioned and admirably scored. This work also is available on rental from the Leeds Music Corporation in the United States. The work was originally intended to consist of one movement only (the first); Miaskovsky added the three further movements subsequently, when the success of the first movement encouraged him to do so. The Symphony's four movements are: I. Maestoso—Allegro molto; II. Moderato; III. Andante Serioso; IV: Poco maestoso—Vivo. The first and last movements are vigorous and optimistic; the second movement is a symphonic waltz movement, while the third is meditative and serene. Miaskovsky felt that writing a symphony for band was an unusual and difficult task, as he wished, according to his biographer Alexei A. Ikonnikov, to produce a work "which would be equally appreciated by experts and by the general public." No trace of strain is apparent in the work, however, and on the whole Miaskovsky succeeded remarkably well in his objectives. The first *complete* United States performance of the Symphony was given by The Goldman Band on July 7, *1948*. Miaskovsky also composed several marches for band, and an Overture in G minor, Opus *60*, dating from *1942*.

The fact that symphonies can be composed for band, whether the symphonies are masterpieces or not, shows strikingly how very much the character of the band as a musical institution has evolved. And it must be noted that many composers became sufficiently interested in the band as a musical medium at about this time to undertake the composition of large-scale works. In the United States, the first was perhaps James R. Gillette, whose First Symphony ("Pagan") for band dates from *1932*. Ernest Williams' First Symphony for Band was completed in *1938*, and the Symphony for Band of Robert Sanders dates from *1944*.

One of the first important American composers of the next generation to address himself seriously to composition for band was Henry Cowell (b. *1897*). Cowell's enormous musical curiosity, which has led him to explore music of all times and places, and his inventiveness and taste for experiment, must inevitably have led him to this medium. Cowell's *Celtic Set* (*1937-38*) struck a fresh note in band music, as did his *Shoonthree* (*1941*). These two works have a fine freshness of sound and texture, show great imagination in treating the band, and are melodically very appealing. Cowell has since written a great many more works for band, and has made a very great contribution to the growing repertoire.

Jaromir Weinberger's original pieces for band date from about this time. His *Rhapsody, Life on the Mississippi,* was composed for The Goldman Band in *1938,* and was first performed in the following year. This is an interesting work, using the same theme as Delius' *Appalachia,* and shows the skill in instrumentation one would expect from the composer of *Schwanda.* Weinberger subsequently composed a number of other works for band, but none seem to have made a great or lasting impression. Like many other composers of great skill, Weinberger seems to have been unable to resolve the problem of writing fairly "easy" music, on a standardized instrumentation basis, for the consumption of

⟦ ORIGINAL BAND MUSIC, 1760-1960 ⟧

school bands. This problem has been solved, certainly on a technical basis, with greater success by composers who have also been successful "arrangers" and bandsmen, and the literature of original band music contributed by these men, such as Erik Leidzen, Charles O'Neill, Clare Grundman, Harold Walters, Paul Yoder, David Bennett, John J. Morrissey, Bernard Green, Frank Erickson, Philip J. Lang and many others, constitutes a very useful and rewarding portion of the practical repertoire for younger bands.

COMPOSITION FOR BAND SINCE 1940

Since *1940* there has been a steady stream of original works for band by nearly all of the American composers of distinction, and a very great number of works by the best-known composers of Europe, many of whom have written specifically for American bands. This volume of composition is on the increase, and will unquestionably result in a repertoire which will liberate the band from dependence on a diet of transcriptions. The years *1941-42* alone saw the composition and performance of the following impressive list of new pieces by leading composers of the United States:

Roy Harris: *Cimarron Overture*
William Schuman: *Newsreel*
Morton Gould: *Jericho*
Paul Creston: *Legend*
Philip James: *Festal March*
Leo Sowerby: *Spring Overture*
William Grant Still: *Old California*
Aaron Copland: *An Outdoor Overture* (composer's own band version)
Pedro Sanjuan: *Canto Yoruba*
John Alden Carpenter: *Song of Freedom*
Henry Cowell: *Festive Occasion*

⟦ ORIGINAL BAND MUSIC, 1760-1960 ⟧

In the next two or three years, the above list was extended by works of Wallingford Riegger (*Passacaglia and Fugue*), Arthur Shepherd (Overture, *Hilaritas*), Samuel Barber (*Commando March*), Joseph Wagner (*American Jubilee Overture*), as well as by further new works from the pens of Cowell, Gould, James, Sanjuan and others who had already made their debuts as band composers.[1]

From this point on, it becomes difficult to keep track of the activity in this field, and next to impossible even to attempt a complete listing of the available works. In addition, such a list would involve judgments which should not be made at this time, as to which works, or possibly which composers, are of more than passing interest, and also decisions as to what is "concert" material as opposed to primarily "educational" material. There are, for example, many excellent works written by composers who are as yet not nationally or internationally known; and on the other hand, there are some rather poor works by relatively famous composers. An indiscriminate listing would not serve a useful purpose and would, in any case, still involve selection from the vast amount of material.

It should be noted, however, that the new surge of writing for band has not been confined to the United States. In England, for example, there have been original band compositions by John Ireland, Gordon Jacob, Haydn Wood and a number of others; there is a scattering of new works for band in other countries, including Russia (by Khatchaturian and others) and Japan. But none of this is on a scale approaching that which the movement has assumed in the United States. Most of the band works composed by the most celebrated European composers—Schoenberg, Milhaud, Hindemith, Stravinsky—were composed in America for American bands.

The Schoenberg, Hindemith and Milhaud works are all "major" ones in the current band repertoire, and these each certainly require more than passing notice. The earliest of these is the Theme and Varia-

[1] Publisher's Note: We would like to add Richard Franko Goldman to this list of distinguished American composers. Well-known both as a composer of original band works and as an arranger, Mr. Goldman recently was the recipient of the Alice M. Ditson Conductor's Award for 1961.

[ORIGINAL BAND MUSIC, 1760-1960]

tions for Wind Band, Opus *43*a, of Arnold Schoenberg (*1874-1951*), which was composed in *1943* for the Goldman Band, and first performed by that organization under my direction on June *27, 1946*. (In the meantime, Schoenberg had arranged the work for orchestra and it was performed in this version by the Boston Symphony Orchestra under Serge Koussevitzky in *1944*.) The Theme and Variations, it goes almost without saying, is one of the most important and one of the most uncompromisingly serious works yet composed for band. It is not a twelve-tone work; it hovers about the key of G minor, and is rather wanderingly chromatic in a manner slightly reminiscent of Reger. The theme itself is of a dignified march-like character, constructed of ingenious motives which are used with immense technical skill in the variations, of which there are seven, with a Finale. The voicing is complex, and the rhythms subtle; touchy solo passages are abundant, and the work requires careful preparation and the finest balance and care for detail. It is not a work that is ever likely to be widely popular with band audiences, and it may, in fact, be questioned that it ranks among the best of Schoenberg's works; nevertheless, it remains a monument of contemporary band music and a composition which, for seriousness of tone and concentration of musical thought still stands alone in this field.

Darius Milhaud's *Suite Française* was written and first performed in *1945*. This beautifully scored and immediately appealing suite is already a band "classic," on which the composer himself has given us the following comment:

The Suite Française *was originally written for band. The parts are not difficult to play either melodically or rhythmically and use only the average ranges for the instruments. For a long time, I have had the idea of writing a composition fit for high school purposes and this was the result. In the bands, orchestras, and choirs of American high schools, colleges, and universities, where the youth of the nation will be found, it is obvious that they need music of their time, not too difficult to perform, but nevertheless keeping the characteristic idiom of the composer.*

The five parts of this Suite are named after French Provinces, the very ones in which the American and Allied armies fought together with the French underground for the liberation of my country: Normandy, Brittany, Ile-de-France (of which Paris is the center), Alsace-Lorraine, and Provence.

I used some folk tunes of these Provinces. I wanted the young American to hear the popular melodies of those parts of France where their fathers and brothers fought to defeat the German invaders, who in less than seventy years have brought war, destruction, cruelty, torture, and murder, three times, to the peaceful and democratic people of France.

The Symphony in B♭ of Paul Hindemith was composed in *1951*, and received its first performance on April 5 of that year by the United States Army Band in Washington, with the composer conducting. This is an altogether typical Hindemith work, fluent, expertly put together, and perfectly suited to its medium. As with the Schoenberg, it may be questioned that it ranks, in the quality of its ideas, with the composer's best works, but it is certainly a substantial, serious and solid work that is completely characteristic and vigorous. Its three movements are: I. Moderately fast, with vigor; II. Andantino Grazioso—Fast and Gay; III. Fugue.

The practice of commissioning new works for band has proven a great stimulus to the broadening of the repertoire, as has that of instituting contests and competitions. Clinics, or meetings, for the reading and discussion of new works have also proven valuable. The first regular series of band commissions was inaugurated by my father in *1949*. These commissions, awarded at first through The League of Composers and later through the American Bandmasters Association, were awarded during Dr. Goldman's lifetime as follows:

⟦ ORIGINAL BAND MUSIC, 1760-1960 ⟧

1949: Virgil Thomson, *A Solemn Music*
1950: Walter Piston, *Tunbridge Fair*
1951: Peter Mennin, *Canzona for Band*
1952: Robert Russell Bennett, *Mademoiselle*, Ballet for Band
1953: Vincent Persichetti, *Pageant*
1954: Howard Hanson, *Chorale and Alleluia*
1955: Paul Creston, Overture, *Celebration*
1956: Morton Gould, *Santa Fe Saga*

Since the death of my father, I have continued this series of commissions as a memorial; the works in this series since *1956* have been:

1957: William Bergsma, *March with Trumpets*
1958: Vittorio Giannini, *Praeludium and Allegro*
1959: Douglas Moore, *The People's Choice*
1960: Norman Lloyd, *A Walt Whitman Overture*

Through the American Bandmasters Association, there has been since *1956* an annual award given by the Ostwald Uniform Company in memory of Ernest Ostwald, for the best composition submitted to a jury of the Association. Winners have been:

1956: Clifton Williams, *Fanfare and Allegro*
1957: Clifton Williams, *Symphonic Suite*
1958: Mark Quinn, *Portrait of the Land*
1959: Maurice Weed, *Introduction and Scherzo for Band*
1960: Florian Mueller, *Overture* in G

[ORIGINAL BAND MUSIC, 1760-1960]

There have been many important single commissions awarded by musical organizations since 1952. Among these have been Vincent Persichetti's *Psalm for Band*, commissioned by the Pi Kappa Omicron Fraternity of the University of Louisville in 1951, and William Schuman's brilliant Overture, *Chester,* commissioned by the same group. Persichetti's Symphony for Band, Opus *69* (which will be discussed below), was commissioned by the band of Washington University of St. Louis in *1956*. The United States Military Academy Band at West Point commissioned Morton Gould's Symphony for Band in *1952,* and also Darius Milhaud's *West Point Suite.* The Duke University Band commissioned Vittorio Giannini's Symphony for Band in *1959*. All of these works were thus written as a result of direct, practical encouragement in the form of commissions, a most meaningful development in the field of band music. These commissions are typical, and the list is of course by no means complete. The commissions cited are representative, and indicate what may be anticipated in the future.

The symphonies by Gould, Persichetti and Giannini are all fine works, of which any repertoire might be proud, and which are of special significance in the modern American band repertoire. Gould's is a two-movement work of large proportions and is, in my opinion, one of the finest works he has composed in any medium. The scoring for band is extremely brilliant; it ranks with the scores of Grainger as an outstanding example of original and imaginative treatment of band sonorities. It is highly recommended for study. This is a "virtuoso" piece in that it makes considerable demands on the band, and it should not be attempted by any but the best performing groups. But all of the writing is effective and the sound is dazzling.

This Symphony was composed for the West Point Sesqui-centennial celebration. Captain Francis E. Resta and the West Point Academy invited Mr. Gould to contribute a work for this event. Mr. Gould felt that the occasion warranted a major work and wrote this Symphony in the early months of *1952*. The work was premiered on April *13th* at West Point with the composer conducting. It is the composer's Fourth Symphony, but his first for band.

The first movement is lyrical and dramatic. It starts with a quiet and melodic statement of the main theme and motifs that are used and expanded through the entire piece. The general character is elegiac. There is contrast between sonorous brass statements, and poignant and contemplative reflections in the woodwinds.

This resolves into a broad and noble exposition of one of the motifs, followed by a transition to what serves as both an extended coda of the movement and a transformation and peroration of the preceding sections. The form here is a passacaglia based on a martial theme, first stated in the tuba. On this is built a series of variations that grow in intensity. They mount to a dynamic peak, and after a final climactic variation the movement recalls the previous lyricisms, but with the passacaglia motif hovering in the background. The movement finishes quietly.

The second movement is lusty and gay in character. The texture is a stylization of marching tunes that parades past in an array of embellishments and rhythmic variants. At one point there is simulation of a Fife and Bugle Corps which, incidentally, was the instrumentation of the original West Point band. After a brief transformed restatement of the themes in the first movement, the work finishes in a virtuoso coda of martial fanfares and flourishes.

Persichetti's Symphony for Band is his Sixth Symphony, and his first composed for band. This work, in four movements (I. Adagio-Allegro; II. Adagio Sostenuto; III. Allegretto; IV. Vivace) also represents a major contribution to the art of writing for band. In its way, it represents how greatly the concept of band sound and texture has changed in recent years. In general, Persichetti's score is spare in texture, with carefully calculated balances, and an important (and subtle) role assigned to the percussion. The movements are generally taut and rhythmic, the slow sections full of a sustained lyrical inspiration.

The Symphony by Vittorio Giannini is his second work for band. Like the Persichetti, it is in four movements: I. Allegro energico; II. Adagio; III. Allegretto; IV. Allegro con brio. It presents fewer performance difficulties than either the Persichetti or the Gould Symphonies, and its idiom is somewhat more conservative. It too is beautifully conceived and scored in wind band terms, with a full and generally rich sound. It is skillfully designed and most rewarding to play and to hear.

I have singled out these three works not only because they are full-scale symphonies (and not merely *called* symphonies), but because they are first-rate pieces which would have distinction in any repertoire. There are many other excellent works of large dimension in the new repertoire; H. Owen Reed's *La Fiesta Mexicana* may be cited as one. It is not that size makes a determining difference; but the fact that large-scale works can today be considered *practical* for bands again marks the distance that bands have travelled musically. And on this point, an observation of Vincent Persichetti's (in a letter to the author) is pertinent and interesting. Persichetti commented that having bands anxious to play what he writes, makes the effort both spontaneous and worthwhile, and adds, ". . . it seems to approach the relation of composer and performer in other, happier centuries." I think all bandsmen may take this as a heartfelt and important tribute to their interest in the new repertoire of original music for band.

Among the other distinguished American composers (not mentioned previously) who have produced interesting works for band since the end of World War II, one should certainly cite Robert Ward, Don Gillis, Mel Powell, Ulysses Kay, Jack Beeson, Gerald Kechley, Walter Hartley, Elie Siegmeister, Gardner Read, Normand Lockwood, Ingolf Dahl, William Russo, Dai-Keong Lee, Alfred Reed, Ellis Kohs, Gail Kubik, George F. McKay, Herbert Haufrecht, William Latham, Henry Leland Clark, Alec Templeton, Julian Work, Robert McBride and Philip Lang. This list is by no means complete, and there are unquestionably many good and interesting concert works, both published and in manuscript, that I have not had the opportunity of seeing. Many of the composers whose names have been cited in preceding paragraphs have produced other compositions for band than those named. Thus, for example, Vincent Persichetti, whose Symphony, *"Psalm and Pageant for Band"* have been mentioned, is also the composer of a *Divertimento for Band* (*1950*), which is not only his earliest band work, but also his best

⟦ **ORIGINAL BAND MUSIC, 1760-1960** ⟧

known and most popular. Clifton Williams, too, has written many fine pieces besides the two that won Ostwald Awards, and Morton Gould, Henry Cowell, Paul Creston and Robert Russell Bennett, among others, are by now fairly prolific composers of band works. As no list can keep up with current production in the field, one can only suggest that the works mentioned to this point will give the reader a basic idea of what he can begin to look for in the original band repertoire.

part four

IMPROVING

the

BAND

Practical Problems

A N D

s·u·g·g·e·s·t·i·o·n·s

⟦ PROBLEMS AND SUGGESTIONS ⟧

A combination of musicianship and common sense has always seemed to me to be the answer to most of the problems that arise with bands and band performance, and I believe that this is just as true of work with school bands at any level as with college or professional bands. I am not a great believer in methods as such, certainly not in any single method or formula, or in solving problems by going out and buying more equipment. On the other hand, I am not an expert on problems of administration and organization in the school band field, or on problems connected with marching bands, and I would not, under any circumstances, presume to offer advice or suggestions in these areas. There is a large literature on these subjects, and many relevant courses are offered in departments of Music Education.

I shall therefore confine my observations to those areas in which I have had experience, and will attempt to discuss those problems about which I am asked most frequently.

TUNING

The first of these problems is that of tuning and intonation. Everyone agrees that this is the basic problem with most young bands (and with many older ones as well), and there is an immense amount of time and effort devoted to ways and means of improvement and control. Almost every issue of the magazines devoted to school band affairs carries a paper on the subject, and we read constantly of new devices, surveys and charts supplied in an effort to provide "scientific" aid. My own position may be described as a conservatively radical one; I do not think that there is any substitute for old-fashioned ear-training, and I doubt that any short cuts or mechanical devices will produce really satisfactory results.

In my travels through the United States during the last thirty years, I have listened to school bands tuning up in a variety of ways, and in general I have felt that the whole tuning up process was largely wasted time. Whether the players tune to a B♭ played by the teacher

[ILLUSTRATION XLVI]

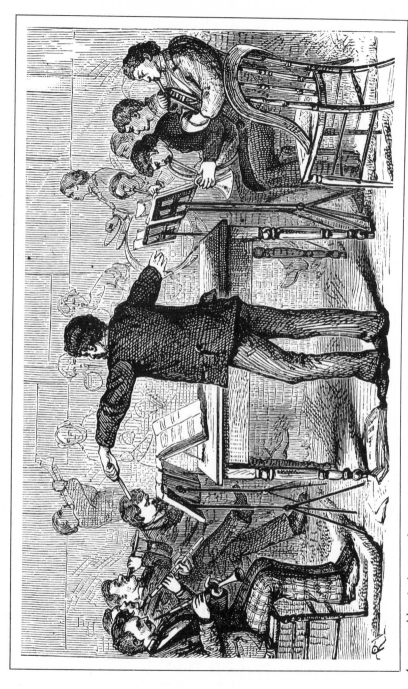

An ensemble of nineteenth century bandsmen show the lost art of band practice.   *Courtesy, The Bettmann Archive*

⟦ PROBLEMS AND SUGGESTIONS ⟧

or by a member of the band, or produced by a stroboscopic checking device does not, it seems to me, matter at all. The fact that the player can match his B♭ to another one simply is no guarantee that he can play C or D in tune, because *in most cases he has never learned intervals.* To be sure, the band must start with some fixed and settled tuning note. But that is only the beginning! On many occasions I have watched the bandmaster going down his clarinet section, one player at a time, checking the B♭, and wondered why he worked so hard to so little purpose. Often, by the time he reached the last clarinetists, the first ones had already strayed well off the pitch. On the other hand, I have often started a rehearsal with a strange school band, and asked the second clarinet to play a note a perfect fifth above the B♭ of the first clarinet. Most of the time I get no response but a blank stare; the student doesn't know what a perfect fifth is, and if he did he would probably not know if it were in tune.

This, it seems to me, presents the whole problem in a nutshell, and the solution is to provide fairly rigorous elementary ear-training as a required accompaniment to any instrumental instruction. The student must know simple intervals and chords before he can play in tune.

My own method, for what it is worth, is to tune in thirds and fifths. I find that the octave is quite unsatisfactory for students with undeveloped ears. Thus it is usually difficult (often impossible) for the average tuba player to get his B♭ in line with the clarinet B♭ several octaves higher, or for the baritone to tune in an octave with the oboe, and so on. I will often start by asking the band to play a major triad— usually any major triad *except* B♭ or E♭. This has often necessitated explanations on my part as to what a major triad is. Once that hurdle has been cleared, one can explain that the bass instruments will play the root of the triad, and that the other instruments can choose either the third or the fifth. It should be fairly random. The players must *hold* the triad as long as they can produce a tone, making adjustments as they listen to the others. On the second try, the instruments that played the third will take the fifth, and vice versa. Then, if one has patience, one does a triad in first inversion, using the same changes. When I use

⟦ PROBLEMS AND SUGGESTIONS ⟧

this technique, I change the root of the triad frequently, from F to C to A♭ and so on. The next step is to take any triad and to have the band attack it pianissimo, building gradually to fortissimo, and returning to pianissimo. This helps the band *retain* the pitch and control the tone, and the whole process works remarkably well in a short time. During several years in which I conducted amateur bands, I used no other method of tuning, and I think I can claim without boasting that these bands, considering the very mixed levels of ability among the players, were normally very satisfactory as to intonation. We also saved hours of rehearsal time!

In using this method, one must of course start with a fixed note. One can take the B♭ of a tuning bar or other device. But the important thing, I think, is that one must get the players to *think,* or perhaps to *sing, accurately,* not a B♭, but a D or an F *before they pick up their instruments.* I am convinced that a bit of time devoted to this sort of drill will work wonders and, as I stated above, will result in hours saved for other work.

SEATING

For some reason, the question of "properly" seating the players in a band seems to be an absorbing one, and I am almost invariably asked, when I appear as a guest conductor, for my opinion on the subject. But this again seems to me to be an open matter, on which no single answer is possible. The best effect, so far as seating is concerned, depends on a large number of variable factors. These include the size of the band, the size and shape of the stage, the nature of the auditorium or band shell, the quality of the players and the band's own style of playing.

The conclusion that there is no "best" way would seem to be clearly indicated by the fact that our greatest bandmasters have not been able to agree on one, and in fact many of them changed their minds about seating arrangements several times during the course of their careers.

⟦ **PROBLEMS AND SUGGESTIONS** ⟧

The old style in band seating was to have all the clarinets immediately at the conductor's left, and the cornets immediately at his right. This practice has generally been abandoned in favor of a more "orchestral" seating, with flutes and oboes in the front ranks, clarinets behind them, and the cornets placed somewhere approximately at mid-center of the group. But there are infinite variations. In general, percussion and "heavy" brass (baritones, trombones and tubas) will be at the rear, and lighter instruments of higher range toward the front. The problem is always how and where to place the band's great variety of middle-register instruments.

There is no gainsaying that this does constitute a difficult problem in many ways, not so much because of the ranges and timbres of the instruments themselves, but because of the way band music is written, and the manner in which parts are distributed. Thus, for example, a melodic part in the tenor register may be assigned to baritone, saxophone, bassoon and bass clarinet. One would like to have them together, because what the composer or arranger is trying to get is probably a group sound such as the sound that would be produced in the orchestra by all of the 'cellos. But it is hard to place these instruments in this fashion, because each has other demands made upon it, and each belongs to a different family or group within the band. One normally wants the baritone with the other brasses, the bassoon with the double reeds, and the bass clarinet with the rest of the clarinet family.

There is also the matter of the direction in which the instruments point. Here the acoustical properties of the stage or auditorium are most important. (Draperies at the back or side of the stage will, for example, make a considerable difference.) But by and large, the sound of a properly proportioned band will not be too greatly affected by the angle at which trombones, or any other instruments, are seated with respect to the audience.

Many conductors prefer to have all the clarinets together, usually on the left, while others prefer to have first clarinets on the left and second and third clarinets on the right. In former times, one usually found orchestras following the pattern of placing first violins left and second violins right, but even in the orchestral field this seating is by no means universal today. With my own band, having tried various plans, I have reverted to the practice of having clarinets both right and left, but I am not at all convinced that this is the only, or the best, way of placing them. It does, however, seem to work out better with the size and shape of the bandstand on which we usually perform.

The determining considerations, when all is said and done, should be: (*1*) Does the seating give the conductor a feeling of control so far as blending various parts of the band is concerned? Can he (the conductor) hear proper balances between sections? (*2*) Is the seating rational for the players? Are concerted passages often distributed among players who are so far apart that they cannot hear one another properly? (*3*) Does the seating make a presentable picture for the audience? And will someone seated in the middle of the audience not feel that he is hearing too much strength in any one part of the band?

DISTRIBUTION OF PARTS

It is still common in school bands to have all of the better clarinetists or cornetists playing the first parts. At times, there is a far too noticeable difference between the playing of first and second parts, not only insofar as the technical agility of the players is concerned, but also in matters of tone quality and intonation. This is obviously not a satisfactory musical situation. Of course the morale and "prestige" of the players, especially young players, must be considered; the better players feel that they are entitled to play the first parts, and they are justified. It is perfectly obvious that any band needs competent and responsible first-chair players or section-leaders. But it is also true that the rest of the band's performance must be considered. I do not think that the "morale" problem is a difficult one. Morale can be kept high by developing a sense of responsibility all through the sections. Good players in each section (among the third clarinets, for instance) help the weaker ones, and everyone benefits. On printed programs, it is now usual simply to list "clarinets" or "cornets," not identifying first, second or third players, except for the principal of the section. Equal prestige can be maintained in this way without difficulty.

A sensible practice followed in many school bands and orchestras is the rotating of parts. A youngster will play first violin or first clarinet in one selection, but will play second violin or clarinet in another. This is a practice much to be recommended, even though it may mean a bit of shifting, and perhaps extra work for the librarian. But it pays off in results, both musically and in terms of morale.

But what is the school band conductor to do when he knows, for instance, that he has far too many saxophones in proportion to the rest of the band? This situation often arises, and is, of course, a delicate one, since the problem is not only a musical but also a diplomatic one. If the bandmaster *must* use all the youngsters who play saxophone, there is probably little he can do about it. He might try having the players take turns, but he will have to be unusually persuasive to bring this about. Otherwise, he will probably have to get along as best he can, and his wisest solution can only be to choose repertoire in which an over-balance of saxophones will be the least objectionable or noticeable.

The same situation often arises with the percussion. A good many school bands I have visited simply have too many percussion players on hand. Here, I think, the situation can really be solved only by rotation. Most band scores do not require more than four percussion players; the others are just adding confusion in many cases. And it is also sadly noticeable that the percussion is almost invariably the weakest section of the band in terms of ability. More rigid standards might certainly be applied in most cases. Two or three fairly good percussionists will always produce a far better effect than seven or eight inept ones.

GENERAL MUSICIANSHIP

The school band is a part of a general program in music education, and this fact, I feel, should not be forgotten. It is not enough to train or to drill youngsters to play notes on an instrument. This is a mechanical acquisition, although a valuable one, and represents specialized training rather than general education. Children are not trained seals who, as it happens, can *also* be taught to blow notes. The band can be an extremely valuable adjunct to general education, provided the participants receive some idea of what their skills are meant to serve, and acquire some familiarity with the art of music itself.

This is a point on which I feel quite strongly, as I have indicated in earlier portions of this book. Performers exist to serve an art, and not vice versa; nor do performers exist primarily to serve an audience, except insofar as that audience is also interested in *why* the performer is there: that is, in the pursuit of some artistic, and not merely exhibitionist, ends.

It is, of course, only in a limited way that one can talk of "art" in connection with the average school band. Nevertheless, this is an end and a goal that should not be lost from view, and it should be approached as closely as circumstances and abilities will permit. It has always saddened me to hear a school band play well, but unmusically, often like a well-drilled group of automatons, and I have felt on these occasions that this is not education in any sense except the most useless and limited one.

It is my firm belief that school band work should be accompanied by instruction in elementary musicianship including, as I have pointed out above, elementary ear-training. The student musician in high school should recognize and reproduce intervals, be able to identify major, minor and dominant seventh chords (as a minimum), and should also be familiar with the elementary aspects of harmonic motion and tonality. Beyond this, he should have a general elementary knowledge of music history, and an awareness that there is other music besides band music. (This is a *minimum* goal!) It may be objected that this kind of program would consume too much time; but the only answer that can be given is that there are certain things for which time *must* be found.

(In this connection, I should like to observe that the finest elementary school orchestra I have ever heard did *no* rehearsing at all on school time. The children reported three-quarters of an hour before their first class, *five mornings a week*. This was only because they loved it and wanted it. In their regular school hours, they had general music lessons.)

The school band program should, under optimum circumstances, include a number of other activities conducive to general musical development. The school band should not concentrate on a few pieces to be played at a competition or concert. There should be time set aside for sight-reading, to broaden the students' knowledge of repertoire as well as to increase reading proficiency. For the same reasons, and also to improve tone and musicianship, as many players as possible should be required to play in smaller ensembles: woodwind quintets, brass groups, and other combinations. Nothing is more effective in developing independence, reliability, sensitivity and responsiveness in the player.

It is quite possibly Utopian to suppose that all of this can be accomplished in most cases. But I do believe that effort should be made in all of these directions.

REPERTOIRE

Repertoire is obviously a basic consideration in the musical development of the band and its players. Choice of repertoire must depend on two factors: difficulty and musical value. It is of course senseless to have the school band attempt music which is far above its level either technically or esthetically. In general, my observation has been that most school bands tend to attempt music too difficult in a technical sense, but too unambitious or unrewarding in a musical sense. A happy balance should be found.

On the technical side, the problem is easier of solution. The bandmaster simply must be realistic about what his band can play well, and not be led to compete with larger schools or more proficient groups. A simple number played well should give musical satisfaction in many ways. It is understandable that both the bandmaster and the students should be ambitious about what they can play, and in fact one would not want it otherwise. But there are limits, as one realizes from time to time when one hears a moderately good band obviously struggling with a work that would be taxing even for a top-notch college organization. There is today so much good music available at all levels of difficulty that there should be no real problem here at all.

This, however, points up how necessary it is for the bandmaster to know what is available. The bandmaster's first responsibility here is not so much choosing the music to be played, as knowing what he has to choose from. One cannot rely on most local music dealers to keep up with everything that is published. But publishers are always happy to send catalogs, and local dealers are always happy to order what the bandmaster wants, provided the bandmaster can tell him. Aside from the publishers' catalogs, which are the primary sources of information about materials of this sort, there are the many periodicals which review new publications; these will, however, not provide the necessary information about older publications. But whatever means or combination of means he uses, the bandmaster must give himself the advantage of knowing what materials he can obtain.

On the musical or educational side, the lines with respect to repertoire are much more difficult to draw. All educators will agree that the musical taste of the students should be improved, however slowly or imperceptibly, and that the use of cheap or vulgar material should be avoided. But who defines what is good and what isn't? Here again, it is the musicianship and common sense of the director that alone can provide a standard. One thing is certain from an educational viewpoint: very little education will result, as a rule, from playing only what the youngsters or their parents like. But we would be giving up all hope in education if we did not think that they can be persuaded to like better things. And indeed we know that this is so.

The bandmaster should exercise the greatest care in the selection of repertoire—even more than he exercises in the choice of uniforms and other appurtenances. Every band, no matter how undeveloped, should have a respectable library; here again, at least as much should be spent on music as is spent on uniforms and equipment. The basis of the library should be proper band music: marches, and such of the repertoire of original band works as is within the musical range of the band. A selec-

⟦ **PROBLEMS AND SUGGESTIONS** ⟧

tion of the best original band music is the indispensable foundation of a good modern band library. And the music should be treated with at least the same respect as is given to instruments and to other property. For it is, although replaceable, the most valuable property the band owns.

EQUIPMENT

Many bands today are so extraordinarily well supplied with property of one sort or another that their management becomes a large business enterprise. Aside from instruments, uniforms, music stands and other items which may be considered basic, the band has tuning devices, tape-recorders and all manner of equipment that would have been unbelievable only a short time ago.

All this is well and good, provided that it does not become an end in itself, and that all of the equipment is put to some profitable use. It might, on occasion, simply be recalled that bands and other musical organizations did manage to exist, and fairly well, before all of these things appeared on the scene.

My only suggestions or comments here involve types of "equipment" which do not normally receive as much attention as tape-recorders, spotlights, amplifiers and all the rest. I should like to suggest that a fraction of the money spent on mechanical equipment be devoted to library facilities for the students. A selection of both books and music should be a part of the band's service to its members, as well as a collection of recordings to which the students may have access. There should, for example, be histories of music and biographies of composers among the books; solo and ensemble compositions among the music; and selections of orchestral, operatic and chamber music among the recordings. There should of course also be a selection of the best band recordings. All of this is to stimulate and encourage the musical growth of the band players. Many will not take advantage of the opportunities, but those who will should be given the chance.

THE

CONDUCTOR

AND

Teacher

⟦ THE CONDUCTOR AND TEACHER ⟧

All of the problems that have been discussed, particularly in the preceding chapter are, of course, the problems of the bandmaster himself. In some respects, conducting a band is more difficult than conducting an orchestra; and in nearly every respect, conducting a school band is a more difficult job than conducting a professional one. One must therefore give all the more credit to the thousands of dedicated men and women who have accomplished such wonders with school bands in the United States over the past forty years.

The school bandmaster is not only a conductor; he is primarily a teacher, responsible to the students in his charge, to the educational system in which he works, to the parents of the students, and to the community at large. He has, in addition, his deep responsibility to the art of music, which is his reason for being a music teacher in the first place. These are his primary responsibilities. But even beyond his musical functions, he must be an organizer, morale-builder, drill-master and parade marshal. The complete school bandsman must be versatile and adaptable, equipped with the energy of a dynamo and the patience of a saint.

Most of the school bandmaster's problems—all of those concerned with the marching band, for example—lie outside the province of this book. But the bandmaster's musical problems are numerous enough, and we have already touched on most of them. We have not, however, discussed the art or the technique of conducting itself. It hardly needs to be emphasized that this is a subject of some importance if we are to consider seriously the status or improvement of the band as a musical institution.

The easiest way of disposing of the subject would be simply to say that in most cases the band is as good as its conductor. This would be perfectly true, but not necessarily helpful. The corollary would be that better training in the art and technique of conducting would be desirable. But here again, there are only a small number of practical steps that can be taken. The sad but inescapable fact is that beyond a certain rudimentary point, conducting cannot be taught. The art of conducting, in its most fundamental sense, depends on a combination of musicianship and temperament. Anyone can learn to beat time, and

⟦ THE CONDUCTOR AND TEACHER ⟧

to master the simple repertoire of gestures that will convey basic meaning to a group of players. This, however, is but the barest beginning of conducting.

It is not absolutely necessary to have a vigorous, fiery or even "artistic" temperament to be an effective conductor; one does, however, need to have a real devotion—one might even say an addiction—to music. Beyond that, the growth, development or stature of a conductor is a matter of his innate and acquired musicianship. In practical terms, this means that he must have good physical equipment to start with: a good ear first of all, a good sense of rhythm, good motor co-ordination and quick reflexes. His musical training must be thorough in every branch: he must know instruments, be familiar with a wide variety of musical literature, understand at least the principles of harmony, counterpoint and musical form, and be able to read scores with some degree of facility.

These are technical qualifications that are reasonable and easily understood. Most of them can be acquired through practice and hard work. Even physical co-ordination can be improved, as can the ear, by well-conceived exercise and practice. There are many methods, and any one of them that works is good. (It must be emphasized that what is effective for one person is not necessarily effective for another, especially in the matter of developing physical poise or an accurate ear.) The serious conductor must of course strive constantly to improve his ear, his command of expressive gesture, and every other physical characteristic that will help him.

Conducting is not a democratic art. The conductor is right, even when he is wrong. When he is wrong, the band (or orchestra, or chorus, or ensemble) has to be wrong with him. It is therefore the conductor's responsibility to be right as often as possible, in those matters where a definite matter of right or wrong can be established. Most matters in the province of the conductor's authority are not so clearly defined. How loud is *mezzo-forte,* for example, or how fast is *allegro con spirito?* But the point is: they are exactly what the conductor determines they are, and he is responsible for his decision.

⟦ THE CONDUCTOR AND TEACHER ⟧

Thus most of the matters for the conductor's decision are in the area of taste and musicianship or, more broadly, in the realm of *style*. The conductor obviously must have musical taste and experience above that of his students or audience. He must be a leader, not a follower, in matters of taste, style and repertoire. A bandmaster who knows only band music is very limited in scope, and cannot offer the most helpful musical guidance to either his students or his community at large. He should be familiar with the masterworks of our great musical heritage, and not in a superficial way. These works should really mean more to him than most of the band works that he will be playing most of the time. If they do, he will be a better bandmaster and educator, certainly a better musician and conductor.

There is every opportunity for the bandmaster today to develop his experience and knowledge of music. The long-playing record has brought the entire musical literature within easy reach, and the serious conductor who wants to learn can have invaluable free lessons from all of the greatest conductors whose performances have been recorded. With my own students at Juilliard and elsewhere, I have always insisted that at least two recordings of a given work be studied from this standpoint. The conducting student should analyze what Toscanini does with the Second Symphony of Beethoven; then compare this with perhaps Bruno Walter's recording, or Scherchen's, or Beecham's. This is a marvelous way to learn! One can study not only obvious matters, such as tempi and dynamics, but also the subtleties of molding phrases, the balancing of chords, the nuances of expression. And such study develops at the same time the student's discrimination and taste; he will prefer what one conductor does in such a passage, what another conductor does elsewhere, and will instinctively formulate justifications for his preferences. He adds to his knowledge, and gains the courage of his own convictions. This knowledge and these convictions will somehow be transmitted to the young musicians he directs, even in a simple march or an elementary piece for sight-reading.

It is obvious that the bandmaster-teacher has a primary responsibility for developing the taste, knowledge and sensitivity of the students entrusted to him. Making music is not merely a matter of physical skill. It can contribute many values in general education, appropriate to all ages, circumstances and degrees of training and background. It is an important part of the school bandmaster's job to realize these values and to make them effective. In other words, his students should achieve something beyond technical proficiency and a sense of "togetherness"; their participation in music must provide some esthetic pleasure—no matter how simple—and more important, must provide the groundwork for future growth: intellectual, artistic, and even moral. And only the attitude and ability of the bandmaster himself can make this possible.

Repertoire is a central consideration in this aspect of the bandmaster's responsibility. Repertoire for the school band will always be determined in part by the grade of difficulty, but there is still great range of discrimination to be exercised in the choice of material at any level. Added to this there are the questions: how is the music approached? What values are sought in and through it? A most important consideration is the connection of the band repertoire with other music and, speaking idealistically, always better music. The important thing educationally is to convey to the student, however limited his background or ability, some sense of music as an art.

At the risk of being repetitious, it must be stated again that the bandmaster must know the repertoire, *and know it thoroughly*. He must not rely on information that reaches him second-hand, or trust that at some clinic or regional meeting he will hear something that he thinks he can use. It is his obligation as a teacher and a musician to be well informed. He can do this easily enough. First of all, he should know *all* the music publishers who bring out band music, and he should have their catalogs, which they are very happy to send. Most publishers will also send sample scores, or scores on approval, for examination. The bandmaster should have a good notion as to the *type* of band music in which a given publisher may specialize. Which publishers have large catalogs

⟦ THE CONDUCTOR AND TEACHER ⟧

of standard works? Which publishers are reliable for good-quality easy material? And the bandmaster should not forget that his dealer can order music from *any* publisher who has a work that the bandmaster may want.

Beyond this, the bandmaster should be able to compare and evaluate different editions or arrangements of standard works in the public domain. Even Sousa marches are now available in many editions! (Original copyrights are good in the United States for twenty-eight years and are renewable for another twenty-eight. Thus any works published earlier than *1904* were in the public domain by *1960*.) It is not necessarily true that there is a *best* arrangement of any given piece; but there may be a best arrangement for a particular band. And there may be (and indeed there are!) some arrangements that should not be used even by bands at race-tracks.

Reviews of new publications in the many good periodicals devoted to music education are very helpful, and the bandmaster should know these periodicals as well as the standard texts in his field. However, no review is ever intended to be a final word on a given subject, and although the reviewer's experience and judgment may be very valuable, the bandmaster must still supplement this by his own experience and judgment, as well as by the knowledge of his own special circumstances or requirements.

Ideally speaking, every band director should be a competent arranger. Not only does such competence aid him in judging published arrangements, but it is an invaluable asset in the many unpredictable emergencies that always seem to arise with bands. Ability to arrange helps solve many repertoire problems, for the bandmaster can arrange, for the use of his own band, any useful material that is in the public domain. (The bandmaster must be cautioned against the arrangement of copyright works, however. An unauthorized arrangement of a copyright work, even for private or educational use, constitutes an infringement of the copyright law.) It is evident that a special arrangement, made with the capabilities or the limitations of a given band in mind, is always the most satisfactory musical solution of the problem of difficulty or adaptation.

⟦ THE CONDUCTOR AND TEACHER ⟧

No emphasis is needed to underline the fact that the responsibilities of the bandmaster-teacher are many and varied. In large school systems, he may have assistants to help him with the actual job of teaching instrumental techniques, or to assist him in others of his many duties. But in most cases, he goes it alone, and is responsible for everything. In most cases, also, he is held responsible for what administrators and parents loosely call "results." All too often, what is meant by "results" is not some intangible and hard-to-assess musical or mental growth and development, but merely the successful performance of a showy concert or entertainment. The bandmaster in such cases eventually realizes that he is being judged by what he can make the students *do*, rather than by what he has taught them; these are not necessarily the same thing, and they are not of equal value in education. But even at best, the bandmaster knows that the band is his show and that he is in a particularly vulnerable spot; he is *on view* at concerts and all of the other events in which his group participates, and he is constantly being judged in a public way to which most teachers in other areas are not exposed.

It is no wonder, therefore, that there is inevitably a great value placed on showmanship in the field of band music. The bandmaster is expected to be a showman, for he is working in a field that is heir to a long tradition of display and entertainment. This must be balanced against his function as an educator. The two functions are not necessarily antithetical, but they may be. The most successful school and college band directors are able to resolve this antithesis very skillfully and effectively, but many find themselves trapped by demands to which they are not equal. The outstanding band directors in schools and colleges have certainly been effective educators in a real and vital sense; and they just as certainly have been excellent showmen as the term is commonly understood. What is important is that the showmanship be conceived not as an end in itself (which it may be for the military or professional director) but as a means to help achieve the proper aims of music education.

The basic work of the conductor-teacher is done at rehearsal, and in the day-to-day work with students. The public performance may demonstrate the value of his work, or it may demonstrate the opposite; but the students, in either case, are not being trained primarily to develop ability as public performers. If this distinction seems subtle, it is because the teaching-performing situation itself is full of difficulties and contradictions. Explained another way, the public performance is a demonstration of "results," but it is not in itself the essential or unique result. It is the essential result only in schools whose aims are specifically directed to the training of *performers:* in other words, in schools devoted to more or less pure vocational or professional training. But general education is another thing.

This is another reason why the rehearsal is so important in the work of the band director in the school or college. For the rehearsal is not only the working period devoted to practising pieces for a performance; it is also the teaching period in which the bandmaster can communicate most immediately and effectively with his students. Here again, the outstanding school and college band directors are marvelously effective in their rehearsals, and the student, or aspiring director, should avail himself of every opportunity of observing the techniques of the directors whose bands play most musically. The school or college band rehearsal is not like the professional rehearsal. In the latter, it is assumed that every musician can play any part put before him, with no difficulty; the conductor should be concerned only with technical matters of ensemble (balance, phrasing, volume) and with interpretation. He does not have to worry whether or not the players like the music or understand it; they are being paid for their skill and their time, and the conductor is under no obligation to educate them.

Rehearsal techniques vary enormously, in both professional and amateur situations, depending on the character of the group, the nature of the repertoire and the personality of the conductor. The one important consideration in all rehearsals is to accomplish an objective with no loss of time. It is necessary to concentrate on essentials first, and to pace the session or sessions so that time remains available for detail.

With school bands, or amateur bands in general, it is seldom wise to worry about details, or even about such things as wrong notes, at too early a stage of preparation. Sectional rehearsals or individual coaching will iron out many if not most of these early problems, and it is in general more rewarding to let the band as a whole get a good idea of the shape and content of a new piece. The manner in which a director approaches a new work often determines very quickly how the students will react to it, and their enthusiasm or indifference will usually make a considerable difference in the speed and ease with which the problems of the piece are worked out. The director must come to the first reading of a new piece with a secure knowledge of the entire work. He must know ahead of time the "shape" he wishes to give it as a whole, and he must be able to hear it in his mind. He must, of course, be familiar with the details of the score, know which parts are likely to be difficult or troublesome, know when he must give definite cues, where there are attacks or release that may need special care. He cannot learn the piece along with the band! This is not only time-wasting, but usually results in a performance that sounds only half finished.

When a full score is not available, the conductor's work is sometimes made more difficult. (This is not always true; for many simpler works a condensed score, if well made, is entirely adequate.) But a conscientious conductor, faced with a condensed score that is not completely clear in its indications, will spend the necessary additional time looking over the parts themselves, and noting passages to which the conductor must give special attention. Even so experienced and busy a conductor as my father would invariably do this, thus saving precious hours of rehearsal time, and bringing to his work an exact knowledge of what each instrument was doing. With full scores, this extra preparation is naturally not necessary, as everything is there for the eye and ear of the director. The full score should always be available at the early rehearsals. Later, when notes have been learned and the shape of the work is clarified, the conductor may prefer to use the condensed score in order to save page-turning; it is there simply as a memory-refresher, for most if not all of the score should be well established in the conductor's mind.

Many conductors have a gift with words; others do not. Verbal explanations may save or waste time; one cannot make a general rule about

⟦ THE CONDUCTOR AND TEACHER ⟧

this. Other conductors can achieve results by singing, gesturing or facial expression. In general, with student groups, clear and concise verbal explanations help a great deal, not only in specific technical matters (where the conductor must be able to give precise professional advice) but also in giving ideas and information about the work itself. I believe that students should know as much as possible about what they are playing, from every conceivable angle. In my experience, they play better, with more enthusiasm as well as with more understanding, when this sort of instruction is added to the rehearsal routine. Needless to say, the rehearsal cannot become a lecture; the director's remarks and comments should be interesting, brief and to the point. If they are, they can make a substantial contribution not only to the students' education, but to the efficiency of the rehearsal as well.

The inexperienced conductor will often waste much time going over small things that would right themselves in due course, and will sometimes pass over things that will get worse if not corrected immediately. With most high school bands that I have conducted, there is not much point in letting most of the band sit idle while one attempts to work out a passage with weak players. They will not improve rapidly enough to make it pay; the proper amount of work needed can be done only in a sectional rehearsal or with individual coaching. If the players (for example, the third clarinets) cannot master the passage, then the work is too difficult for the band as a whole, for the band is really only as strong as its weakest part. If one is committed to the performance of the work, one must devise some manner of "faking" these passages, and an experienced conductor can usually find some way of doing it.

Amateur players will often "freeze" to a mistake that they have made once. They may become very self-conscious or nervous, and if the conductor works over the passage too insistently during a rehearsal, the player may go from bad to worse. I have seen this happen often enough. Here again, the experienced conductor will make a rapid estimate of the situation, and should try to make things easier for the player and the band by turning his attention to something else. Often a relaxing of tension—even a joke, or a humorous comment (though not, of course, at

⟦ THE CONDUCTOR AND TEACHER ⟧

the player's expense)—will set matters right more quickly than an insistent effort to correct the player then and there.

Unless one has a truly proficient band—and by this I mean proficient players right on down to third clarinets and second bassoons —one should generally try for overall movement, "shape" and spirit rather than for perfection of detail. The latter is almost impossible to attain except on the top levels of college or professional band work. One must be aware that students as a rule play as well as they can all the time. In many instances, they will be able to play a passage materially better only after two more years of study—not after fifteen minutes of sweating over the passage in a rehearsal. The conductor of the band with players at varying levels of ability must know what they can do, and how far he can expect them to go.

The band director must have a clear idea of the kind of band sound that he wants to obtain. Bands vary in character perhaps even more than orchestras, not only because of their variation in size and in instrumental make-up, but because of their lack of an international tradition and repertoire. Add to this the fact that the band is an evolving medium which always demands new works, or at least new arrangements of old works. There is not much agreement on how a band ought to sound, and in fact there is perhaps less agreement on this subject today than there was fifty or a hundred years ago. But the essential point, so far as the conductor is concerned, is that the same band can be made to sound remarkably different with a different conductor. It is the conductor's idea of style and of sound that shapes the sound and style of the ensemble.

It is interesting in this respect to compare band performances of that basic item of band repertoire, the march. Conductors differ not only in ideas of tempo, but in every other detail of performance. This is, of course, even on this relatively simple musical level, a matter of "interpretation," but it is fundamentally a matter of *style:* that is, of an over-all conception of what a band should sound like. Of course every band director, when it comes to marches, also appeals to "tradition"; and one can only say, after hearing a variety of performances "in the Sousa tradition," that Sousa must have changed his mind at least once a week

⟦ THE CONDUCTOR AND TEACHER ⟧

during his more than fifty years of activity. As a matter of fact, taking the testimony of the many men who played under Sousa, that great man *did* vary his interpretations occasionally. But he never varied his *style;* that was *his,* and that is what made the Sousa Band.

It goes without saying that the conductor has to know his trade. He has to be able to beat time, control attacks, releases and dynamics, keep everyone together, hear mistakes and correct them; in short, be a competent technician. But he can be able to do all of these things and still not be a successful conductor. Beyond these rudimentary abilities, he has to be both a musician and a personality, so that the band or orchestra or any other group he conducts takes the style of both his musicianship and of his personality. There is no formula for learning to conduct, and there of course can be no uniform guide to style. The world would be terribly dull if there were. If one watches today's outstanding bandmasters in action, or remembers the great ones of yesterday, one realizes what style is, and how many different styles can be interesting and effective, provided only that they are genuine, and that they remain at the service of music.

The other end of the spectrum is the cultivation of mannerisms, or the emphasis on a style that is calculated to draw attention by its eccentricity. Both the band and the orchestra have seen conductors of this breed, and one must admit that many of them have been phenomenal at the box-office. But this is the triumph of showmanship over music, and not the use of showmanship in the cause of good music. Toscanini, in his way, was a great showman, but no one could ever for a moment have thought that he was not a musician first. Sousa was renowned for his showmanship, but the same is true of him. Anyone who remembers Sousa, or has read any of his writings, is aware that he was a fine musician and a cultivated gentleman, with a deep love of *all* the arts, and with a fine sense of humor and proportion. Sousa's conducting was rather stiff; he never made great gestures, and he was not even especially graceful; but there was a real personality behind the rather awkward baton technique, and this shone through to the players as well as to the audience. The style was the man himself, genuine all the way through.

[THE CONDUCTOR AND TEACHER]

The band today is in good hands. There are many fine band conductors, sincere musicians and good showmen both, throughout the United States. It is to them, and to those who will follow, that we must look for the further advancement of bands not only as serious musical organizations dedicated to a worthy repertoire, but as valuable agencies in the progress of American education.

Selected

bibliography

⟦ SELECTED BIBLIOGRAPHY ⟧

ADKINS, H. E. *Treatise on the Military Band.* London: Boosey & Co., 1931.

BARZUN, JACQUES. *Berlioz and the Romantic Century.* Boston: Little, Brown & Co., 1950.

————. *Music in American Life.* New York: Doubleday & Co., 1956.

BERGER, KENNETH. *The March King and His Band.* New York: Exposition Press, 1957.

BRENET, M. (M. BOBILLIER). *La Musique Militaire.* Paris: H. Laurens, 1917.

BRANCOUR, R. "Musiques Militaires Belges," *Le Ménestrel* (Paris), Vol. 82, No. 36 (1920).

BUCHMAN, C. "Composers Dedicate Works to the Band," *Modern Music* (New York), Vol. XX, No. 1 (November, 1942).

CARSE, A. *Musical Wind Instruments.* London: Macmillan, 1939.

————. *The Orchestra from Beethoven to Berlioz.* Cambridge: W. Heffer & Sons, 1948.

CHIDESTER, L. W. *International Wind-Band Instrumentation.* San Antonio: Southern Music Co., 1946.

CHIDESTER, L. W., and PRESCOTT, G. R. *Getting Results with School Bands.* New York: Carl Fischer, 1938.

CHOP, M. *Geschichte der Deutschen Militärmusik.* Hannover: L. Oertel, 1925.

⟦ SELECTED BIBLIOGRAPHY ⟧

CLAPPÉ, A. A. *The Principles of Wind-Band Transcription.* New York: Carl Fischer, 1921.

————. *The Wind Band and Its Instruments.* New York: Henry Holt, 1911

COLLEGE BAND DIRECTORS NATIONAL ASSOCIATION. *Bulletin of Proceedings,* 1958.

COMETTANT, O. *Histoire d'un Inventeur au XIX siècle* (Adolphe Sax). Paris: Pagnerre, 1860.

CORIBA, L. "As Bandas Portuguesas e as Estrangeiras Comparadas," *Eco Musical* (Lisbon), Vol. I, No. 47 (1911).

COURROYEZ, G. *Étude sur les Musiques d'Harmonie.* Paris: Andrieu Frères, 1931.

DARLINGTON, MARWOOD. *Irish Orpheus* (Gilmore). Philadelphia: Olivier-Maney-Klein Co., 1950.

DAVID, HANS T. *Musical Life in the Pennsylvania Settlements of the Unitas Fratrum.* Winston-Salem: The Moravian Music Foundation, 1959.

DEGELE, L. *Die Militärmusik.* Wolfenbüttel: Verlag für Musikalische Kultur und Wissenschaft, 1937.

DICHTER, HARRY, and SHAPIRO, ELLIOTT. *Early American Sheet Music.* New York: R. R. Bowker Co., 1941.

DVORAK, R. F. *The Band on Parade.* New York: Carl Fischer, 1937.

ELLIOT, J. H., and RUSSELL, J. F. *The Brass Band Movement.* London: J. M. Dent, 1936.

⟦ SELECTED BIBLIOGRAPHY ⟧

ESPINOSA, M. DE *Toques de Guerra del Ejercito Español.* Burgos: 1939 (reprint of original, published at Madrid in 1769).

FARMER, H. G. *Memoirs of the Royal Artillery Band* (An Account of the Rise of Military Music in England). London: Boosey & C., 1904.

———. *Military Music.* New York: Chanticleer Press, 1950.

———. *The Rise and Development of Military Music.* London: W. Reeves, 1912.

FENNELL, FREDERICK. *Time and the Winds.* Kenosha, Wis.: G. Leblanc Co., 1954.

FFOULKES, C. *Notes on Early Military Bands.* London: Society for Army Historical Research, 1938 (Vol. 17, pp. 188-200).

FIBULA, L. "Per Una Partitura Unica di Banda," *Musica d'Oggi* (Milan), Vol. 2, No. 11 (1920).

FRIES, J. H. *Abhandlung vom Sogennanten Pfeiffer-Gericht.* Frankfurt, 1752.

GALLO, S. *The Modern Band.* Boston: C. C. Birchard, 1935.

GEIRINGER, KARL. *Musical Instruments.* New York: Oxford University Press, 1945.

GILES, RAY. *Here Comes the Band.* New York: Harper & Brothers, 1936.

GODFREY, D. *Memories and Music.* London: Hutchinson, 1924.

GOLDMAN, EDWIN FRANKO. *Amateur Band Guide and Aid to Leaders.* New York: Carl Fischer, 1916.

[SELECTED BIBLIOGRAPHY]

————. *Band Betterment*. New York: Carl Fischer, 1934.

GOLDMAN, RICHARD FRANKO. *The Band's Music*. New York: Pitman Publishing Corp., 1938.

————. "Bands in War-Time," *Modern Music* (New York), Vol. XIX, No. 3 (March, 1942).

————. *The Concert Band*. New York: Rinehart and Co., 1946.

GOLDMAN, RICHARD FRANKO, and SMITH, ROGER. *Landmarks of Early American Music*. New York: G. Schirmer, 1943.

GRAHAM, ALBERTA. *Great Bands of America*. New York: Thomas Nelson & Sons, 1951.

GRIDER, RUFUS A. *Historical Notes on Music in Bethlehem, Pa.* Winston-Salem: The Moravian Music Foundation, 1957.

GRIFFITHS, S. C. *The Military Band*. London: Rudall, Carte, 1896.

HAYES, G. *King's Music*. London: Oxford University Press, 1937.

HINDSLEY, M. H. *Band . . . Attention!* Chicago: Gamble Hinged Music Co., 1932.

HOBY, C. *Military Band Instrumentation*. London: Oxford University Press, 1936.

————. "Wagner and Military Music," *Musical Progress and Mail* (London), October, 1953.

HOWARD, JOHN TASKER. *Our American Music*. (Rev. ed.). New York: Thomas Y. Crowell Co., 1939.

⟦ SELECTED BIBLIOGRAPHY ⟧

HUME, J. O., and ZEALLEY, A. E. *Famous Bands of the British Empire.* London: J. P. Hull, 1926.

JONES, ARCHIE N. (Ed.). *Music Education in Action.* Boston: Allyn & Bacon, 1960.

KALKBRENNER, A. *Die Organisation der Militärmusikchöre Aller Länder.* Hannover: L. Oertel, 1884.

————. *Wilhelm Wieprecht, Sein Leben und Wirken.* Berlin, 1882.

KAPPEY, J. A. *Short History of Military Music.* London: Boosey & Co., 1894.

KASTNER, J. G. *Manuel Général de Musique Militaire.* Paris, 1848.

KOCHNITZKY, LEON. *Adolphe Sax and His Saxophone.* New York: Belgian Government Information Center, 1949.

LAHEE, HENRY C. *Annals of Music in America.* Boston: Marshall Jones, 1922.

LANG, PHILIP J. *Scoring for Band.* New York: Mills Music, 1950.

LEINBACH, JULIUS. *Regiment Band of the Twenty-Sixth North Carolina.* Winston-Salem: The Moravian Music Foundation, 1958.

LEIDZEN, ERIK. *An Invitation to Band Arranging.* Bryn Mawr: Theodore Presser Co., 1950.

LINGG, ANN M. *John Philip Sousa.* New York: Henry Holt, 1954.

McCORKLE, DONALD M. *The Collegium Musicum Salem: Its Music, Musicians and Importance.* Winston-Salem: The Moravian Music Foundation, 1956.

⟦ SELECTED BIBLIOGRAPHY ⟧

MAHAN, F. A. "Military Band: History and Organization," *Journal of the Military Service Institution of the U.S.* (Governor's Island, N.Y.), 1908.

METCALF, FRANK J. *American Writers and Compilers of Sacred Music.* New York: Abingdon Press, 1925.

MILLER, G. *The Military Band.* London: Novello, 1912.

NEUKOMM, E. *Histoire de la Musique Militaire.* Paris: L. Baudouin, 1889.

PANOV, P. *Militärmusik in Geschichte und Gegenwart.* Berlin: K. Siegismund, 1938.

PERRIN, A. *Les Musiques Militaires.* Paris: Alcan-Lévy, 1882.

PORTEOUS, R. *The Bandmaster's Atlas.* London: R. Cocks, 1854.

ROUSSEAU, J. J. "Sur la Musique Militaire," in *Ecrits sur la Musique.* Paris, 1838.

SACHS, CURT. *The History of Musical Instruments.* New York: W. W. Norton & Co., 1940.

SCHEUNEMANN, G. *Trompeterfanfaren, Sonaten und Feldstücke . . . des 16/17 Jahrhunderts.* Kassel: Baerenreiter Verlag, 1936.

SCHWARTZ, H. W. *Bands of America.* New York: Doubleday & Co., 1957.

———. *The Story of Musical Instruments.* New York: Doubleday & Co., 1939.

⟦ **SELECTED BIBLIOGRAPHY** ⟧

SONNECK, OSCAR G. *Bibliography of Early American Secular Music.* Washington: McQueen, 1905.

SOUSA, JOHN PHILIP. *Marching Along.* Boston: Hale, Cushman and Flint, 1928.

————. *Through the Year with Sousa.* New York: Thomas Y. Crowell & Co., 1910.

THOMSON, VIRGIL. *The Musical Scene* (especially chapter on "Transcriptions"). New York: A. A. Knopf, 1945.

————. "What Shall Band Music Be?" *Etude* (Philadelphia), July, 1942.

THOURET, G. (Ed.) *Musik am Preussischen Hof.* Leipzig: Breitkopf & Härtel, 1896.

VESSELLA, A. *La Banda dalle Origini. Fino ai Nostri Giorni.* Milan: Instituto Editoriale Nazionale, 1935.

WAGNER, JOSEPH. *Band Scoring.* New York: McGraw-Hill Book Co., 1960.

WATERS, EDWARD N. *Victor Herbert.* New York: Macmillan, 1955.

WHITE, W. C. *A History of Military Music in America.* New York: Exposition Press, 1944.

Note: No attempt has been made to provide a complete list of relevant articles in periodicals. The reader will find many articles of interest in the files of publications such as The Instrumentalist, The School Musician *and other periodicals devoted to instrumental music and music education.*

Index

⟦ INDEX ⟧

[INDEX]

〖 INDEX 〗

⟦ INDEX ⟧

⟦ INDEX ⟧

[INDEX]

〖 INDEX 〗